POWER PUBLIC RELATIONS

SECOND EDITION

How to

Master the

New PR

LEONARD SAFFIR

NTC Business Books
NTC/Contemporary Publishing Group

Library of Congress Cataloging-in-Publication Data

Saffir, Leonard.
  Power public relations: how to master the new PR / Leonard
Saffir. — 2nd ed.
    p. cm.
  Includes index.
  ISBN 0-658-00060-8
  1. Public relations.   I. Title.
HD59. S315   2000
659.2—dc21   99-24839
                                                          CIP

Published by NTC Business Books
A division of NTC/Contemporary Publishing Group, Inc.
4255 West Touhy Avenue, Lincolnwood (Chicago), Illinois 60712-1975 U.S.A.
Printed in the United States of America
International Standard Book Number: 0-658-00060-8

99 00 01 02 03 04 XX 19 18 17 16 15 14 13 12 11 10 9 8 7 6 5 4 3 2 1

To Samantha, Michelle, and Andrew Saffir.
Now, finally, you can answer your friends'
question, "What does your father do?"

And to my wife Eleanor, who, for sure,
knows what I do.

And especially to the late John Tarrant,
who assisted me in the first edition of
Power Public Relations. Jack was a
talented writer, a friend, and a strong
believer in Power Public Relations.

Contents

Acknowledgments

I would like to thank those whose contributions made this book possible.

My agent, the late Anita Diamant, deserves major thanks for believing in this book.

Many thanks to Danielle Egan-Miller for her valuable editorial support.

Thank you to Karen Schenkenfelder for her skillful copyediting.

I am particularly indebted to Richard Weiner, a friend, mentor, and a Power Public Relations leader for many years first at Richard Weiner, Inc., and then, upon its sale, at Porter Novelli International.

Special thanks for assistance are also extended to Bob Seltzer, who worked with me at Richard Weiner and Porter Novelli and then went on to become president of Ogilvy Public Relations Worldwide.

To Bob Dilenschneider, head of his own firm and a long-time Power Public Relations leader, my thanks for his support and assistance.

There are many more who helped. They include Larry Aasen, Roger Ailes, Charles Black, Fred Bona, Laurel Callahan, Jay DeBow, Kevin DeMarrais, Susan Donovan, Doug Durrett, Roger Durrett, Jean Farinelli, David Finn, Peter Gorman, Veearni Gunavardhana, Ed Halloran, Peter Hannaford, Paul Jacoby, Fritz Jellinghaus, Rita Katz, John Kramer, Marti MacKenzie, Margo Mayor, Ed Stanton, Robert Stone, Dorothy Tarrant, Leon Theill, Judy Twersky, Eleanor Unger, Lisa Vale, Steve Winston, Jon Zilber, and all my colleagues in public relations.

Finally, thanks to all the clients I have had the good fortune of working with, who gave me the firsthand knowledge to write this book.

Foreword

Twenty-eight years ago I sat across a conference room table making a presentation to a self-made man who had decided that he was ready to spend $1 million selling his brand of cigarette lighters. It was clear that he had no idea what advertising could do and was desperate to run through his money as fast as he possibly could, so that he could tell his friends at the country club he was an advertiser.

As gently as I could, I tried to lead him in another direction. I said, "I don't know if you need an advertising agency. I think what you need is PR. It would cost you a fraction of what you're planning to spend, and you'll achieve exactly what you want to achieve."

"PR," he said disdainfully, "Why do I need PR?"

"Because if your objective is to become well-known, you haven't got the ad dollars to sustain a campaign. And, frankly, your competitors, Gillette and BIC, are outspending you ten-to-one."

"But what does PR do?"

I said, "For one thing, it'll get people to know you."

"Oh, forget it," he replied. "I definitely don't need it."

"You definitely don't need PR?"

"No, it's a waste of time. If all PR does is get people to know me, I don't need it."

"Why not?" I asked.

"Because *everyone* I know knows me."

Such is the client ignorance that Len Saffir has had to live with most of his professional life. And yet, when you read the following pages, you'll see that he approaches this business with an enthusiasm and love (yes, I said love) that makes him the best in the business.

Public relations is the last free thing in America. One can develop a new product, give an existing product a shot in the arm, or resurrect a dying product—all it takes is a mind, a pen, and a fax machine.

My favorite experience with PR came in 1967 when my agency was a breath or so away from bankruptcy. No one knew us. No one would answer our calls. And we couldn't afford to advertise. So, I decided to try my hand at PR. I picked up the phone and called the editor of *ANNY*, a well-read ad publication of the time.

"Joe," I said to the editor, "I'm just calling to tell you that Della Femina, Travisano is not going to get the Panasonic account."

"You're not getting Panasonic?" he asked.

"No, I'm not getting Panasonic. I want to formally deny the rumor."

"I hadn't heard that rumor," he said.

"Well, the story is yours exclusively," I said.

That week, the front-page headline was "Della Femina Not Getting Panasonic." The next week I denied that I was going to get the Borden's account. Another front-page headline. "Borden's Says 'No' to Della Femina." The third week brought another denial and another front-page headline. Our agency was made. Everyone was talking about the new hot agency that had come so close to getting three major pieces of business.

A year later I ran into the marketing director of Panasonic. He looked puzzled. "We never talked to you," he said.

"That's true," I said.

"We never were going to give you our account," he said.

"That's what I told the press," I replied.

He paused and smiled and said, "I think your agency's going to do all right."

So I can say, firsthand, I owe a lot to PR. And PR owes a lot to Len Saffir. Picture this headline in a PR trade paper: "Len Saffir Denies That His Bestselling Book Is Getting Him the General Motors PR Account."

Jerry Della Femina
Chairman
Della Femina/Jeary and Partners

Preface

Take one week in the present-day business world. A number of things happen:

- A large company, planning an important new-product introduction, entrusts the campaign to the public relations department rather than to the traditional marketing apparatus.
- Public relations practitioners orchestrate a new stock offering by a struggling corporate giant.
- The White House retains public relations professionals to facilitate the confirmation of a high-level nominee or fight impeachment.
- A corporate vice president is recruited to fill a CEO job, substantially on the basis of visibility achieved through PR techniques.
- Facing off in a major lawsuit, the opposing sides hire public relations counsel at the same time they retain legal counsel.
- A convicted murderer launches a public relations campaign to get out of prison.
- A large advertising agency announces that its new head comes from a public relations rather than an advertising background.
- For the first time in its history, a marketing giant budgets more for public relations than for advertising.

What is going on here? Has public relations become "The Blob," oozing into every aspect of our lives?

Not quite. But public relations has certainly grown up. Once a kind of corporate office boy, relegated to odd jobs in the communications area, public relations is now a giant, with massive strength and wide versatility.

This giant is here and will not go away. Those who know how to handle it will profit. Those who ignore or mishandle the giant will get hurt, perhaps badly hurt.

This book is a look at the powerful and pervasive discipline that public relations has become, from the point of view of a leading practitioner of corporate public relations who has also been deeply involved with public relations on the political, legal, and social fronts.

Public relations is full of paradoxes. It is a discipline devoted to messages—yet few people outside the industry really understand what it is and how much it is capable of doing. In a related paradox, the discipline, which is so good at making clients, products, and causes seem important, seems to conspire to make itself look unimportant. But that may be, to an extent, deliberate. A number of thoughtful public relations professionals worry about the consequences of letting the general public know just how extensively public relations is calling the shots.

The most dangerous paradox of all may be that this most pervasive of disciplines is still considered by most non-PR managers to be of only passing concern.

Today, all of us ignore the emergence of Power Public Relations at our peril. Managers and organizations need to be *PR literate and PR competent.*

Public Relations Literacy

Most successful managers excel in at least one discipline but are "literate" in all important disciplines. The executive who wants to head the organization remains preeminent in finance while keeping up to speed on developments in marketing, research, production, etc.

When one attempts to rise out of the realm of the particular into the general, "illiteracy" in any important branch of organizational functioning is a decided liability.

Public relations is the latest discipline to become a major branch of organizational functioning. However, not everyone has fully realized this—and therein lies the opportunity for those who do. Some managers still think of public relations as a low-level function pursued by an ink-stained drudge who has recently discovered the Internet, sends out releases, and tries (unsuccessfully) to keep bad news out of the papers. Some managers still confuse public relations with advertising.

Power Public Relations is a research-based matrix of sophisticated techniques that are being used today to influence thinking and shape public reaction in ways undreamed of a few years ago. This book describes the awesome size and diversity of public relations and tells where it will be going tomorrow.

Public Relations Competency

The practitioners of Power Public Relations have developed certain techniques that may be adopted by managers and entrepreneurs. These techniques—some of them new, some enhanced versions of older tools—add up to a potentially powerful arsenal of tactics for the *aggressive engineering of perception.*

Old-style public relations is reflexive and reactive. The new public relations is innovative. Traditional public relations was always soothing and positive; the new approach is realistic, admits mistakes, conveys balanced information rather than just puffery. While public relations used to be confined to a limited number of fields, the new techniques are deployed in proxy battles, lawsuits, and campaigns for personal advancement. Professionals—doctors, lawyers, consultants, financial advisers, and others—who are limited in their freedom to advertise and promote are now able to use public relations techniques to create images that attract clients. Ambitious men and women are using PR strategies to help shape successful careers.

Some of this book is *what is happening*—case histories illustrating the scope, pervasiveness, and power of public relations today. Some of it is *how-to*—the strategies and tactics that make Power Public Relations work. Public relations professionals will agree or disagree with what they find here—but will, I hope, find something of interest. For those outside the public relations field, the case histories will help to draw the outlines of this new colossus. And the behind-the-scenes, how-to material offers a shortcut to PR literacy.

So let us take a trip through the bizarre bazaar of modern public relations. We will meet some strange people and see some strange things.

Above all, though, we will become better acquainted with a giant whom we had better be friends with, if we know what is good for us.

The Art of Making Up Minds

New Roles, New Precision, New Importance

In the corporation of the twenty-first century, public relations will rank higher than advertising. CEOs of major companies will come out of the public relations field. Executives in all disciplines will take it for granted that a grasp of the essential tools and principles of public relations is as important as computer literacy. Business schools will teach modern public relations as an essential course. Instead of separate advertising agencies and public relations firms, we will have "sell shops," which combine the disciplines.

These things, and more, will happen because public relations will have emerged as the dominant force in what is fundamental to success in business and politics: the engineering of perception.

The most spectacular recent examples of the handling—and mishandling—of Power Public Relations involve President Bill Clinton and Independent Counsel Kenneth Starr, as well as former Speaker of the House Newt Gingrich, whose career disintegrated over his choice of appropriate strategies regarding President Clinton's problems. Whether or not you like these three, their experiences exemplify the vast power of present-day public relations to boost you to the heights and hurl you to the depths. Historians will determine how their use of Power Public Relations might have altered how one century ended and another began.

Power Public Relations Has Arrived

Power Public Relations is here—and it is bigger than it has ever been. The public relations industry experienced the most incredible growth in its history in the middle and late 1990s. By the turn of the century, fees of many millions of dollars were commonplace as many large firms doubled in size.

This fantastic growth should in no way discourage the small company. Yes, the pie is bigger, but there is still room for the small guy. Creativity and ingenuity still drive public relations.

PR's importance is undeniable. When the topic of public relations comes up, the reaction is no longer, "So what?" The reaction is more likely to be, "Now what?" Recognizing the power of new-millennium public relations is one thing; harnessing it is another.

Public relations is now big in raising capital, creating billion-dollar market-capitalized companies from start-ups almost overnight, effecting mergers and takeovers, dealing with communities, influencing governments, and fighting presidential impeachment.

The year 1998 was dominated by anti- and pro-Clinton public relations forces battling each other to get their message someplace, anyplace, on the new twenty-four-hour news cycle. In President Andrew Johnson's time, and even President Richard Nixon's time, the impeachment fights were not fueled by massive public relations wars. But in 1998, activists on both sides of the political spectrum openly declared Power Public Relations war in newspaper and network and cable television interviews and on the Internet. From the first mention of Monica Lewinsky's name on the then relatively unknown Drudge Report in early January 1998, PR practitioners and lawyers fought together side by side.

Public relations will be one of the most important businesses in the new century, simply because of the power of public opinion. Robert Dilenschneider, head of The Dilenschneider Group and former CEO of Hill and Knowlton, says, "Public opinion is everywhere, from businesses relocating to new situations, to politicians being elected, to the sale of products, to the sustaining or humbling of reputations." He adds, "Those who know how to deal in public opinion are ahead on the power curve. Certainly those who do not are almost always going to encounter problems that are difficult, at best, to reach their objectives."

Public relations has grown into a full-fledged discipline with the power and reliability to influence perception in ways that make it a strong and supple tool. And modern public relations has an additional advantage for those who know how to use it. Many business leaders have not yet fully realized the potential of the discipline. Those who do can enjoy a substantial competitive advantage over those who don't.

This goes for countries as well as businesses. Kuwait hired the PR giant Hill & Knowlton to promote U.S. military action against Iraq.

Public relations has matured, just like advertising. Advertising changed from a knack into a discipline. The field was dominated by people with the wit and flair to create copy that worked: "They laughed when I sat down at the piano"; "They Satisfy"; "It Floats." Advertising was seat-of-the-pants. You had no benchmarks—you tried an ad, and if it didn't work, you tried something else.

One important thing that happened to advertising was research. Practical psychologists devised reliable methods of identifying the people who were most likely to buy a product or service, testing the effectiveness of various possible appeals to these people, determining the channels through which they could best be reached, and testing the impact of advertising after it was launched.

Advertising changed. Creativity was still paramount, but the creators were no longer shooting in the dark. Results were quantifiable and, to a markedly greater degree, predictable.

In the earliest days, ads were created in-house by wordsmiths. But as advertising became a discipline, the agency emerged as the entity that could gather all the necessary skills in one place and create advertising far better than the company could do on its own. Nowadays, we take the advertising agency for granted. There are giant agencies and smaller, specialized shops. For most companies, marketing success pivots on how well the company chooses and works with its ad agency.

Public relations has passed through a similar transition. Sixty years ago, there were few public relations practitioners selling their services to industry. The craft had been around since the first decade of the twentieth century, when Ivy Ledbetter Lee, celebrated as the father of public relations, began to advise various large interests like Bethlehem Steel and the Pennsylvania Railroad. (The railroads, oil companies, steel companies, and utilities had discovered that they needed all the image improvement they could get.) Lee's great coup was to have John D. Rockefeller, the epitome of the hard-hearted, tightfisted industrialist, hand out shiny dimes to deserving youngsters.

A number of brilliant—and sometimes flamboyant—successors to Ivy Lee sold their services to companies throughout the first half of the century. One of these men was Edward Bernays, a public relations genius who started one of the first PR firms. In 1991—at the age of 100—Bernays was still defending and explaining public relations practitioners in our society. (He died in 1995.)

On the whole, however, public relations was an in-house function, largely confined to issuing releases and writing speeches for executives. There were, of course, bolder ventures, but these tended to focus on "publicity stunts" rather than coordinated campaigns executed in accordance with a clear-cut strategy.

After World War II, public relations began to become a science. More practitioners appeared, larger PR firms were formed, and more companies began to pay serious attention to public relations. But the discipline was still insignificant compared with advertising. It was, by and large, a one-way function, devoted to generating output that, it was hoped, would get into print and on the air. And while the heads of major corporations were now deeply interested in their advertising, public relations usually impinged on the consciousness of CEOs only when they had speeches written for them.

What Is Happening: The Growth of Planning

The picture has changed in some very significant ways. Today, because of improved research, every stage of a public relations campaign can be planned and directed with a rigor never before possible. As a result, public relations has become a versatile power tool, capable of performing a number of jobs that are vital to the enterprise in the competitive environment of world business today.

Most PR organizations and consultants have integrated research into their major functions. It starts with the planning stage. I can remember the freewheeling days of PR, when the "planning stage" consisted of making sure you spelled the client's name right. Today we are set up to access on-line computer databases to find out about past coverage of an issue, product, or service in the press, including specialized magazines and trade journals; consumer surveys and public opinion polls; demographic, economic, and industry trends; wire service stories; house organs and newsletters. When the PR planners have thoroughly marinated in the background of the issue, they are better able to make sound decisions.

"Who are we talking to?" This is a perennial question for PR professionals. Today we are able to probe and segment our audience as never before to get information on customers, prospects, opinion leaders, constituency groups, shareholders, etc. This means a lot in shaping the message, and it makes public relations a powerful marketing tool.

Once public relations was a shotgun operation. You fired broadsides of releases, hoping some would get used. That was simple. It was also very wasteful. There is no point in edifying folks with your message if they cannot do anything for you. So now we undertake careful statistical analyses of attitudes, lifestyles, purchasing patterns, etc., to define our audience. For instance, a target audience profile for a maker of carpet fiber identified a high-potential group of carpet buyers among those who had recently moved from one type of home to another. This segmentation made it possible to focus on a prime group with less wastage.

Media planning has revolutionized advertising. It is now a key factor in transforming public relations. Computerized databases select print and broadcast vehicles that reach the target audience most efficiently. We have come a long way from the days when the idea was to try to get all the press you could.

Media planning can make as big a difference to the PR client as it does in advertising. For example, a *Fortune* 500 company wanted to run a corporation-image PR campaign directed to four very different business sectors. The traditional way would have been to target each segment separately and develop four different campaigns, with varying approaches. The client was ready to do this. But a media-planning analysis disclosed virtually no differences among certain media that reached executives in each of the four industries. A single PR campaign was created, and it did the job.

Even the time-honored PR practice of buttering up editors and program directors has been affected by the march of progress. These gatekeepers control the content and flow of information reaching the target audience. It is now possible to find out a great deal about the knowledge, preferences, biases, and perceptions of individual gatekeepers through systematic research. We still butter them up, but now we can do it more effectively.

When we have identified the target audience and the media most likely to reach it, we can then undertake a "baseline survey," which tells us how much the audience knows about the issue, what it thinks, how deeply it cares. Sometimes, the baseline survey discloses that a campaign should be greatly reduced in scope or is not necessary at all. Occasionally the baseline research becomes a tool for the PR campaign. The research turns into the message.

We test everything today. We test the concepts to be used in the campaign; we measure the tactics as they are being deployed; we assess the results at every step of the way. A PR campaign is not only more relevant to the actual need and situation, but is flexible enough to be adjusted as results come in.

When I started, the seat of your pants was often your road map. Public relations practitioners tended to place a lot of material in a particular newspaper, for example, because they were friendly with the editors of that newspaper. Advertising professionals sneered at public relations as press agentry compared to their own precise mechanisms. (Many still do not understand public relations, but they don't sneer at it anymore.) On the whole, public relations was considered a frill.

Public relations is emphatically no longer a frill.

Public Relations: A Two-Way Function

Modern public relations is also different from the older version in another fundamental way: old-style PR was primarily devoted to publicity. Now, to some, publicity is a four-letter word. ("Oh, he's just a publicist or a flack.") Publicity in itself is a useful and important function; it is now part of the larger function—modern-day Power Public Relations. These days the main job of public relations may be the shaping of the broader context within which the public in general—or, more likely, specific target publics—forms opinions and makes decisions. When used right, public relations is a two-way function, feeding back readings and predictions on public perception as well as executing plans to affect that perception. This makes public relations a useful tool in the setting of policy as well as the implementation of policy.

The measurement and influencing of opinion is as important to the small firms as it is to the big ones. Frequently, it's more important. Favorable image is as vital to the newly fledged manager as it is to the chairman of the board or the President of the United States. The only difference is scale. Take a look at the White House.

On August 28, 1991, in the wake of the stunning coup and countercoup in the Soviet Union, the Baltic nations were throwing off their chains. Country after country had recognized Latvia, Lithuania, and Estonia as the independent nations they had been before being taken over by the Soviets in World War II.

President Bush was delaying U.S. recognition of the Baltics, and the *Wall Street Journal* was lamenting that we were behind the curve:

> We wonder whether the problem here doesn't have more to do with public relations than policy. Faced with a public event of the grandest historical scale, no one currently in the White House inner circle can come up with the right words to surround it. And lacking the words, they end up not quite having a policy, or at least not one that anyone outside the White House can comprehend.

The *Wall Street Journal* had a suggestion: "What the White House needs is someone skilled in the *arcane but necessary art of putting the Bush presidency in sync with the public mood.*" The *Journal* went on to suggest that the administration enlist the services of Roger Ailes, the legendary political PR and media operative, as "President Bush's Personal Plenipotentiary for Major Historical Phenomena."

The *Journal* was writing with tongue partially tucked into cheek. But the point is an important and timely one. The emerging role of the new public relations professional is putting and keeping an organization "in sync with the public mood."

The ability to articulate policy is a determinant of policy. Public relations should be represented in the highest reaches of policy making for several reasons. One is to warn of disaster: "That just will not fly." Another is to help sell the policy by planning, right from the beginning, the engineering of perceptions about that policy.

And still another role is to put the policy into words. As most of us in advertising and public relations know, it is often the case that when you sit down to write about a policy, the policy's contradictions and confusions emerge. The discipline required by clear communication is a test of soundness. So, from the White House on down, the infusion of PR thinking into high-level deliberations is a healthy and useful advance.

Since public relations is now an intelligible discipline with a set of principles, effective PR can be applied in many situations and at many levels.

In 1998, an army of public relations specialists—or "spin doctors," as they were labeled by the media—declared "war" against President Clinton's opponents and were quite effective.

I would like to tell you some stories about contemporary public relations that illustrate these principles and to offer observations you will find useful.

Let's begin.

2

Integrated Marketing

PR Blends with Advertising

In the broad sense, you could say that just about every aspect of public relations relates to marketing. Today there is a more sharply defined category of public relations that involves the use of public relations to support the marketing of goods and services.

This category of public relations is defined and analyzed in Thomas L. Harris's book *The Marketer's Guide to Public Relations* (John Wiley & Sons, 1991). Harris calls this subspecialty "marketing public relations" (MPR). He explains its role this way:

> The growth of public relations and its acceptance as a valuable, sometimes essential, marketing practice is practically universal. Companies assign public relations staff specialists to their product marketing teams and engage public relations firms to help them get maximum mileage from product introductions, to keep brands prominent throughout the product life cycle, and to defend products at risk.

Harris has spotlighted a vital manifestation of the maturing of public relations. A few years ago, most corporate decision makers would have dismissed the idea that PR practitioners should be part of the marketing effort. Now there is widespread recognition of the importance of public relations. It is not just a generalized notion that good publicity can help sell products. It is the acceptance of public relations as a *necessary* part of the successful marketing mix and the identification of specific elements of the marketing mission that should be carried out by public relations—that, in fact, cannot be accomplished *without* public relations.

Marketing public relations is an idea whose time has come—but the reality is still in the process of arriving. A multitude of companies now acknowledge the power of the new public relations, but they are having trouble applying it. And a lot of public relations practitioners are finding that their confidence in the discipline is being confirmed—but these practitioners have not yet found ways to adapt their skills to the new situation.

Public relations has been admitted to the corporate family. But like many recent additions to a family, public relations has had trouble fitting in. There are jealousies and frictions. The most common form of the strain is the difficult question of relations between two entities: marketing and public relations.

Two scholarly observers of the discipline, Philip Kotler and William Mindak, wrote an article in the October 1978 *Journal of Marketing*, pointing to growing confusion between marketing and public relations. The first news—and it is bad news—is that the points made by Kotler and Mindak are still timely. The strains and confusions between the two areas have not gotten straightened out. If anything, they are worse.

How PR and Marketing Can Work Together

Kotler and Mindak discussed five possible ways in which marketing and public relations can relate.

Separate but Equal

Marketing and public relations may be treated as two separate disciplines. Marketing identifies customer needs and satisfies them at a profit. Public relations produces goodwill among various publics whose goodwill (or at least lack of bad will) is important to the organization.

So why the separation? Marketing practitioners dislike and misunderstand the PR practitioners and vice versa. Marketing sees public relations as press agentry and flackery. Public relations sees marketing as number crunching and hucksterism. Therefore, management keeps them apart from each other, gives each its own mission, and lets each fight for its share of corporate resources.

Separate and Unequal: Marketing Dominant

A second possible view is that public relations exists in its own right but is subordinate to marketing in every way. Marketing defines the objectives and devises the strategies. The main forces in executing these strategies are old-line functions like advertising and promotion. Public relations' role is to support and further the impact of these other techniques.

Separate and Unequal: Public Relations Dominant

An unequal setup in which public relations dominates is far less prevalent. It does, however, exist in some organizations that depend heavily on how they are viewed by all their publics, not just customers. Take, for example, the recent evolution of such institutions as art museums. A museum may have had an active public relations function for some time. More recently marketing has entered the picture, through retail, mail-order, and e-commerce. The marketing function may find itself tucked into the public relations function.

Equal but Overlapping

The two functions also may be maintained as separate entities, equal but overlapping. However, since they share common ground in such areas as publicity for new products and service operations, they are expected to draw on each other and cooperate with each other. Marketing calls in PR practitioners for advice on such matters as handling customer complaints. Public relations calls on marketing for such things as effective benefit stories that can be worked into releases, and for lists of important prospects who can be targeted for publicity.

Integrated

Finally, the two functions may be integrated, brought together under a senior executive with a title like vice president for marketing and public relations. Practitioners of the two disciplines share information, go to meetings together, and are expected to sing off the same page and harmonize to maximize profit.

The Substance Is More Important than the Form

Corporate organization charts are rarely one hundred percent logical. They have been formed over the years by a process of accretion. As new disciplines come along—like management information services—they get onto the chart, but there's often a lot of uncertainty and friction over where they belong and how high up they should be. Most important new functions (like pop songs) start low in the charts and work their way up. The same is true for old functions that acquire broader functions and greater importance. In many companies, the personnel department used to consist of an executive who was not a line manager anymore, plus a couple of employees dozing over dusty benefits files. Now, under the new banner of human resources, the function has gradually picked up more clout and authority.

However, the organization chart usually lags reality. When a function becomes more important, it may remain stuck in an inappropriate organizational slot for a long time.

The particular slotting of public relations in the organization is important, but it is less important than the actual role the discipline is allowed to play. Depending on the nature of the organization, public relations and marketing may be formally treated as equal but overlapping, integrated with marketing, or some other (and less likely) version of the Kotler/Mindak quintet of possibilities.

Wherever it is stuck on the chart, public relations must be allowed to do its job. One part of that job is to coordinate with the other functions involved in selling, so the organization can do the most complete selling job possible.

Breaking the Mind-Set

In talking about integration, let's first try to break out of the mind-set implied by using the labels "marketing" and "public relations." Public relations is a *discipline*. Marketing is a *task*, which is to be accomplished by a number of disciplines in cooperation—sales, sales promotion, merchandising, marketing research, advertising. And public relations.

Public relations is part of the marketing team when it is doing a marketing job. It happens that public relations does other things that are not directly connected with selling goods or services (although in a sense everything public relations does is more or less connected with selling). Unfortunately, the fact that public relations handles other assignments besides marketing seems to make public relations a perpetual outsider, the "man without a country" of the corporation. To use this discipline effectively, corporate executives must get used to the idea that it does not fit entirely within the marketing box, or the community relations box, or any other box on the traditional chart.

It is all right to make public relations part of marketing. It has to go somewhere. The important thing is to let the function do all the things it is capable of doing.

Publicity, Promotion, and Positioning

The most obvious use of public relations with a product is to publicize it. Stories in the trade press keep the industry informed about developments. Stories on the air and in the newspapers and magazines attempt to present the product or service in a favorable or intriguing light.

Publicity is particularly important in launching a new product. You are starting from zero, so the aim is to let the maximum number of potential buyers know about the new development in the shortest possible time. Publicity is highly desirable when there are changes in an existing product or service—modifications, new applications, broader markets.

When public relations is used to obtain publicity, it is, in a general way, supporting the brand, and its messages are created to tie in with advertising and other marketing messages. The media are in the driver's seat in deciding if and when stories will run. Line management does not always understand this. They tend to demand that the "placement" of stories be as predictable and plannable as the steps in an advertising campaign.

This sort of misunderstanding comes with the territory. Public relations professionals should waste no time wringing their hands over it. The mission is to do the job while gradually reducing the level of misunderstanding.

The larger problem with publicity is that too many organizations settle for it as the be-all and end-all of public relations. Publicity is still the central activity of public relations, but it is not always the most important activity. The discipline can be used in other effective ways to support a brand.

As I discuss elsewhere in this book, public relations can go beyond publicity into planned promotion—developing activities and events that bolster brand identification and image. This aspect of public relations is more controllable than the quest for editorial coverage. It can be integrated more smoothly with other marketing activities.

At yet a deeper level, though, public relations can be used in ways that have a major impact on future sales. When public relations is used as a positioning tool within the context of a long-range strategy, it can achieve remarkable results. This application of the discipline— unlike the more rudimentary task of sending out releases and seeking editorial coverage—requires a high level of understanding within the organization. Everybody involved needs to know what public relations is all about. Given a satisfactory level of PR literacy, it is possible to obtain close cooperation among marketing, advertising, and public relations executives, along with the right kind of support from top management.

Feeding a Fad

One of the most spectacular marketing successes in the 1980s was the Cabbage Patch Kids, those squishy-looking little creatures who swept the country. Richard Weiner, one of the most innovative and resourceful exponents of Power Public Relations, was a driving force behind the phenomenon. He says, "Of all the coups we ever achieved, the sweetest was the Cabbage Patch Kids. It was not anticipated by anybody, not even Coleco, the manufacturer. And the success of the Cabbage Patch Kids was achieved without advertising." In fact, when ads were introduced later in the campaign, they were canceled because there was no need for additional selling. As *PR News* reported in 1983, shoppers were engaging in disorderly fights to buy the Kids that were available in stores.

When these strange-looking dolls—lumpy, blank-faced, utterly unbeautiful—were first introduced, they were sold only on a "tailor-made" basis. Working with Xavier Roberts, who created the dolls, and the Coleco Industries marketing team, Weiner devised a plan. The plan was based on considerable research, including consultations with child psychologists, psychiatrists, pediatricians, educators, and others. One key point, as the *PR News* case study points out, was that "most children don't consider themselves beautiful, and that their parenting instinct is aroused more by the homely Kids than by glamorous dolls." Not that all dolls were made to look beautiful; the impish Kewpie doll had been a rage in the early part of the century, and Raggedy Ann was a longtime favorite.

What gave the Cabbage Patch campaign its distinction was the thorough and serious procedures through which the youngster "adopted" a Cabbage Patch Kid rather than just receiving it. Each Kid was accompanied by an "adoption form" (blue for boy dolls and pink for girls) indicating the doll's name. There was a space for adopting children to fill out their names and addresses, promise to take good care of the adoptee, and become members of the Cabbage Patch Kids Parents' Association. Coleco would follow up with a congratulatory note and, a year later, a birthday card to the adopted Kid.

The adoption feature was carefully studied before the campaign started. Was the idea a negative? Did children fear it? The advice of experts was that the idea of adoption, if handled right, was positive. A central element of the campaign was to make the Cabbage Patch experience valuable for the adopting children. Working with a child psychologist, Weiner prepared the Cabbage Patch Kids Parenting Guide, full of helpful guidance.

Weiner's efforts generated tremendous awareness among retailers and potential licensees for tie-in products. The program continued in this vein, driven by public relations aimed at the trade and the general public. At the height of the craze, Coleco was producing 200,000 dolls a week but could not keep up with the demand.

The big toy fads to come along in the 1990s were Tickle Me Elmo, Furby, and Beanie Babies. In December 1998, just before Christmas I saw $39 Furby dolls being sold for $200, and I watched a middle-aged woman—seemingly in her right mind—spend slightly over $2,500 for a half dozen Beanie Babies at a Beanie secondary market sale in a local mall.

With the exception of Beanie Babies, the toys copied the Cabbage Patch success. The producers started with the product, and then they planned, planned, and planned some more. Tickle Me Elmo and Furby launched traditionally, early in the year at the Toy Fair, and then their makers followed with massive PR programs. By Christmastime, they had already created a huge impact in the marketplace, with sales running high and unplanned shortages adding to the PR story. Christmastime riots were commonplace and fueled the PR fires.

Defying the Norms

Beanie Babies were a completely different story, one that rates among the great marketing successes of the last two decades of the twentieth century. And public relations had a part to play—but not the usual one. First, Beanie management—the Ty Company—planned shortages with both small and large runs. Then, sometimes very quickly without warning, Ty stopped manufacturing (or "retired") specially selected Beanie Babies, thus creating demand over short supply. With a great understanding of marketing communications, theirs was an outstanding independent strategy. Instead of choosing mass retailers typical of the toy industry, Ty chose smaller independent retailers such as greeting card stores.

In contrast to the strange, lumpy, and blank-faced Cabbage Patch dolls, Beanie Babies are cute and adorable, and they captured the hearts, minds, and pocketbooks of both young and old. Some might argue that the Beanie story is a much bigger one than Cabbage Patch, and it's an open debate how long the Beanie phenonomenon will last into the twenty-first century. How many of us—seasoned professionals or ambitious upstarts—would have believed only a few years ago that a collection of some 200 cute creatures would be valued at about $100,000 or more—though each retails for $5 to $7?

The majority of Beanie fanatics started buying and collecting in the late 1990s—and 75 percent are adults. The Beanie boom has been fed by more than 850 Web sites, selling and trading Beanies, and countless Beanie-themed magazines. The largest is *Mary Beth's Beanie World,* a slick 250-page monthly with a paid circulation in excess of one million.

Is this the PR planning and the work of Dick Weiner or a new Dick Weiner? Trained as an investigative reporter, I went looking for the story. I had an impossible time trying to crack the Beanie fortress, Ty's headquarters outside of Chicago, to learn how the phenomenon came about.

First off, the good folks at the secretive Ty Company delisted their telephone number. Even resellers have difficulty reaching the company. Then the person handling public relations never responded to a half dozen telephone calls and faxes. Wise or nutty policy? It's hard to fight it when Beanie collectors are buying $1,500 riders on their homeowners insurance policies or are logging on to a new Web site that will simultaneously search listings at several auction Web sites to find sales of Beanies you might want and then link you right to them. And the publicity keeps flowing, though owner Ty Warner doesn't do interviews.

Still, in March 1999, he paid $275 million to buy the Four Seasons, the tallest hotel in Manhattan.

The delisting of the Beanie telephone number reminds me of how a friend and I once started an upscale restaurant in the affluent Hamptons section of New York. Part of our PR planning was not to install any signage in front of the restaurant. Patrons calling for reservations were directed to the restaurant's nearest landmark. That declaration of independence led to an item in Liz Smith's popular gossip column, and it, along with good food, ensured our success.

There's a revolution under way in the toy industry, so PR planning must be considerable and precise. In the twenty-first century, with semiconductor companies like Intel designing toys, toys will behave more like humans and public relations practitioners should behave more like Power Public Relations practitioners. The Cabbage Patch and Beanie Baby successes underscore certain points. They show the importance of research in building successful campaigns. When your concept is solidly grounded, you can build flights of fancy on your foundation.

These experiences also show that, in the right situation, public relations can do more than advertising to create and sustain such triumphs.

When the Ads Become the News

Today, more and more, the idea of integrated marketing is being demonstrated by the use of advertising for public relations purposes—and indeed, the production of ads primarily as hooks on which to hang a publicity campaign.

Starting in 1984, with its commercials built around Michael Jackson and Lionel Richie, Pepsi-Cola became especially adroit at making its advertising campaigns a legitimate news story. Now handling a new ad campaign as news has become standard practice in many organizations.

This can be done when the ads feature celebrity endorsers: Edward Koch promoting a diet aid, Bob Dole for Viagra, and the scores of celebrities with milk moustaches. Writing in the *New York*

Times, Randall Rothenberg quotes Phil Dusenberry of BBDO on using advertising for public relations:

> When you get this kind of publicity, it's like someone coming along and handing you a whole pile of money you didn't have. It takes on more value because it's being mentioned in a non-advertising context. You're not thrown into that cluttered commercial pod. Your commercial is being voiced-over by the local announcer.

When I was at Richard Weiner, Inc., Pepsi-Cola hired us to promote its first three-minute television commercial with Lionel Richie. Rebecca Madeira, Pepsi's head of public relations, gave us our charge: Get more publicity than for the previous year's Michael Jackson commercial. Jackson's publicity, already huge, got even bigger when he accidentally set fire to his hair. Nevertheless, we were able to outdo the Michael Jackson coverage.

Big celebrities help, but there are other ways to give a public relations dimension to a new advertising campaign. One way is to use the advertising strategy to illustrate significant developments in lifestyle, tastes, or society. The PR team looking for a hook on which to hang a campaign built around the advertising should take a look at the research on which the advertising is based. Usually the research is simply treated as "working papers." Some research is guarded jealously, with its defenders repelling efforts to violate the confidentiality of the findings.

But, for example, if the research seems to point to some facts or trends that are interesting in themselves, then they may lend themselves to a public relations campaign that does three things:

1. Gets publicity for the product and the sponsor
2. Preconditions audiences to be more alert to the ads
3. Strengthens the credibility of the ads

In 1989, MasterCard—long identified with its "Master the Possibilities" slogan—launched its Master the Moment campaign. Porter Novelli was asked to promote the campaign, under my management. At the time, MasterCard was being squeezed downscale by competitors like American Express and Visa Gold. More and more, Master-Card was perceived as a "blue-collar" card.

Credit cards are part of everyday life. They are tied in with megaforces that affect everyone: the economy, demographics, lifestyles. Therefore, a new advertising campaign by a major credit card company could, possibly, be turned into news. We searched through the upcoming campaign, and the research that underpinned it, to find possible news hooks. We studied every legitimate possibility, including the landslide victory of George Bush.

The most likely target audience was a business audience, although we thought there might be certain aspects of the new campaign that could interest the public at large. But MasterCard was interested in the business audience, so we tried to identify reasons why the new campaign might be presented as important to business. Among them were the following:

- *New trend*—America's attitudinal shift toward "kinder, gentler" values is of keen interest to a wide variety of businesses.

- *MasterCard's authority*—MasterCard is positioned as a leader in what might be called "consumerology"—the science of spending. When MasterCard detects an important development, the business world listens.

- *High-stakes conflict*—Credit card competition is a high-profile struggle. When a major player makes a significant move, many people watch with interest and enjoy a hard-fought contest.

- *Broader sociological implications*—MasterCard's societal seismographs have signaled a shift that tells us something about where we are going as a country and a people.

- *Classic competitive strategy*—This campaign is a dramatic example of a competitor identifying a large opening and moving quickly and decisively to fill it.

- *Marketing ground rules*—Americans are redefining "prestige" in terms of personal mastery and achievement. Since prestige is a central factor in marketing in a broad range of industries, the development has interesting implications for marketers.

Applying these potentially newsworthy angles, we prepared a prototype release:

Mastercard Launches New Ad Campaign Keyed to "Kinder, Gentler America"

Spotting a neglected market in the affluent, responsible center of the consuming public, MasterCard has created a new Master the Moment campaign directed at the "kinder, gentler America" evoked by President Bush in his pivotal campaign speech. The campaign, in broadcast and print, will be unveiled on the March 29 Barbara Walters special preceding the Academy Awards.

The Master the Moment approach uses warm, unusual vignettes to emphasize MasterCard's distinctive prestige and features the vital role of MasterCard in family pleasure, personal growth, sharing, and the solving of problems.

Two fundamental assumptions provide the basis for the new campaign. MasterCard anticipates further escalation of the "gold wars"—the fierce competition for domination of the premium card market. And MasterCard, keenly sensitive to the consumer environment within which billions of buying decisions are made, perceives America as turning away from an intense concentration on self and status, and turning toward traditional values and the pleasures of caring and loving relationships.

"These two assumptions intersect to point the way to our new direction," says Peter Dimsey, president of MasterCard International. "In pushing further and further into the big-ticket, high-prestige quadrant, premium cards tend to become associated with hard-driving careerism and splashy but brittle values. The America we see is rediscovering the joys of family, friendship, and quiet pleasures. We Americans take pride in making every moment of life a success, big or small."

The Master the Moment theme positions MasterCard as the "enabler"—the "power for leisure" that simplifies and enhances life in many important aspects.

Is "prestige"—a pervasive theme in credit card marketing—no longer a persuasive appeal? "On the contrary," says Mr. Dimsey, "prestige is as important as ever. But America is forging a new working definition of prestige. It's not just something external, intended strictly to impress others. True prestige lies in the power to achieve big and small satisfactions by managing your life well. Personal worth is no longer simply asserted; it is demonstrated by the effortless achievement of pleasure, for you and for those who are close to you."

"MasterCard is spontaneity," says Joanne Black, a MasterCard marketing vice president. "Snapping up that great dress you see on sale. Treating friends to lunch without worrying about the check. Picking up a spur of the moment surprise for the kids."

MasterCard advertising sells "more steak with the sizzle." The steak is MasterCard's undisputed reach and power. The sizzle is using that reach and power to command everyday enjoyment. "That makes us feel good about ourselves," says Ms. Black. "That's what prestige means today."

MasterCard research shows that uncertainty and stress are growing factors in shaping the values and attitudes of American consumers. People worry about their jobs; about drugs; about AIDS. In response, consumers are reacting by gaining more control over their lives, asserting their individuality, and humanizing their environment. Simplicity, comfort, beauty, and personal relationships are becoming more important.

The Master the Moment campaign is designed to show that MasterCard works best in enhancing family pleasure, sharing, and personal growth.

The new advertising campaign underscores MasterCard's superiority as an enabler of pleasure by contrasting it with the competition. One typical commercial assures the viewer that, "You can count on MasterCard to help you master the moment in three times the number of places as American Express."

"When George Bush talked about a 'kinder, gentler America' and 'a thousand points of light,' he was not just campaigning," says Mr. Dimsey. "He was tapping in to a fundamental shift in the viewpoints and values of America. Viewpoints and values shape lifestyles, and lifestyles mold spending patterns. We are positioning MasterCard along the lines we see in the new pattern."

In this way, developments in advertising can be made into news. To apply this concept to your own objectives, analyze the research. Look for unusual angles. Focus on the most significant changes. Then handle the new campaign like an important product change, company reorganization, or other major development, with news and (if appropriate) video releases and, maybe, a news conference.

Converting Controversial Ads into Publicity

A recently developed and intriguing nexus between advertising and public relations is the PR exploitation of controversial ads.

Sometimes advertising makes people mad. Once, when this happened, the PR function would be called upon to smooth the ruffled feathers or at least to control the damage. Offending *anybody* was a cardinal sin in advertising. When it happened, the objective was to keep it out of the press.

Then somebody woke up to the possibilities of turning a liability into an asset by using the controversial ad's misfortune to generate stories. After that, it was perhaps logical to move on to the next step: deliberately creating offensive, startling, or controversial ads primarily for the purpose of mounting a PR campaign.

The brilliant Roger Ailes claims to have started the trend in 1984, when he was working for A. Mitch McConnell, Republican candidate for the U.S. Senate in Kentucky. (McConnell won the election.) Ailes's commercial showed hound dogs frantically seeking Walter Huddleston, the incumbent Democrat. The ad evoked cries of rage and pain. It was shown on the *Today* show and got publicity far and wide. And will anyone ever forget Ailes's Willie Horton commercials for George Bush?

There are other candidates for recognition as inventor of this ploy. According to Randall Rothenberg of the *New York Times,* some political pros give the credit to Arthur J. Finkelstein, a talented conservative Republican strategist who created a number of news-making ads in 1982. "Still others," reports Rothenberg, "say that Ronald H. Brown, the chairman of the Democratic Party, developed the strategy when he managed the California primary campaign for Senator Edward M. Kennedy in 1980 and flew around California hold-ing press conferences to unveil ads that he had no money to run."

It may have begun among political strategists, but the calculated crafting of too-hot-to-handle advertising for PR purposes has spread to certain areas of the private sector. Take the brouhaha over Drixo-ral, a cold medicine made by Schering–Plough. When Drixoral came out with a commercial using footage of Bush and Gorbachev without their permission, two networks refused to run it. Was this a disaster? Quite the contrary. It was all according to the plans dreamed up by Howard J. Rubenstein Associates, the public relations firm that helped to create the ads, and that went into gear immediately when ABC and CBS refused the ads. Almost instantly, dozens of network and local news shows were carrying the story, which included parts of the commercial. Schering had budgeted $100,000 to broadcast the commercial; the company received "millions and millions of dollars' worth of free time," reported a partner in Drixoral's advertising agency.

No Excuses jeans took the tactic further. No Excuses garnered tremendous amounts of attention by creating outrageous ads, espe-cially ads featuring notorious celebrities. Predictably, when they hired Marla Maples—at the height, or depths, of the flap over her rela-tionship with Donald Trump—two networks refused the commercial. This, of course, led to much publicity. The interesting point here is that No Excuses had not bought any network time in the first place. The whole point was to get the ads rejected. When this happened, numerous TV stations, including some that had rejected the ad, fea-tured the story. The New York daily *Newsday* ran a full-color picture of the ad on its front page. (Imagine what it would cost to buy a color ad on the front page, if the front page were for sale.)

When you run a controversial ad to attract attention, you have to be ready to handle the heat. In 1988, the Roy Rogers fast-food chain did a powerful commercial featuring grotesque ladies serving school cafeteria food. The ad worked, but there were complaints by the American School Food Service Association. Roy Rogers, which at that time just wanted a commercial with impact, pulled the ad. In 1990, with the exploitation of controversial commercials on the rise, Roy Rogers ran it again. A spokesperson said, "We're sorry if any group is offended by this. . . . It's a fun commercial that's done in good taste." Predictably, the cafeteria workers protested again—and Roy Rogers pulled the ad after five days. There was some publicity, but not all that much. Roy Rogers just came off looking indecisive.

In 1991, Mars, Inc., ran a commercial poking fun at private schools for girls. In this case, the PR exploitation of the controversial ad was carried on by the purported victim. The Coalition of Girls' Schools and the Coalition of Girls' Boarding Schools, according to the *Wall Street Journal*, instantly hired a public relations firm, which orchestrated the response with maximum favorable publicity for girls' schools. Mars quickly pulled the ads, muttering lamely that all the daughters of the Mars family graduated from private girls' schools. Mars expressed resentment of the ploy: "It is unfortunate that the coalition did not see fit to contact somebody in the company before utilizing the resources of a public relations counselor." It is barely possible that the company was also chagrined that it did not recognize and capitalize on the publicity possibilities of the imbroglio.

Stroh Brewery ran a headline-generating campaign in 1991—but seemed to be flabbergasted by the headlines it generated. Stroh's created the "Swedish Bikini Team" to sell Old Milwaukee beer. From the beginning, the sexism of the blonde bimbo ads drew fire. Then the Swedish Bikini models went off on a tangent—they appeared nude in a *Playboy* spread. Callers got the chance to dial 900 numbers and hear women use phony Swedish accents to talk sleaze. A spokesperson said the free publicity had been phenomenal but that there was a lot of "negative baggage."

As public relations and advertising blend into a new configuration, companies will be better able to anticipate the possible fallout from controversial campaigns and to modify or eliminate them if necessary.

During the days before the Senate hearing of Judge Clarence Thomas's nomination to the Supreme Court, a pro-Thomas conservative group produced a commercial that questioned the ethics of Democratic Senators Edward Kennedy of Massachusetts, Joseph Biden of Delaware, and Alan Cranston of California. The sponsors of the commercial said they had hoped to show what was in store for these senators and others if they engaged in what the conservative groups called "character assassination" of Judge Thomas during confirmation hearings.

Actually, the commercials were intended to stir up the publicity pot. Less than $40,000 of air time had been bought for the commercial, which cost around $15,000 to produce. But the value of the exposure achieved from the publicity ran in the millions. Every television network ran the commercial in prime time and throughout the day for many days. Every newspaper in the country covered the news of the commercial in depth. This included a three-column head, a lengthy article, and a photo on the front page of the *New York Times*.

The ploy of the deliberately controversial ad for PR purposes can work. The creator of the campaign has to be able to stand some heat. The ad should not offend truly powerful interests or pick on victims who naturally attract sympathy. Above all, the campaign had better be clever and good-natured. Editors and news directors are wise to the ploy and will not let themselves be used by clumsy efforts at exploitation.

Maybe the most significant thing about this phenomenon—which will never be useful beyond a very limited field—is that it is an offshoot of the growing recognition that advertising and public relations can work with great effectiveness when they are yoked together.

They Don't Like Ads? Use Public Relations!

When the Berlin Wall crumbled, marketers from all over the world exulted at the prospect of reaching millions of new consumers. To reach those consumers, they deployed the familiar armament of modern marketing. But it did not work the way they expected.

On October 4, 1991, the *Wall Street Journal* ran a story headed, "Eastern Europeans Deeply Distrust Western World's Ad Campaigns." The story said that East Germans were not buying: "They overwhelmingly mistrust advertising and are already fed up with Western product offers that have blanketed their part of the country since Germany's reunification."

These are consumers who have had forty years of antiadvertising conditioning. The *Journal* story quoted Marylin Silverman, executive vice president of the ad agency Backer Spielvogel Bates Worldwide, who said the East Germans had been hearing since childhood about "the evils of capitalism—and advertising is one of those evils."

Marketers who have big plans for the former Eastern Bloc nations have to stop and think carefully about the implications of this development. While there was no decisive indication of whether other Eastern Bloc countries would share this mistrust of advertising, it could be a reasonable bet that conventional advertising will not work as well in that part of the world as it does here.

Here is where Power Public Relations comes in. In Chapter 8, I show how public relations has been able to replace advertising and do the same job advertising does. This has happened in extreme cases like that of cigarettes, whose ads are banned from the airwaves. In a far greater number of cases, public relations is working alongside advertising but is making up a significantly larger percentage of the marketing mix.

What the *Wall Street Journal* story says is that the East Germans resist advertising simply because they perceive it as advertising. The quality of the ads does not matter because the target audience is not letting the message get over the threshold.

Public relations—through a variety of sophisticated means—sells without being labeled as paid advertising. And that can make all the difference. The fact is that there are considerable pockets of resistance in the United States and the Western world, where people mistrust and reject advertising.

Advertisers are responding in various ways. Near the end of 1991, various sources reported that big corporations were cutting back on advertising that focused on the image of the company itself rather than the merits of its products. General Electric, Philip Morris, and others were shying away from corporate campaigns. There was a growing feeling that advertising just can't do that much to influence the public perception of the firm.

Besides corporate advertising, audiences are manifesting higher resistance to ads in general. This leads advertisers to get more strident and outrageous. When a new gimmick comes along, advertisers everywhere use it until its impact is quickly neutered. The movie *Terminator 2* featured a new computer technique called morphing, in which one object metamorphoses into another. Soon commercials were morphing all sorts of things, turning cars into animals, juke boxes into rock singers, and so on. Advertisers complained that, with everybody using the idea, there was no more bang for the hefty bucks it cost.

Thinking up new gimmicks is not enough. The increasing ineffectiveness of advertising often is rooted in its very essence—*paid* promotional messages. The public is opting for reality. Reality-based television shows proliferate. People would rather see real cops in action than another fiction show about cops.

Here's where public relations comes in. Good PR slips over the threshold, wearing the cloak of utility. It is not labeled, "I am a paid ad to sell you something." It is reality-based. Some advertising people see this. On January 9, 1992, Stuart Elliott (in the *New York Times*'s "Media Business" column) reported on "The 15 Best Ideas for Improving Media and Marketing Effectiveness in 1992," a report put together by Myers Marketing and Research. The column noted that the recommendation that could possibly touch off the most debate was to place products in movies.

Getting products into movie scenes is an old public relations ploy that formerly involved under-the-table payments. Now there are established fee schedules. The compilers of the "15 Best Ideas" were surprised at how often movie placement was mentioned during their research. This is just another example of how messages are being morphed out of the conventional advertising form.

Advertising and Public Relations Should Be Partners, Not Rivals

The advertising profession has acknowledged the status of public relations in a number of ways. One of the most significant ways is by voting with their wallets. Many ad agencies are hiring PR firms to promote themselves. Typically, the *Wall Street Journal* quotes Sheldon Marks, vice chairman at AC&R, a Saatchi & Saatchi agency:

> We've never had top-of-mind awareness. We felt a public relations company might be able to concentrate on that fulltime. . . . The marketplace is very competitive and everybody is looking for the best way of positioning themselves.

However, as public relations becomes a recognized and increasingly important part of the marketing mix, some advertising practitioners feel threatened. They fear that their budgets will decline as those of the PR practitioners increase. That trend will continue until there is greater equity between the two.

The fears of some advertising professionals are fed by suggestions that public relations will totally replace advertising. This is a rash claim that may, on occasion, be made by PR practitioners just to bug their advertising counterparts. The fear of the ad battalions is fueled by stories like one that ran in the *Wall Street Journal* in August 1990, headed, "When Economy Slides, PR May Get a Boost." The story asks, "Does PR stand for Pending Recession?" It goes on to suggest that "in a softening economy, the public relations side of a marketing program gets more attention" because of its cost-effectiveness. "The PR business booms at times like this," says the head of an executive search firm that locates PR professionals. The story suggests that when times are tough, public relations is better than, say, taking out a full-page ad because "editorial mention is free."

The story appears to be based on a release from the executive recruiter, who is adroitly promoting his own business. But the points it makes are dubious ones, calculated to increase friction between the disciplines. "Editorial mention" is not free. Public relations costs money. Furthermore, if PR is so cost-effective when things are bad, why isn't it equally cost-effective when things are good?

Public relations cannot replace advertising, at least not usually. (Nor can advertising do the job of public relations.) There are exceptions caused by exceptional circumstances. In Chapter 8, I cover the extraordinary uses of public relations by the cigarette industry, which is banned from broadcast and much print advertising. In quite a different area, note the touching announcement by the Maritime Center in Norwalk, Connecticut. Strapped for funds in the early 1990s, the Maritime Center candidly announced that it was shifting its focus from paid advertising to public relations:

> Rather than paying for extensive ads on radio and television, we are using publicity, and publicity has a very high credibility and can be produced at lower cost.

For a public or semipublic facility truly short of money, such a move can work. Local newspapers and radio and TV stations will run the stories. But a profit-making organization had better not try it.

There will always be rivalry between advertising and PR. That is healthy—as long as it stops short of paranoia.

The Bumpy Road to Integration

Melding advertising and public relations is often a painful process, punctuated with shrieks of anguish and growls of enmity. The biggest problems, as you might expect, involve people and money.

Public relations and advertising forces should work closely with each other. This cooperation can and should be expedited by structural arrangements. When it is necessary, the two disciplines ought to be given the same information, brought in on projects at the same time, invited to the same meetings.

However, just getting public relations and advertising people to sit down with each other does not begin to solve the problem of bringing about fruitful interaction. The road to cooperation is often blocked by misunderstanding, mistrust, and rivalry. Two of the biggest obstacles are PR illiteracy and billing.

Public Relations Illiteracy

Everyone knows, more or less, what advertising is, but there is much ignorance and confusion about public relations, even among people who should be better informed. It is—unfortunately—not uncommon for an advertising agency account supervisor, meeting with the client and the PR agency, to demand that the PR agency "place" the publicity in precise coordination with the ad campaign and to expect that the PR material will parrot the key selling lines of the advertising. Worse, the client also is not up to speed on public relations, so the PR practitioners have a problem with the other two angles of the three-cornered meeting.

When this happens, the members of the public relations team are forced into a defensive posture. First, they are trying to conduct an instant adult education course on their discipline; second, they have to explain why they cannot do what the others expect them to do. This is not a comfortable position. It leaves the PR practitioners open to the suspicion that they are making excuses in advance for lack of performance.

Public relations literacy should be a job requirement for corporate executives and advertising professionals.

The Bugaboo of Billability

"Is it billable?" This question is—unfortunately—central to the public relations business, and it lies at the heart of some of the most serious difficulties between public relations and advertising or public relations and client.

The typical public relations agency charges on an hourly basis, in contrast with the advertising agency, which gets paid a percentage of billings (the amount paid for the advertising that is placed) or on a fee basis or through a combination of percentage of billings and fees. The advertising agency does not have to sit around worrying about how much to charge the client for a meeting or a lunch.

Hourly billing is one of the dirty little secrets of the PR industry. It is open to abuse and to suspicion of abuse. Worst of all, it can damage the ability of the public relations agency to do its best for the client.

Take the kind of meeting we have been talking about, at which people from the ad agency and the PR agency meet with client representatives to forge a productive blend of the disciplines. The concept of the meeting is fine. In actuality, the conference table at the meeting tends to be an uneven playing field because the advertising people carry more weight.

One reason for this is that the client is probably budgeting a lot more for advertising than for public relations. A second reason is that the client knows what advertising is all about but is still somewhat in the dark about public relations. A third reason is that the ad agency is apt to be able to send higher-ranking people to the meeting than the PR agency.

Here is the situation. The advertising agency is being paid through a percentage of billings, so it feels justified in sending its heavyweights to the meeting. If the meeting works out right, there will be more advertising and greater billings. Or the ad agency makes its money from a fee that is generous enough to justify the dispatch of senior people to the meeting.

However, when the meeting is scheduled, the public relations agency faces a dilemma. It could send a team headed by one of its highest ranking associates. However, he bills $250 an hour, and each member of the team also bills a substantial amount. The agency, in pitching for the client's business, has probably lowballed the amount necessary to do a super job. The logical thing would be to send a PR heavyweight, but then the client will scream about the bill, and there may be less money available to execute the campaign. Or, at the client's insistence, the PR agency will eat the cost. But that could lead to the road to ruin.

So the PR agency sends a couple of people whose time is billed at $125 per hour. This compromise assures the worst of all possible worlds. The PR professionals may be bright and competent people, but they are not top rank. They are outweighed by the ad agency's representatives, who can push them around with impunity. The client is not thrilled at saving money. The client is insulted. The worst abuse of hourly billing is not $250 per hour for a competent senior. It is $125 an hour for a learner or a hack.

Even if the public relations firm wants to send senior people to more important meetings, it is hard to do. The time available is finite. And, in the typical agency, the top-echelon executives may spend no more than 25 percent of their time in servicing clients. The rest is spent on pitching new business and administrative work. The ugly truth of it is that to have a chance of getting new business, the agency *must* involve senior officials; once the business has been secured, there is a constant temptation to service the account with lower-paid people.

Lower-paid does not necessarily mean lower-skilled. It is often quite the contrary. Clients can get a lot more out of young, ambitious people than the seasoned pros, who may be sitting around thinking about how to pitch the next potential account. But, face-to-face with advertising professionals who draw more water, the lower-level PR practitioners are at a disadvantage in asserting themselves.

The hourly billing practice exacerbates a situation that is bad to begin with. Public relations agencies should have the guts to insist on getting paid in a way that enables them to do a good job of client service. This means a fee arrangement, at least in part. And if the PR agency is reluctant to suggest the arrangement, the client ought to bring it up. Hourly billing may look like a bargain, but it leads to a bottom-line mentality.

When I was executive vice president of Richard Weiner, Inc., we billed all of our clients on a retainer fee basis. We worked hard for our clients. For the most part they were very pleased with our work. We were very pleased with our work. Dick Weiner, the sole owner of the agency, was pleased with our work and the year-end bottom line. If we did 15 percent of our gross billings on the bottom line, champagne corks popped, and fat bonuses were distributed to all.

After Weiner sold the agency to BBDO, it became a part of Omnicom, a holding company (BBDO, DDB Needham). Next, it merged with Porter Novelli. Porter Novelli had its start in Washington. There it served, for the most part, public affairs clients. It was acquired by the Needham Harper advertising agency, which, in turn, was acquired by BBDO and moved into Omnicom. The ad professionals woke up one day and discovered that they owned Porter Novelli and Richard Weiner, as well as a third PR agency, Doremus. They merged them all. Doremus, subsequently, went its own way under the Omnicom banner.

We were forced to switch to hourly billings. Pencil pushers and advertising professionals decreed that this was the best for bottom-line results. It was not the best, in my judgment, for clients. Our turnover increased substantially. We now had a big corporate overhead, and Omnicom demanded appropriate profits. If we did not make 25 percent of gross income or close to that—compared to the 15 percent we made with Weiner—heads would roll.

Only Philip Morris, a longtime client of mine, refused to go along with hourly billing. According to Tom Ricke, a Philip Morris vice president, they had been burned in the past. They were one of the few clients in the agency on a fee basis. They profited. So did we.

Hourly billing need not be a horror show. It can work—*if* the procedure is thoroughly discussed in advance, with all the tough questions brought up. ("Do you bill for lunch?") If the client docs not bring up these questions, the PR firm should. And any bill that might seem doubtful should be accompanied by an explanation. Moreover, there should be a reasonable procedure for talking over differences.

Ultimately, though, fee-based billing is the better answer. It is professional, and it is understandable.

3

Using Surveys as a Publicity Tool

Measuring Public Opinion

In the current era of pollsters and "instant" market research, conducting surveys about interesting and controversial topics has become more than a way to measure public opinion. It's become one of the most powerful communications tools available. Simply put, the media love data. We live in a *USA Today* world in which every issue can be unveiled in a snapshot. Tying a statistic to a story can make it come alive. Whether you are considering the fashionable or the substantive, the use of surveys in company, product, and cause-related publicity is a potent force for telling a story.

Organizations can use surveys to promote topical and product linkages, establish organizational credibility, and broadast general consumer feelings to target audiences. A survey can subtly promote a product's assets or the need for a particular service without ever naming a brand. If a survey of mothers says a telephone call is the best present they can get for Mother's Day, phone companies will want to get that information out. If cola is voted the most refreshing flavor of soda, the Coca-Cola Company will want to remind people of that.

Better still, surveys can be used to support very specific product messages that encourage consumer behavior. For example, in a survey that Ogilvy Public Relations conducted in 1997 for the Society of American Florists, the data uncovered that 60 percent of women prefer receiving roses to other flowers on Valentine's Day. Merely pointing to this preference for roses, as Ogilvy did for the society just a week before Valentine's Day, would help to keep not only roses, but all flowers, top-of-mind for gift givers.

Often a survey need only support its sponsor by tying the sponsor's name to the issue the survey clarifies. For example, in 1997, Alexander Communications conducted a Digital Citizen Survey that teamed its client Merrill Lynch with *Wired* magazine. The survey, which found that technologically connected Americans are more likely to be socially savvy than the commonly perceived "slackers" and "computer geeks," allowed Merrill Lynch to position itself as a firm that is well connected to the digital pulse and truly understands the on-line user.

Current research techniques make the gathering of data relatively easy. Overnight omnibus surveys allow companies to plug into consumers' minds and report their findings almost immediately. The options for how to conduct surveys are many and include mall intercept, random telephone sampling, preexisting panels of ready-to-order respondents or those organized by global research firms. Web surveys can also collect and analyze consensus opinions instantly and allow companies to focus on what self-selected, interested people may think about an issue, product, or concern.

Surveys as Legitimate Research

In a survey conducted for publicity purposes, it is critical that the data be truly valid. Ironically, although the media may often publish data that are suspect, PR and research professionals understand and expect that the samples used are representative and honest, and that the results accurately describe the entire population sampled.

For generating valid data, one requirement is a large enough sample. According to A. Turner Price, senior vice president for Research International, one of the world's leading research firms, an adequate sample to represent the general population of the United States is 800 to 1,000 people. Price says a sample of this size "will provide statistically significant data with a margin of error of plus-or-minus 3 percent. You do not need to have a more accurate sample than that for publicity purposes, and if you do reduce the number of people by half to 500, your margin of error only rises to plus-or-minus 4 percent."

As an alternative to straight statistics, qualitative surveys can be another excellent way to generate media interest. Informally polling a clearly defined, newsworthy target group (for example, 100 CEOs, members of Congress, mayors of small towns) can be more akin to developing qualitative focus group results than quantitative opinion data. Qualitative surveys provide an informed opinion, but they lack the statistical validity and definitive conclusions about a generally held opinion that could be used as evidence with the media for further product or policy positioning.

For Credibility, Align with Independents

If you come out with a research finding on behalf of your client that speaks favorably about the client's product, it is likely to look suspicious and self-serving. But if a recognized research organization is responsible for finding the same data, this lends third-party objectivity to the research and assures the media that even if it is self-serving, it is still fully credible. By aligning with the Gallups and Research Internationals of this world, public relations agencies and their clients can have the validity of a known brand to back up the data.

You can choose from many tactical formats for surveys, depending on your budget, need for speedy results, and the depth of information you expect to receive from your respondents. Research firms conduct weekly and nightly omnibus surveys that poll general population samples, usually by telephone or in mall intercepts, using an assortment of collected questions from firms seeking to measure public opinion about numerous specific topics. If you ask the right question, inserting your specific query into these regularly conducted surveys costs only a couple of thousand dollars and can yield you immediate, valid results. On the other hand, creating your own custom questionnaire and fielding an in-depth survey will likely yield a richer body of data and allow you to more substantially examine the issues that can be used to fuel and perpetuate marketing campaigns.

Beyond the credibility of the technical research being conducted, a survey can also serve as an occasion to form and promote advantageous bonds to related organizations. For example, going back to the Digital Citizen Survey conducted by Alexander (now part of Ogilvy Public Relations), Merrill Lynch was seeking to position itself as an expert in e-commerce and on-line financial services. Who better to align with than one of the arbiters of the new digital media, *Wired* magazine? This gave Merrill Lynch automatic cachet in the digital arena, as well as immediate access to the segment of consumers represented by *Wired*'s readers.

Ask the Right Questions

As with any research, the questionnaire instrument must be phrased with precision. When you are producing a survey whose results you want to use for publicity purposes, how you phrase the question is often more important than the topic itself.

A survey was the perfect method for Nestlé, producer of Toll House Morsels, to remind consumers how much they love chocolate chips. Already the market leader in chocolate chips for homemade cookies, Nestlé stood to benefit simply by reminding people about what makes a chocolate chip cookie taste good. The question Nestlé posed was simply, "How many chocolate chips should be in a perfect one-inch-wide chocolate chip cookie?" The answer cited most often, "twelve chips," is far more than any one-inch cookie could hold, but the data clearly suggested America's love of the chocolate chip, and encouraged bakers to use more.

Nestlé's PR agency maximized the value of this survey when it sent the data to local television stations. The agency suggested that one co-anchor ask the other how many chips he or she thought folks said belong in a one-inch cookie. That tactic not only got the survey mentioned but launched the TV anchors into a vivid discussion of the number of chips they would like to see and their personal love for chocolate chip cookies.

The style of question you ask can influence your results as well. Open-ended questions are more difficult to tabulate but can provide excellent sound bites. But although verbatim results occasionally give valuable and printable color commentary, they can also end up being an unwieldy volume of wide-ranging personal opinions that are more trouble than they are worth to interpret for a general audience. In contrast, ratings and ranking questions (e.g., "On a scale of 1 to 5 . . ." or "Rank the following from first to last . . .") are useful strategies that will generate good comparative data from which to make claims and give authoritative insights.

Another advantage of closed-ended questions with a set of responses to choose from is that you can focus the answers. You can force your audience to think about solutions to problems in the way that you want, so you know that people at least consider each possibility. For example, in 1998 Ogilvy Public Relations conducted an Information Resource Study that was designed to analyze media usage habits and behaviors. It included a question that asked people who use the Internet, "If you weren't using the Internet so much, where might that time be utilized?" Answer choices included "watching TV," "relaxation," and "talking on the telephone." In addition, because Ogilvy was more interested in using the data to demonstrate its own understanding of the media than to arrive at any particular finding, the survey question had a response choice that would provide an excellent media hook: "having intimate relations." Only 14 percent of respondents selected that choice, but even a small number showing that the Internet is replacing sex would raise the media's eyebrows. And it did.

Carefully think through the exact nature of the responses you seek. To be certain your questions can lead in the direction of the desired response, construct the questions backward from your hoped-for end point. Then pretest the survey by fielding it as a pilot among a limited sample group. If preliminary results go the wrong way or if the answers to questions will refute other points you are trying to make through the survey, then kill or change the problematic questions. Unsavory response data cannot be hidden if the integrity of the entire survey is to stand, so pretest it first. Research rules mandate that you must provide the full set of data if the media request it.

Publicity Survey Planning

As with any marketing communications campaign, the clearer the program goals at the outset, the more compelling the results and the conclusions that can be drawn from them. Use surveys to focus on needs, advantages, or unique distinctions, or to confirm the proven popularity of a product, service, preference, or need.

Know your communications objectives, including the messages you would like to convey, your strategies for conveying them, and the target audiences you want to reach. All of these insights will help you focus the research, survey the right populations, and design the questionnaire in a way that will elict the kind of response you seek.

Select and commit your resources according to your budget, time pressure, and the level of scrutiny you expect to undergo. All research must be sound and statistically valid.

Putting Your Survey in Context

Before you embark on a publicizable survey to take a target audience's current temperature, it's important to know what's already been said about a subject. More important still is to know how to exploit the opportunities of what has not quite been said around a subject. Old tried-and-true topics (e.g., preferences of payment methods in retail banking) can be given whole new life by building on the body of information already established on the subject. To do this, look for ways to refresh the topic and give it a new, unique relevance. For example, a 1998 study conducted for Europay/MasterCard explored anxiety that exchange rate hassles would accompany introduction of the euro as a European currency. The study was able to link alleviation of this anxiety to the use of credit cards.

A survey that successfully revived an issue that had become tired and overexposed was conducted on behalf of the nonsedating antihistamine Seldane. For years, Seldane had been promoting the fact that it was nonsedating, in contrast to over-the-counter antihistamines, which could cause drowsiness. To find data that would make the story come alive once again, researchers asked allergy sufferers to pinpoint the dangers of medication-induced sedation. A two-part question asked first, "Are you aware that the OTC medication you take now advises you not to drive when you use it?" The 49 percent of subjects who responded "yes" were then asked, "Have you driven a car anyway while taking your current antihistamine?" A whopping 61 percent said they had. The new data—that 61 percent of all OTC allergy medication users *admit* they have ignored package warnings and driven anyway—made the issue of the availability of nonsedating antihistamines come alive again in national media such as *Newsweek,* the *New York Times,* and *CBS Evening News.*

Conveying the Data

When providing information to the media, an organization should expect to answer all sorts of probing questions as they arise. And the organization should welcome such inquiries. Provide the research methodology, the questionnaire instrument, and the topline report of survey results to anyone who requests them. For the survey results to have impact, the organization must stand by them and defend their credibility. Offering interpretation of the data via quotes allows you to pull out the most critical points for your perspective and to make sure they are not overlooked.

You can aid in the pickup of results by supplementing a press release about the data with graphic interpretations of some of the most exciting findings. Distribute prepared, camera-ready illustrations of data highlights as charts and graphs. Identify the source of the information (i.e., you or your client) directly in the prepared illustrations, making it easy for publications to give you the credit in ink.

Measuring Results

Bob Seltzer can be counted among the true believers of using surveys for Power Public Relations. First as a top executive at Richard Weiner and Porter Novelli and now as president and chief executive officer of Ogilvy Public Relations Worldwide, Seltzer lists surveys as one of the major tools in the public relations mix.

"A good survey can lay the foundation for a replenishing supply of future publicity," says Seltzer. "It can become a benchmark against which results from the same survey in future years can be compared. This evergreen situation yields consistent publicity by using a platform that, by repeating it annually, builds on its own credibility. It also can serve to give the sponsoring organization associated with it a strong hold on future discussion regarding the topic. Surveys that generate publicity and credibility are ones that have fulfilled their promise."

So, if you haven't gotten your feet wet, maybe now is a good time to jump in the survey waters. And remember, surveys can be as short and simple as you want to make them. At Richard Weiner we conducted what we called a minisurvey of one question, only four words long. We asked *Fortune* 500 chief executive officers, "How tall are you?" The answers showed that the majority of CEOs are over six feet tall. The results, quoted by the Weiner client, made the front page of the *Wall Street Journal*.

4

PR as a Strategic Weapon

No Customers? No Partner? No Problem!

"Public relations is not for us."

That is what a lot of CEOs say. They have their reasons:

- Our markets are limited.

- We just sell to industry.

- All we make are widgets—publicity has nothing to do with it.

- That's not the way we do things in our business.

This is what a lot of CEOs still say, and a lot of them are wrong and getting wronger every day. Power Public Relations can handle a variety of heavy-duty jobs far beyond those that conventional wisdom assigns to the discipline. Corporate leaders who grasp this development are using public relations to achieve big results in ways that other company heads consider outlandish and, sometimes, absolutely crazy.

Take the case of Gordon M. Anderson, president and CEO of Santa Fe International. Santa Fe builds and contracts oil-drilling rigs. Based in Alhambra, California, the company has operations in South America, Asia, Africa, Europe, and the Middle East. In 1981 Santa Fe was bought by the Kuwait Petroleum Corporation, an arm of the Kuwaiti government.

Gordon Anderson is unusual in a number of ways. One of them is that he has spent his entire career with one company. Anderson joined Santa Fe part-time while he was a student at the University of

Southern California in 1951, and he rose steadily through the ranks until he reached the top.

The oil-drilling industry is not noted for fanciful innovation. Historically, drilling contractors and vendors do little to promote their products except through the tried-and-true channels: ads in trade journals, displays at trade shows, direct contact with prospects. In recent years, as the oil business struggled, even these activities were cut drastically, especially by companies in the hard-hit Southwest.

There would be no particular reason to think that Gordon Anderson, a lifelong, dyed-in-the-wool, oil-drilling man, would have anything but the most conventional approach to selling. But Anderson's mind was open to a world of new ideas, even the off-the-wall notion that public relations was more than just sending out releases.

Anderson's entry into major public relations—for the first time in his nearly forty years with Santa Fe—began at the Indy 500 over Memorial Day weekend in 1989. I was there, representing the Ganassi Racing Team.

Bruce Barnes, an auto-racing marketing consultant, said he had an account for me. According to Barnes, Gordon Anderson, his former college roommate, had ambitious plans for Santa Fe. He knew it would take more than business as usual to bring these plans to fruition. He sensed that there were important new dimensions to public relations, and that the discipline might just be a power tool to help him execute a bold strategy for Santa Fe.

We made a presentation to Anderson and his key staff. He liked what he heard, and we agreed on a two-year plan. Santa Fe was assigned to Jay DeBow & Partners, a wholly owned PR subsidiary of Porter Novelli. Jay DeBow is chairman of the agency; I was its president. A longtime client of DeBow's is Ashland Oil, giving us some experience in the oil industry.

Jay DeBow became an important strategic element in Santa Fe's plans. The next couple of years would be even more tumultuous than any of the principals had envisioned. During the Persian Gulf War, some of Santa Fe's employees were held prisoner by the Iraqis. Anderson and the Jay DeBow team found themselves discussing various options. The hostages were freed before any direct action was taken.

Meanwhile, Santa Fe was at the center of one of the most remarkable public relations campaigns ever conducted.

Ferocious Competition

The contracting of rigs for offshore oil exploration is a fiercely competitive business, with vast amounts of money riding on executive decisions. Every step is risky, so companies in the industry prepare for every step with extreme caution and maximum safeguards. They make detailed arrangements with suppliers. They enter necessary partnerships. And, above all, they have ironclad deals with their customers before building a drilling rig. Without that kind of assurance, the thinking in the industry goes, the risks are unjustifiable and the potential losses catastrophic.

Or at least that is the way it was up until the moment when Gordon Anderson took his momentous gamble. Anderson committed Santa Fe to building the world's largest jack-up rig *without having a potential customer lined up.*

There were great benefits to be reaped—if the gamble paid off. The rig would be state-of-the-art, containing considerable technological advances over anything ever built before. When complete, it could be sold to customers at a higher price. That is, it could be sold more profitably *if* the project were completed, *if* Santa Fe's suppliers were willing to participate and share the risk, and *if* there were indeed customers lined up to use the new rig when it was finished. The new rig had to attract enough favorable attention, long before its completion, to accomplish a pair of objectives:

- Persuade vendors to go along on a speculative and—to them—highly unorthodox venture
- Secure a contract before the rig was complete

Anderson was sure Santa Fe could build a great rig, better than anything ever done before. But quality was not enough. The *perception* of quality had to be established and maintained throughout the project. Before the rig was anywhere near complete, it had to be attractive enough to make hard-boiled, oil-business people be a part of it.

Gordon Anderson realized that this task required sophisticated public relations techniques—an approach that would be a new and daring departure in the oil business.

Taking a Tip from Auto Racing

We came up with an approach. We adapted our strategy from the auto-racing arena, in which Bruce Barnes and I had extensive experience.

The program was given a name: Team Galaxy. We called the huge rig Galaxy I. In auto racing, companies finance the cars and teams, and share in their success. The racing car is a kind of Christmas tree on which to hang the backers' promotions. Team Galaxy would bring together principal vendors, each sharing equally in financing the public relations project and receiving an equal opportunity to promote its products. "We wanted primarily to draw attention to the rig, and the quality technology that was going into its construction," says Kevin DeMarrais, DeBow vice president. "But one of the important side benefits was that the vendors really felt as if they were a part of the program, and as a result, they had a greater commitment to the project. We would visit vendor companies and find people wearing Team Galaxy baseball caps."

How many participants? Twelve was the optimum number—small enough to retain exclusivity and large enough to provide a sufficient budget (at $40,000 per vendor).

Participants could not just buy their way into the project. First, a number of vendors were selected on the basis of the quality of their equipment and services. Then, three key vendors were sounded out. They reacted positively, so participation was offered to others. In all, $480,000 was raised from the vendors to cover the two-year budget of the program.

Coming Up with a Strategy

The PR team planned strategy and tactics with two principal objectives:

1. Impress on potential oil company customers the significance of this dramatic project and its technological advantages
2. Act as a vehicle for vendors to publicize their latest and best products

The program would try to reach decision makers directly, through mailings and events, and indirectly, through oil trade media and business media. The common theme would be to position Santa Fe and the vendors as innovators on the cutting edge of technology, delivering the best and most productive equipment in the industry. Team Galaxy would be a kind of oil industry version of a moon landing, with Galaxy I as the spaceship.

The program was planned over a two-year timetable. It had three phases:

1. Sell the program to vendors
2. Get the program off to a successful, highly visible start
3. Keep Team Galaxy and Galaxy I top-of-the-mind with industry decision makers over the two years from start of construction to completion

We created a distinctive Team Galaxy logo. One use of the logo was on baseball caps given to vendors, workers in the plants, and the media, to emphasize the team concept. Key players got windbreakers with the logo.

Participants in racing-car teams are often promoting their products to a very wide audience. They want millions to see the logos of their motor oil, tires, beer, etc. on national television. The target audience for Team Galaxy was much smaller. True, extensive coverage by the general media would be a definite plus, but the PR group did not know how widespread the coverage would be.

So, to make sure of reaching the targeted public with maximum impact, Jay DeBow went to the *Oil Daily*, the industry's most important publication, offering the story on an exclusive basis. The story ran on page one. On the day the story appeared, a press conference was held in Houston, the center of the American oil industry, to announce the creation of Team Galaxy. The news conference was attended by representatives of other important industry media, including *Drilling Contractor, Offshore, Offshore Rig Newsletter, Offshore Data Services, Oil & Gas Journal, Ocean Industry,* and *Offshore Engineer,* along with general print and broadcast media. The *Houston Post* carried a front-page story in its business section, and AP and UPI moved the story on their national wires.

Beginning immediately after the launch, and continuing throughout the year, the PR cadre continued to generate coverage through direct contact with media. Newsletters were published and sent directly to decision makers, as well as being distributed to the media.

Filling the Dead Spots

When a public relations plan stretches over two years and focuses on a developing program, there is, inevitably, a dead period in the middle months. The initial surge is past; it is too early to announce definite results. To an extent, the PR group can try to generate feature coverage, but without news hooks, this is a lot of effort for not much payoff. Media people do not take kindly to pure puffery. So, during this period, Team Galaxy ran a limited advertising program to keep the name in front of the target public.

Two months after the launch of the program, the annual Offshore Technology Conference (OTC) was held. OTC draws more than 30,000 of the most influential people in the industry to Houston in May. Team Galaxy was prominent at the conference. Team banners were displayed, and promotional materials were distributed. An advertorial was placed in *Key,* a magazine distributed in Houston hotels and at the conference.

The Team Galaxy program had a budget of $480,000, all paid by the participating vendors over two years, with 64 percent assigned to media relations, 21 percent to newsletters (sent out quarterly), 12 percent to advertising, and 3 percent to conference activities.

The media relations program of regular mail, telephone, and personal contact worked. Visibility was maintained to such a degree that Team Galaxy became a familiar topic of discussion and speculation in the industry. At strategic points along the way, the campaign was given a boost. For example, *Ocean Industry* was given first usage of an artist's rendering of Galaxy I for the cover of its September annual rig-directory issue, which is kept by decision makers throughout the year. Within its area, the program was creating the kind of curious interest displayed on a broader scale over the unveiling of a new car model. A four-color advertisement was developed, with each of the Team Galaxy members featured, along with a quote from Santa Fe president Anderson, highlighting the technological advances incorporated in Galaxy I.

The media attention garnered by the program, as measured by clippings, was impressive. But, as the Jay DeBow group said in its evaluation summary, success must be more than mere attention:

> Publicity is great, but means little by itself. In implementing the Team Galaxy program, we never lost sight of our two goals:
>
> Secure a contract for Galaxy I before construction is completed, by impressing upon the potential oil industry customers the significance of this dramatic project
>
> Act as a vehicle for vendors to publicize their latest and best products to generate additional business

By these measures, the program was an unqualified success, as *Inside PR* reported in its March 1990 issue:

> Within two months of the launch and 15 months before the completion of the project, Santa Fe was already in negotiations for a contract expected to be at the highest rate for a jack-up rig in industry history. The vendors, meanwhile, have reported increased awareness of their products and several major orders, one for several million dollars.

Early in 1991, industry media proclaimed the successful culmination of the program, as Santa Fe closed on a long-term contract for Galaxy I. Industry reports, as in *Offshore Rig Newsletter* and *Gulf of Mexico Newsletter*, said the Galaxy I would generate over $90,000 per day. The going rate at that time for similar rigs was reported as $50,000 to $55,000 a day.

There were other benefits for the participants. Santa Fe was solidified as a power in the industry and a spearhead of technological advance. Vendors, apart from actual orders, received favorable attention and heightened visibility. *Inside PR* commented, "Several of the smaller participants gained instant recognition as major players in the industry."

Additionally, Jay DeBow said, "Vendors have reported increased awareness of their products, an improved team spirit on the workshop floor," and, across the board, there was the life and drive that come with taking part in a really important event.

The Keys to Success

A number of points can be made about this success story.

The "team" concept is useful and adaptable. Teamwork is an attractive idea. It conjures up pictures of athletic achievement and winning. People like to be part of a team. They like to wear the caps, the T-shirts, the jackets—the uniforms that proclaim them as team members.

Team involvement is a factor that can be exploited well by expert public relations. It is quickly grasped. It engages attention and, more important, it evokes participation. When you are a team member, you are an active doer, and you are proud of it. This is why Team Galaxy had a positive effect on internal morale as well as marketing success.

Media like the team idea. They do not have to explain it. It is fun. And it permits colorful coverage.

Public relations techniques developed for broadscale programs can be adapted for narrow-focus programs in different areas. The team concept was most familiar, as a PR device, in the auto-racing area. We are all familiar with the pictures—a car, with its hooded driver in the cockpit, surrounded by the team, with logos identifying team members. We took an oil rig instead of a racing car and built a campaign around it, using many of the fundamental approaches used in auto racing. It worked.

When appropriate, advertising can—and should—be used as an auxiliary to public relations. Traditionally, advertising takes the starring role in a campaign to introduce a product or implement a marketing effort. Until recent years, there has been good reason for that. Advertising, with tools like consumer attitude testing and market segmentation, was the well-developed, reliable workhorse, and public relations was the specialized implement, to be applied only in the restricted areas where it had already been applied.

Now it is different. Public relations has come of age. Today, it is legitimate to look objectively at advertising and public relations and to assign to each its proper role—even if that approach results in public relations taking center stage. Previously, a general mind-set simply would not permit advertising (or other marketing tools) to act in a supporting role for public relations. For one thing, the ad professionals would be insulted if it were suggested. Today, advertising professionals may well be found resenting the augmented importance of public relations, but there is no longer a rationale for making advertising the star automatically.

In this case, the program had to be PR-driven. Advertising was an effective tool for buttressing the PR effort and for filling in the blanks. The two disciplines should be considered equally in putting together a campaign.

Persuasion is what this effort is all about. When you come right down to it, campaigns are persuasion—getting people to think a certain way, changing their minds. A campaign—to market a product, win a proxy fight, get a law passed—will be most successful if it makes optimum use of the persuasion tools available. Power Public Relations adds a powerful persuasion tool, to be used where appropriate. This tool will come into wider use. And, more and more, it will be the predominant tool in the persuasion mix.

The Team Galaxy campaign tested public relations in a new and vital role in an industry where public relations had never been much of a factor in marketing equipment. It is a forerunner of things to come, in two ways. Public relations will find an important place in areas where it has been used little. And public relations will be used for a surprising variety of purposes, far beyond the ones conventionally regarded as the province of the publicity people.

5

Power Public Relations in the Making of a President

Get It Right and Write It Right

Here's a pop quiz to see if you are heading down the straight and narrow:

> Your client (or boss), the chief executive of a public company, tells you to release biographical information to the business media, but you are not sure it is true. What do you do?

(1) procrastinate

(2) be loyal and release the information; after all, the rent is due on the first of the month

(3) do some due diligence and then question your client

If you answered (2) as I once did, you might be heading for trouble. The correct answer is (3).

At one time, I unknowingly disseminated information about a client that not only duped the media, but was also accepted as gospel by the Department of State and Central Intelligence Agency.

Let me explain how I was taken in . . . and how a relatively unknown politician used public relations alone to get elected president of his country and to ultimately become one of the richest men on Planet Earth.

The Saga of Ferdinand Marcos

In the early 1960s, I was retained by a young Filipino senator named Ferdinand Marcos and his attractive wife, Imelda. He was very clear about my assignment: make him president of the Philippines, his wife the first lady.

I sat with the Marcoses for days in their modest home in a walled residential area of Manila, listening to fascinating tales of his heroism in World War II and a long list of other accomplishments. I didn't know it at the time, but the stories were all lies.

For seven days, I was taken in by the charming, ambitious couple. Imelda, a former beauty queen who claimed to have sung for General Douglas MacArthur during World War II, was a most gracious hostess. I bounced Ferdinand Junior, "Bong Bong," and daughter Imee on my knee, dined on roast pig and wine, and listened in awe to Ferdinand Marcos's tales of his wartime valor as a guerrilla officer alongside American soldiers; his capture and torture by the Japanese; and his commendations from General MacArthur—who, Marcos noted proudly, once said that Bataan would have fallen much sooner had it not been for Marcos's courage.

I heard the saga of how he had been convicted of murder while a student, refused a pardon, scored the top grade in his bar examination while out on bail, and then was acquitted by the Supreme Court after arguing his own appeal before the bench. Above all, I heard about his political ambitions.

The Marcoses became comfortable with me and soon were convinced of my skills in public relations and contacts with the media. Whatever little money they said they had, it would be used for the campaign. I would be compensated with at least two PR accounts.

The Good Housekeeping Seal Campaign

It would not be an easy job. Ferdinand Marcos was not exactly a household word outside of his own northern province of Ilocos Norte. The media had never counted him among future presidential hopefuls. The president at the time, Diosdado Macapagal, hoped to run again and was not in any serious trouble.

I knew the overall objective. I outlined my public relations objective and strategy and the tactics to accomplish it.

My strategy—I called it the Good Housekeeping Seal campaign—was to establish the Marcos image in the Philippines by executing most of the tactics in the United States. In those days, no country, no people, loved America and everything about America the way the Filipinos did. If you made it in America, you could make it anywhere, certainly in the Philippines.

Having heard Marcos's incredible—though, unknown to me, untrue—life story, I felt a biography was a must. I was not the only one, though; Marcos was ahead of me on that idea—almost. He told me that he had a Filipino writer and a publishing house ready to go on his biography. Bad idea, I told him. It didn't meet my Good Housekeeping Seal standards. I wanted an American author, and I wanted the book published in the United States by a top-drawer publishing house. It was agreed that the book would be top priority when I returned to the United States in a few days.

Back home I planned Marcos's first trip to the United States. He met with editorial boards at the *New York Times,* McGraw-Hill, and others. McGraw-Hill's director of public relations would later write, "It was a great pleasure, as well as an honor to have Senator Marcos and his party here last week." I arranged dozens of one-on-one interviews for Marcos with important media, including Tillman Durdin of the *New York Times,* Bill Jessup of *U.S. News & World Report,* Warren Young of *Life* magazine, syndicated Hearst columnist Phyllis Battelle, Sid Goldberg (husband of the famed Lucianne Goldberg of Clinton/Lewinsky fame), editor of the North American News Alliance, and many others.

We kept Imelda Marcos busy, too. She met with editorial groups at several women's magazines, had a photo session at *Mademoiselle,* and went to a Halloween party at the New York City Shelter for the Homeless, where she followed through on our idea to present the shelter with a fully stocked aquarium.

I also set up speaking engagements for Ferdinand Marcos. His most important speech was delivered at the Overseas Press Club of America, the nation's oldest and largest association of journalists engaged in international news. (Some twenty years later I became the club's president.) He addressed the all-girl student body of exclusive Finch College, which sat attentively throughout a ninety-minute talk.

The trip to the United States was a great success. Daily front-page articles, many with banner headlines, ran in newspapers throughout the Philippines for days, covering every personal appearance of the couple. The relatively unknown Marcos was treated back home like a chief of state traveling abroad.

The Biography

Meanwhile, after a lengthy search, I found the writer I wanted for the Marcos book. He was Hartzell Spence, a bestselling author, highly respected and a longtime editor of the armed forces newspaper *Stars & Stripes,* who was widely admired in the Pentagon. He loved the Marcos story and accepted the assignment to write the biography for $15,000.

Next I needed a prestigious publishing house. After meeting with many publishing companies, I settled on McGraw-Hill. They had been impressed with Marcos during his earlier editorial board visit. They agreed to publish the Spence book on Marcos for our commitment to the purchase of 10,000 books at $2 each.

Marcos agreed to the terms and conditions I had arranged with both the author and publisher. He wired money to Hartzell Spence at his Old Lyme, Connecticut, home and signed the McGraw-Hill contract.

Meanwhile, back in the Philippines and aided by all the publicity from his New York trip, Ferdinand Marcos went into battle for the Senate presidency against the incumbent president's handpicked candidate. Marcos pulled off his first political coup and was somehow elected president of the Senate. The strategy was working.

Soon the battle for the presidency would get under way. Marcos's rival for his party's nomination was Vice President Emanuel Palaez. Marcos won the nomination on the second ballot at the party's nominating convention.

(Ten years later while serving as chief of staff to U.S. Senator James L. Buckley, I was on a Vietnam War fact-finding trip in Southeast Asia with Senator Buckley. Our first stop was in the Philippines. We met with Vice President Palaez, who once did legal work for Buckley's family oil business in the Philippines. Palaez told Senator Buckley, "If Len Saffir can do for you what he did for Ferdinand Marcos, you'll be President of the United States."

Halfway into the presidential campaign, McGraw-Hill published the Spence biography of Marcos, *For Every Tear a Victory*. Marcos quickly saw to it that copies in English and the native Tagalog language were distributed throughout the Philippine Islands. One of Marcos's chief political operatives made a movie from the book. Thousands of copies of the book were distributed to the American media, members of Congress, the White House, Department of State, and CIA.

Veteran journalist Sterling Seagrave, in a 1988 book on Marcos for Harper & Row, aptly summarizes the impact of the Spence biography:

> Naturally [because of the book] Ferdinand was taken to be America's anointed one. Hartzell Spence was an old Pentagon hand and it was only natural for the word to get around Manila, that the C.I.A.—having given up on the candidacy of Emmanuel Palaez—was doing everything it could to boost Marcos.

Spence, the various branches of the American government, and I did not learn of the many falsehoods in the book until many years later. A former Filipino senator who became a foreign minister in a subsequent administration, Raul Manglapus called *For Every Tear a Victory* "the infamous book written in an attempt to disguise with false hyperbole the fake character of Marcos's political career."

The presidential campaign meanwhile had quickly turned into a one-issue campaign. The issue was, of course, the book. President

Macapagal charged that Marcos had paid huge sums of money to Spence to write the book in a scheme organized by an American PR agent. Marcos, however, maintained steadfastly that he had nothing to do with the book. He told the U.S. Embassy that he "wished he had the opportunity to look at the text before it had been published because he would have made a number of changes," and insisted that he had nothing to do with me or the book. Nevertheless, writes author Sterling Seagrave, the book had a powerful impact:

> It was Spence more than anyone else who gave the heroic Marcos legend a ring of validity, when his biography *For Every Tear a Victory* was published. . . . Soon the most respected journals in America were repeating the gospel according to Spence, quoting long passages or summarizing his assertions as if they were palpable facts. After that, who was to challenge the authenticity of the Marcos legend?

A Last-Ditch Effort

President Macapagal worried he would lose the election because of the book. He put his own PR forces to work, fast. He commissioned renowned American author Quentin Reynolds to write the Macapagal biography. However, Reynolds died of mysterious circumstances en route to Manila. The book, called *Macapagal the Incorruptible,* was eventually written by someone else . . . but not in time to have the impact that the Spence biography did.

Marcos, meanwhile, decided it was best not to communicate with me. That included not coming through with any PR accounts, paying me anything for my services, or even reimbursing me for my out-of-pocket expenses. Then, one evening near the end of the campaign, I received a telephone call at my Manhattan apartment. The caller announced that he had just arrived from Manila and asked if I would have breakfast with him the next morning. Finally, I would get compensated for my work, I believed.

At breakfast in the Waldorf Astoria, I learned after ten minutes of opening small talk that my host and his companion were, in fact, not working for Marcos, but for President Macapagal. They told me they knew of my work for Marcos from an acquaintance I had enlisted to try to assist me in getting paid. They offered me $25,000 for copies of my correspondence with Marcos that they knew existed. In those days, that kind of money exceeded my annual earnings. I told them I had no use for Marcos but, because of ethics, the letters were not for sale. By telephone that evening, I was told they understood what I meant by ethics and, accordingly, they raised their offer to $50,000. I declined their second offer of payment and a second breakfast.

The Aftermath

Ferdinand Marcos won the 1965 presidential campaign by 670,000 votes. Marcos had been born, of course, in the Philippines but was definitely "made in the U.S.A." Imelda and Ferdinand entered Malacanang Palace on December 30, 1965—and didn't leave for twenty years.

I saw them again once during my trip to the Far East with Senator Buckley during Marcos's second, and supposedly last, term of office. Shortly thereafter, however, he placed the entire country under martial law, citing the communist menace and remained in office another fourteen years until he was overthrown. He died in exile in Hawaii in 1989, leaving Swiss bank accounts that the Philippine government declared were in excess of $15 billion. Others said he had accumulated even more.

As for Imelda Marcos, since returning from exile in 1991, she ran for the House of Representatives and won, ran for the presidency and lost, was convicted of graft by a Philippine court, and was acquitted on appeal by the Supreme Court. In December 1998, after insisting for years that she and her husband had never stolen a penny and had no money, Marcos announced that she planned to file a lawsuit to recover more than $12 billion in assets that she claimed belonged to her husband.

I have a souvenir of the whole affair: a copy of *For Every Tear a Victory*. It is signed by Hartzell Spence with the notation, "To Lennie, who also suffered."

Remember the little pop quiz at the beginning of this chapter. What if your client asks you to release information to the media, but it may not be true? The correct answer: Check your facts! And then check them again!

6

The Power of Internet Public Relations

Faster than a Speeding Bullet

The Internet age has arrived in a big way. You'd better get with it or get out of PR!

There are some 50 million people—probably growing to 100 million people by 2003—on the Internet, and with a few keystrokes you can send information to millions of them in an instant.

The Internet showed its power as a medium for news in the new age during the Clinton-Lewinsky saga when the House Judiciary Committee released the Starr Report and the president's video testimony. Wired computer users from every country on the planet had immediate access to text and video over their own PCs.

The cost for distribution by the House was zero. The cost for postage was zero. The time it took for worldwide distribution was less than it takes most PR practitioners to have lunch. That's public relations Internet style. Pop quiz: How much would it cost to mail press releases to the top 500 newspapers, 1,000 television stations, and 6,500 radio stations in the United States?

These applications of the Internet force us to gather and distribute news throughout a twenty-four-hour news cycle.

When I worked for the INS wire service in Asia, my competition was the Associated Press and United Press (now UPI after its takeover of INS). We competed ferociously around the clock principally to be first to reach radio stations that had twenty-four-hour newscasts. "Get it first, but first get it right and write it right," was our motto.

One day I was on assignment for a few days in South Korea. The war was over, but the ravaged country was still on high alert. Sleeping in a cold barracks, I woke up at 2 A.M. and took my portable typewriter to a warm area by a potbellied stove to write a letter to my mom. The clacking of keys woke up no less than three correspondents, who literally surrounded me to find out what big story I was working on at that hour.

Now today, look what a Matt Drudge, working out of his Hollywood apartment, can do. Maverick Drudge's first mention of the Clinton-Lewinsky affair drew millions of visitors to his on-line Drudge Report and made him a media power overnight.

Old journalistic rules don't apply anymore, and as such, old public relations rules must be amended—now. Andrea Cunningham of Cunningham Communications Inc., a leader in Internet public relations, says it well:

> Doing the new public relations is like serving as a physical-fitness trainer for companies that want to shape up the right way. We get in there and help companies with their exercise routines, their diets, their habits—all the stuff that will make them a better company. That's a huge change from what public relations used to be: "Here, just wear a dark pin-striped suit, and you'll be fine."

Benefits of Internet Publicity

The Internet is the most amazing communications tool ever invented. Steve O'Keefe, author, syndicated columnist, and the founder of Internet Publicity Services, says that thanks to the Internet we no longer have to pay to deliver information—only to create it.

Say you're the head marketing honcho working on the launch of a new e-commerce Web site. Budgets are tight. You're given $200,000 to tell the world about your company. Your boss wants to be as big as amazon.com. Where do your dollars go? Mine would go to public relations, promotions like advertising specialties, and perhaps billboards, all good for publicity purposes.

Says Larry Chase, one of the first marketers to establish a presence on the Internet for AT&T, "Public relations looms much larger in the communication mix of technology companies because, quite simply, it works better than advertising." Chase bases his opinion on the fundamental principle that high-tech PR practitioners have commercial information that people want to know about—information that can't be given in ads.

In your $200,000-budget e-commerce launch, it will be impossible to advertise all the facts about your new Web business. But if you use PR tools, you will get picked up, and most media will even include your URL, or Web address.

Customize Each Release?

The biggest mistake in on-line PR, according to Chase, is relying on "bot PR." *Bot* is short for *robot*, and it's the industry term for automated PR—sending the same e-mail to thousands of names. PR practitioners are supposed to do public *relations*; they are supposed to establish relationships with people. When you blast the same e-mail to 1,000 people, you're not exactly engaging them in a relationship.

It's hard to customize 1,000 releases, but if you want results, customization for some of the key media will pay off. Let's say you want to get Larry Chase to mention your company in one of his columns. Rather than sending him a long e-mail release with an even longer attachment, you'd be better off to send an e-mail saying, "Larry, I enjoyed your *Online Marketing Digest* column about Celebrity Stores.com. I need to send you information on a new e-commerce company. What's the most convenient way to do that? Fax, e-mail, or snail mail?"

Power Distribution: Putting the Power of E-Mail to Work for You

With Internet PR, you must be doubly careful of your facts; a mistake may be distributed worldwide.

If you've got an e-mail account, you've probably gotten plenty of messages that begin with something like "Hey, don't know if you've seen this yet, but I thought you'd get a kick out of it." Some days your In box may fill up with 20 or 30 copies of the same get-rich-quick scheme, rumor, urban legend, or laundry list of jokes, all forwarded to you from friends and colleagues.

Plenty of e-mails get forwarded around the Net, but relatively few become so widely distributed that they virtually blanket the entire community of e-mail users. Remember the Kurt Vonnegut "commencement speech" that was really from a newspaper column by Mary Schmich of the *Chicago Tribune*? The false rumor about the Microsoft-sponsored free trip to Disneyland? The endless warnings about viruses? (Jon Zilber and John Hlinko, of AlexanderOgilvy, a PR firm specializing in the Internet and technology, are experts in the electronic distribution of PR-developed news. They say warnings about viruses seem to spread much faster that the viruses themselves.)

What is it that propels certain e-mail messages to become "power-distributed"? Is it possible to harness this Power Distribution as part of your PR program?

Hlinko and Zilber tell us that power-distributed e-mail is different from e-mail spam. Spammers send out e-mail directly to an enormous mass-mailing list. Of course, most of these recipients have learned to simply delete the message and hate the recipient. It's not a good strategy for making friends or gaining influence.

When you're sending e-mail, you're not just targeting a recipient, you're targeting a potential redistributor. Your message should be crafted not just to sway the recipient, but to make him or her want to pass it on to friends, family, and anyone else.

What qualities promote Power Distribution? AlexanderOgilvy analyzed ten classic power-distributed e-mail messages, looking for the common threads. The researchers found that the trustworthiness of the source—who sent it—was essential, and humor and a sense of community were helpful. Another common theme among many of the e-mails was an appeal to the recipient's ego, giving him or her a chance to demonstrate either cleverness or righteous indignation by redistributing the e-mail.

Existing Without the Web

In January 1978, I started a daily newspaper called *The Trib* in New York City to compete against the *New York Times, Daily News,* and *New York Post.* There was no World Wide Web or Internet available to get the word out. It's hard to think today how we were able to manage years ago or how we would have fared if the Internet had been around, along with today's twenty-four-hour news cycle.

Because we had a limited advertising budget, most of the *Trib*'s resources went into public relations. We retained two PR agencies for the work. Our few advertising dollars went to limited television, bus advertising, and billboards. We practiced all the Power Public Relations principles described in this book to alert the public to the first new newspaper in New York in decades. And we were highly successful, landing multiple front-page articles in Washington, D.C., Los Angeles, Detroit, and throughout the country—but not in New York.

Something went wrong in the Big Apple on the way to our scheduled January launch: We had the worst winter weather in twenty years. Daily subzero temperatures and raging blizzard upon blizzard for weeks on end kept people off the streets, except for their absolute commuting time. And if they had to walk to a subway stop, it was with head turned down. Bus activity was virtually nil, and newsstand sales even for the venerable *New York Times* were basically nonexistent. You can imagine how sales were for the fledgling *Trib.*

Fast-forward to today. With the World Wide Web, we would have told our story direct to our Internet audience and even published the whole newspaper on the Web. Given the Internet, by winter's end, we would have been a household word in time to stock the newsstands with hard copies of our new tabloid newspaper.

7

Promotional Philanthropy

Cause-Related PR

Bolstered by research and fueled by self-confidence, PR practitioners are promoting their clients in ways undreamed of a few years ago. Some of the new, less inhibited approaches are having a significant effect on society as well as business. Take, for instance, the practice of allying the enterprise with a "worthy cause."

Cause-related public relations is becoming a major element of the business. Companies are tying the promotion of their goods and services to the promotion of causes of all kinds. This development is good for business and good for the causes. Public funding has been severely curtailed. Private fund-raising has gotten tougher as more causes battle for fewer dollars. So when corporations harness their PR power to a worthy enterprise, both parties benefit.

When George Bush, in a celebrated utterance, called for a "thousand points of light," some applauded him for suggesting that the government should get out of the charity business once and for all, and that supposedly worthwhile causes support themselves in the proper way by appealing for charitable donations. Others lamented that Bush was dooming many deserving institutions to the dog-eat-dog ferocity of the marketplace, where hearts are cold and true giving is just a pittance compared to what is needed.

There are not necessarily more worthy causes in America now than there ever were before, but we certainly know about more than we ever did before. Poverty, drugs, disease—we face so many pressing problems, all begging for funding. And what about education? Scientific research? The arts?

Public Relations to the Rescue

The future of philanthropic giving in America is going to be ever more closely tied up with PR strategies. Public relations, in its enhanced role, is serving as a giant lens, focusing the thousand points of light into a beam directed at a variety of philanthropic targets.

Should corporations contribute massively to charity? This has been a subject of debate among management philosophers. Peter Drucker has been cited as saying that giving money to charities or community causes is out of bounds, that the objectives of the corporation are profit and survival. This is not exactly what Drucker says, though. He maintains that managers of businesses must not damage the company's profit and survival chances by giving money away, but he also says, "Management has a self-interest in a healthy society, even though the cause of society's sickness is none of management's making." Milton Friedman takes a more rigidly anti-corporate-philanthropy position, declaring that a business is an economic institution and, as such, must eschew all social responsibility.

Businesses have voted with their bucks on the issue of corporate giving. Corporations contribute billions for all kinds of causes. That they do not do this out of pure altruism is not exactly news. Companies expect to receive benefits right away for what they give. They want to be well thought of in their communities, well regarded by government bodies, and liked by the public at large—not just for the satisfaction of it, but to sell more products and services, make more money, carry out plans without government or community hindrance, and, in general, neutralize the various outside forces (consumer associations and the like) that can make trouble for them.

The philanthropic activities of a lot of companies are a mishmash. Companies make large contributions to "safe" recipients such as universities, especially those attended by the company's high officers; big-name and relatively uncontroversial charities like the Red Cross; high-profile symphony orchestras and ballet companies; and so on. Other companies tend to give defensively, pouring money into areas in which they feel themselves most vulnerable to criticism (and feeling bewildered and hurt when the charity fails to cease the criticism).

The new PR function is giving corporate philanthropy a new look. Public relations people want to get the maximum benefits in favorable perception for every corporate dollar doled out. The expertise of the new PR exponents at doing this has had some surprising and beneficial results.

One result has been a marked increase in corporate willingness to get involved with "unpopular" causes. Once, fearing contamination by association, big-company givers shunned unpopular causes like the plague. They did not know how much of the unpopularity would rub off on the organization, or how much danger there was in the connection, so they went the safe route and confined their philanthropy to the tried-and-true channels where everyone else was giving. There was not much benefit in it, but there was not much potential harm either. The worst that happened was that the money was wasted.

Causes That Are Too Hot to Handle

Companies used to be very careful about becoming linked with causes. Nothing controversial was permitted. Also, depressing or downbeat themes were taboo. Do not permit the corporate name to be associated with anything ugly enough to conjure up bad thoughts. It was all right to be in favor of motherhood or against the man-eating shark, but it was deemed risky to become any more adventurous than that.

Now, however, corporations are getting behind a wider variety of causes. Some of these causes involve crusades in areas that used to cause marketers to avert their eyes. Take the subject of battered women and battered children. Domestic violence has been one of America's shameful secrets, kept in the closet for a long time. The images conjured up by social violence were considered too unhappy and disturbing to associate with a product or company.

In 1987, Johnson & Johnson (J&J) broke the taboo. Working with the National Coalition Against Domestic Violence (NCADV), J&J offered donations to domestic-violence shelters as a way of promoting purchase of such products as Stayfree sanitary napkins and Medipren pain and headache remedy. The project, known as Shelter Aid, was the creation of a number of J&J companies working with the PR agency of Burson-Marsteller.

J&J's association with the cause of battered women and children is one of the most striking examples to date of cause-related promotion. We have seen others, and we will see more. For instance, Tang, a General Foods powdered beverage since 1959, needed help in reviving a fading image and declining sales. In the mid-1980s the Tang March Across America for Mothers Against Drunk Driving (MADD) campaign was created.

The strategy was to set up a major focus for publicity and advertising, using an event specifically directed at the target market for Tang: mothers. Working with General Foods and Young & Rubicam, the ad agency, the Weiner PR professionals made an arrangement with MADD. The big event would be a 4,200-mile march across the country, taking 115 days, and ending in Washington, D.C., in December 1986. It was no coincidence that the route passed through fifteen of the country's top forty retail markets. Coordination of the march was entrusted to the Walkers Club of America. A massive coupon drop was scheduled in the middle of the march, allowing a ten-cent donation to MADD for each coupon redeemed. A large and intricate program of merchandising and publicity was set up to get maximum benefit from the effort.

The Tang march worked very well. Major magazines like *Newsweek* and *Forbes* featured the event. Daily and Sunday papers across the United States ran stories, including around fifty front-page stories. *Good Morning America* and the *Today* show both aired two segments. Local television covered the march copiously, often as the lead story. Mayor Ed Koch and Governor Mario Cuomo, both of New York, announced the program. Mayor Tom Bradley, wearing a "Tang-MADD" T-shirt, kicked off the march in Los Angeles. MADD enjoyed a strong boost in awareness and increase in membership. Tang enjoyed a 12 percent increase in sales during the march period, which the company attributes totally to the event. And Tang, praised by the media and public officials for its concern, got a substantial rejuvenation of its image.

Companies that espouse causes cannot afford to ignore the potential for controversy, however. They should check out all the ways in which the cause might become controversial and should be ready to stick with the cause when controversy springs up. In 1991, Sears ran a pro-animal campaign. For every stuffed animal sold, a contribution went to such causes as the Humane Society. This might have seemed like a blameless area, but there was no such luck. The National Rifle Association assailed Sears for supporting groups with a "radical agenda." Sears dropped the campaign, thus managing to look bad to everybody.

The Cause of the Moment Can Backfire

Now and then a cause of the moment sets in motion a bandwagon upon which everyone tries to jump. The Persian Gulf War was, of course, a stupendously popular cause. American troops in the sands of the Middle East found themselves the recipients of much PR-generated largesse. Even *Business Week* (September 24, 1991) reported on the trek of refrigerated trucks to base camps near the Kuwaiti border, where ice-cold Coke was distributed to thirsty GIs, with film crews on hand to capture the moment, and Coca-Cola's PR representatives getting the pictures to major media outlets.

Since desert heat makes people thirsty, beverages were big in Desert Shield and Desert Storm. Evian Waters of France managed to get network television to show soldiers enjoying the product. Artesia Waters of San Antonio sought help from Texas Senator Phil Gramm in shipping the product to the desert. Anheuser-Busch donated 22,000 cases of beer (nonalcoholic). And so on.

It is a natural impulse. Public relations practitioners want to hook up with huge, popular events. Even more to the point, they do not want to see their rivals get valuable coverage through such an association while they themselves are left out in the cold. But this kind of bandwagon jumping can be dangerous, especially when the cause is a blood-real event like a war, rather than a mock war like the Olympic Games. A company can be perceived as trying to gain commercial advantage out of tragedy. One marketing director of a company rushing publicized donations to the Middle East declared, "We're really just doing this to help the soldiers." People jeer at such explanations. They can backfire.

A Versatile Tool

Cause-related, strategic public relations is a versatile tool. The cause can be big or small. A small business can generate great goodwill and interest in a community by adroit use of the tactic. This means more than just buying an ad in the playbill of the town drama society or just furnishing uniforms to a Little League team. It means espousing a cause that sets the company a little apart from other companies; making skillful, restrained use of the PR opportunities presented; and sticking with it.

Sticking with it is vital. Association with a cause rarely produces a big sales bonanza right off the bat. This is another reason it is better handled by public relations than by marketing, which has to focus on relatively short-term results.

However, when the cause is worthy, appropriate, and well chosen, the company—whether it is a multinational or a neighborhood business—gets results.

Magazines, which are usually the channels of public relations efforts, are finding that they can help themselves through cause-related promotions. The *Wall Street Journal* (September 18, 1991) described how *Vanity Fair* was raising money for Phoenix House's drug rehabilitation programs; *Metropolitan Home* was helping to fight AIDS; and *Town & Country* was raising money to provide cosmetic makeovers for cancer patients.

Magazines can sponsor and promote events. They can also induce advertisers to join them. *Town & Country* notified advertisers it would donate 55 percent of beauty-ad revenue from a special section to the group Look Good . . . Feel Better, which helps female cancer patients.

Helping Education

American education is already benefiting—and will benefit more—from cause-related public relations. Corporations have been contributing to education, in various forms, for many years. Sometimes, they have focused on schools in communities where the company has facilities. In other cases, they have contributed to schools that teach skills the company can use. Still others concentrate on making it possible for the children of employees to get good educations.

Recently, as David Finn, chairman of Ruder Finn, points out, "some companies have discovered that their contributions to education not only help society but also gain visibility for their products and services."

In any giving program, but especially in giving to education, companies have to be sensitive to the danger of being seen as overly self-serving. The firm that looks as if it is messing with the minds of youngsters will encounter a decided backlash. The Citibank Master-Card and Visa division of Citicorp developed a model program, with just the right tinge of self-promotion mixed in with a lot of substance and plenty of high-visibility fun. Citibank adopted a cause: geography. They gave a major grant to the National Geographic Society to develop a school kit. Then Citibank hired "Mr. World"—a former teacher who wears a cape emblazoned with a world map—to put on a geography road show incorporating humor and drama. Each student got a world map and a button highlighting Citibank's sponsorship. Classrooms received teaching aids such as an inflatable globe with a Citibank imprint.

This program provided for tie-ins with local Citibank facilities when Mr. World visited. There was extensive press, television, and radio coverage, all replete with striking visuals. All Citibank's 26 million cardholders got mailings encouraging them to feel proud of being part of the program.

It Is Here to Stay

Some people lament the rise of cause-oriented promotions. In *Business Week* (December 5, 1988), a leading professional fund-raiser is quoted as saying that cause marketing will erode the independence of corporate philanthropy. "No-strings giving" will, the critics say, disappear, because companies will want to derive benefits from their giving.

These complaints are understandable and may have a certain surface plausibility, but they do not stand up to close examination. There has never been no-strings giving. Companies have always expected benefits from their philanthropy. They have not been very good at deciding what those benefits are or in getting the most out of their giving, but the "what's in it for me?" question is still implicit in a great deal of corporate philanthropy, and always has been. (As a matter of fact, private charity is not exempt from ulterior motives or accusations of self-interest. There were outcries when the leaders of a prominent New York crime family funded a cancer wing at a Long Island hospital, but the hospital took the money anyway.)

Professional fund-raisers will obviously complain about the possibility that corporate giving will encroach on their turf. Many charities, fed up with the high fees extracted by these pros, may welcome the self-interest of the corporations. The fact is that corporate giving is probably a much more efficient way of funding causes than fundraising by direct mail or, for that matter, by government support.

Another complaint is that corporations will tend to funnel their money toward uncontroversial recipients. But, as this chapter demonstrates, a lot of companies give a lot of money and support to highly charged, controversial, and sometimes unattractive causes. There is a solid reason for this. When philanthropy is viewed, at least in part, as a PR program, the PR professionals want the biggest bang for the buck. You do not get that by staying with the herd. Advertisers take new and unusual routes to be noticed; so do good PR practitioners. So, if the "safe" contribution field is saturated, the corporate giver receives no particular benefit for more money donated to, say, United Way. The PR professionals look for less-traveled paths, and those paths will lead the organization to less-safe, more-controversial charities.

As with all other aspects of public relations, the giving program will have to fit in with a strategy. That may sound crass, but it is a fact of life. In some cases, the company's giving program will steer clear of controversy because that happens to suit the strategy best. When I was involved in MasterCard's Choose to Make a Difference campaign, we ran consumer polls to determine the most popular charities. In other contexts, I have steered client's contributions toward "hotter" beneficiaries. It is all a matter of strategy.

Strategic corporate philanthropy works better when it is handled by the PR function than when it is handled by the marketing function. Though the marketing professionals will vigorously contest this proposition, there are convincing reasons why it is so. A corporate-giving program almost invariably has other dimensions besides the selling of particular products. The company's image is at issue, not just an ephemeral sales push. Moreover, PR professionals, if they are on the ball, are more adept at self-defense than the salespeople. There are risks in strategic philanthropy. The company that makes a serious mistake can look greedy, cruel, and manipulative. Present-day public relations is geared toward getting the most out of such efforts while avoiding the pitfalls.

One potential problem is the term *cause-related marketing,* said to have been coined by American Express when it started contributing a penny to the restoration of the Statue of Liberty every time somebody used an American Express Card. *Cause-related marketing* is a loaded term. Furthermore, the term is too narrow. Since the giving program should have other payoffs besides marketing—corporate image, internal morale, community influence—it ought to be called something else.

How about *guided giving?*

Generosity Works

Worthwhile causes and artistic endeavors will, to an increasing extent, attract corporate support because what they do fits in with a good public relations program. That is realistic. It is also not as crass as it might sound at first. By tying in more closely with the corporate world, these nonprofit organizations can have a profound effect on the business realm that they may have feared and shunned. David Finn, in a *Harvard Business Review* (July–August 1989) article called "Who Needs Poetry," declares:

> When there is a spark in the soul of men and women who manage our companies, they should use it to light up their business as well as their personal lives, and they should say unashamedly why they are doing it. They will get the satisfaction of contributing to their civilization as well as to their corporations, and they will ultimately earn the gratitude of their fellow citizens as well as their stockholders.

The symbiotic relationship between causes and corporations is here to stay. It will flourish. Corporations should approach it in a spirit of enlightened self-interest. Public relations professionals should be sensitive but unapologetic in using the associations for promotional purposes.

On the whole, the growth of cause-related public relations is an excellent development. To quote Finn one more time, such partnerships "will one day be recognized as one of the most significant contributions of the twentieth-century corporation."

8

How PR Can Replace Advertising

Event Marketing and Promotion in a
Hostile Environment

This chapter analyzes the ways in which one industry has been forced to replace television advertising with public relations. The case study has ramifications for the future, so we will explore it in detail. Readers may enjoy the story while they consider its implications.

What would you do if your products were pronounced to be poison and your advertising banned? Most businesses would fold. Somehow the cigarette makers keep going.

No industry in history has taken the kind of battering that has been meted out to the tobacco industry since the first Surgeon General's report on cigarette smoking. Here is an enormous consumer business, under constant and well-documented assault in the press, in the courts, and in government. Here is an industry that had been extravagantly dependent on advertising and was cut off cold turkey from using TV and radio—its most effective media—and from using many of its most important avenues of print advertising as well.

Whatever you think of smoking and cigarettes, the recent history of tobacco marketing provides vivid and, to some, chilling evidence of the power of the new public relations.

When the umbilical cord of heavy consumer advertising was cut, the major tobacco companies made certain momentous strategic moves. Part of the tobacco strategy involves diversification; R.J. Reynolds's acquisition of Nabisco is one example. However, the real war is being fought by the tobacco-related divisions of these corporations. In this arena, big-scale public relations is being used in unprecedented ways.

Traditionally, public relations has played a secondary role in marketing, especially in the marketing of consumer products. Now PR has been called upon to play a larger role, not only in blunting the assaults and supporting the image of the manufacturers, but in actually selling the products. The results of this experiment so far offer some fascinating indications of the still-untapped selling power of public relations in other industries.

My experience with the tobacco wars has taken me both to the command posts, where the broad PR strategies are devised, and to the front lines, where we fought for direct impact on the market. The overriding factor is, of course, the broadscale attack on cigarettes as a severe health risk.

Philip Morris, which was a client of mine for many years, undertook several bold public relations initiatives. One involves philanthropy. In recent years, corporations in a wide range of industries have found (as we discussed in the last chapter) that there is considerable value in doing good works. But few have conducted philanthropy to the extent of the Philip Morris Companies, which in the last two decades contributed several hundred million dollars to groups working in the areas of health and welfare, conservation and environment, education, nutrition, and the arts.

The computer printout identifying the recipients of Philip Morris's largesse is bigger than a major-city phone book. Among those on the receiving end: the National Urban League, Keep America Beautiful, Women's Research and Education Institute, the Bensley-Bermuda Volunteer Rescue Squad (a Virginia emergency unit), High/Scope Educational Research Foundation, Recording for the Blind, Casa Central (a foster-grandparent program), Sky Ranch for Boys, the Elder Craftsmen. The Philip Morris Family Survey studies the status of the American family, with special emphasis on child rearing. The reach of Philip Morris's giving extends beyond the United States to provide video programs on child care and hygiene in the Philippines.

The arts are big beneficiaries. In 1988, the Tenement, the nation's first urban living-history museum, opened on Manhattan's Lower East

Side, funded by a Philip Morris grant. Philip Morris helped under-write "The Age of Sultan Suleiman the Magnificent," a lavish show about the Ottoman Empire, which was displayed in the National Gallery in Washington and the Metropolitan Museum in New York. Other recipients: the Dance Theater of Harlem, the Greater Louis-ville Fund for the Arts, the Next Wave Festival, the American Museum of Natural History, the Guggenheim Museum, the American Associ-ation of Museums, and "Picasso" at the Museum of Modern Art.

Philip Morris Under Fire

In supporting such institutions, Philip Morris is funding causes that are very important to many people who are the most implacable and vociferous opponents of smoking and everything connected with smoking. This leads to fireworks. In 1987, the Joffrey Ballet under-took a national tour—subsidized by Philip Morris. "How could you take their money?" was the cry. Critics declared that the Philip Mor-ris credit on programs and promotional material sullied the pure artistry of the dance company.

In answer, the Joffrey people said that accepting the funding was not the same as telling people to go out and buy cigarettes. A spokes-person for the ballet company asked the key question: "If Philip Mor-ris didn't help us, who would?"

Paul Goldberger, writing in the *New York Times* (October 5, 1994), says this view is widely held:

> To people in the arts, two of the best words in the English lan-guage for more than a generation have been Philip Morris and never mind if the money comes from tobacco.

The multi-billion-dollar maker of cigarettes, beer, and food has been one of the biggest supporters of culture since the 1950s and unlike many companies, Philip Morris has generally given lots of money and asked nothing in return.

There's the heart of it. The arts run on money. Somebody has to put up the money. Perhaps all of the indisputably good causes supported by Philip Morris would prefer to get their dollars from opponents of smoking and other human indulgences. But that's not the case. Philip Morris is willing to make the contributions. The arts institutions, being realistic, take the money. They benefit. And so does Philip Morris, whose corporate image is enhanced.

That is corporate image building. The same avenue is open to much smaller companies. A suburban advertising agency contributed money to the classical music station at the local university, receiving on-air credit. Establishments from aerobics salons to ice-cream shops pitch in to underwrite a new arts center. A small discount broker buys a new curtain for the community theater. And the list goes on.

Event Marketing on a Massive Scale

Corporate giving on a massive scale is one of Philip Morris's major PR thrusts. A second thrust, even bolder, is the company's innovative work with event marketing as a replacement for traditional product advertising. Here, too, money talks.

The hunger of the press for interesting things to cover is enormous. By taking advantage of this fact of media life, you can win a lot of favorable attention. The technique is basically this: Become identified with a specific event that makes good copy.

You can do this on a grand scale or a small one; tie in with an occasion of worldwide interest or one of local importance. Whether it's the Olympics or a high school band contest, if the identification is appropriate, you can get a lot of mileage out of it.

Event marketing—a wonderful supplement to advertising—has been around a long time. A lot of special events are "publicity stunts" pure and simple: occurrences that are dreamed up and staged exclusively to attract attention. The safe from the sunken *Andrea Doria* is opened before a supposedly breathless audience of millions. A new doughnut shop hires a band and a costumed clown for its grand opening. A chain of delis displays what is purported to be the biggest pastrami sandwich in the world.

Newspapers and TV stations will cover stunts if the stunts are colorful and funny. The media indicate that the events are put on solely to attract attention, but they cover them anyway. In some promotional campaigns, getting the public to know your name is the primary goal. When that's the case, just about anything that draws attention is useful. If all you want is visibility, be outrageous.

Knowing the Name Is Not Enough

Today, though, most marketers are not just interested in name recognition. They want their names to be recognized in a favorable context. Stunts are not enough. So now we have event marketing, which involves not stunts, but real events that have a validity of their own, independent of the public relations uses to which the event is put.

Sports has become the most fertile field for sponsorship of—or association with—events. The contest stands by itself. It has meaning, at least for sports fans. The excitement of the competition and the skill and guts of the competitors can be hooked up with the client's image to good effect. Philip Morris's sponsorship of the Virginia Slims women's tennis tournaments was good for tennis and for Philip Morris. However, antismoking pressure against the women athletes forced Virginia Slims to drop its tennis sponsorship in the 1990s.

"To Get on Television, That's Why"

In 1985, I helped put Marlboro in auto racing. Within four years, Marlboro and its driver, Emerson Fittipaldi, went on to win the Indy 500 and bring millions of dollars' worth of publicity on television and in print to Marlboro.

At a meeting for marketing managers, Hamish Maxwell, chairman and CEO of Philip Morris, asked auto racing manager Mark Hulit, "Why do we buy signage at tracks?" Hulit, of course, knew the answer but was speechless. He didn't know how to answer his chairman. After a long pause, a top-ranking Philip Morris executive answered, "To get on television, that's why."

Since then, under pressure from antismoking forces, Philip Morris has removed from all sports arenas and stadiums any cigarette

advertising that may be seen on telecasts of football, basketball, baseball, or hockey games.

Picking the Right Events

The tobacco business has a lot of problems, but attracting attention
is not one of them. There is no shortage of attention paid to smoking, although most of it is very unfavorable. In such circumstances,
the contrived stunt—no matter how creative—will be worse than inef-
fective. It is apt to backfire. For one thing, journalists, who are good-
natured about the hype of other industries, turn into paragons of
purity when confronted with tobacco hype. While we all know that
the professional journalist is totally unaffected by crass concerns of
advertising revenue, it is nevertheless impossible to ignore the fact
that most of this rectitude has been unleashed by the embargo on
advertising.

So, in looking for events to promote Philip Morris and its products, we sought image enhancers, not just attention getters. Instead
of contriving events, we wanted to attach the company's brands to
freestanding events that have, of themselves, a legitimate reason for
being. These events should, of course, be compatible with the company, the product, and the image we are trying to promote. You would
not promote a new line of gourmet delicacies by sponsoring a motor-
cycle tour by the Hell's Angels. It would not be tactically sound for a
brewery to be identified with a nationwide series of spelling bees for
eighth-graders.

If your product or logo wouldn't look absolutely natural right in
the middle of the event, get another event. It is even better if the freestanding event emits a glow in which you look good. A glow of
integrity, bravery, wisdom, or friendship. In the case I am going to
tell you about, we were able to show our product to the world, bathed
in the rosy glow of sentiment along with the stirring red, white, and
blue of patriotism—*honest* sentiment, *honest* patriotism. The event
already had achieved a serious, imposing stature before we became
involved in it.

And that is the best kind of event: the one that is already accepted as having a good, deep meaning. You cannot create such events; they look phony. But you can attach yourself to them, piggyback on them. How do you make yourself a part of an ongoing event that has achieved stature and become a tradition? You can do it by asking the folks who watch over the event whether they can use a little cash.

It is rare that a project is explained in such detail as I do here, so what follows is actually more than a case study. It is a logbook, a journal to be read and enjoyed. Here's how it happened.

In 1983, Marlboro Country Music was founded to support Marlboro cigarettes by bringing top country-music performers to cities throughout the United States. The connection was a natural. It reinforced the wide-open-spaces theme of the brand image and focused on a prime target market.

Philip Morris retained Regis Boff, a successful music producer with a great many rock-concert credits, to put together the country-music series. Boff created one of the most talked-about shows in the music business. It became the envy of music producers (and sponsors) coast to coast. After Marlboro Country Music was born, Michael Jackson borrowed Marlboro's large screen and other equipment for his Victory Tour, the first rock tour with state-of-the-art production.

The stars who appeared in the concerts gave interviews and appeared on TV shows, generating additional publicity. And the concerts could be tied in with a good cause. In 1987, for example, Marlboro Country Music toured seventeen cities, raising money for Second Harvest, America's largest network of food banks.

I was wondering what we could do next with Marlboro Country Music. We could continue with more of the same, but the novelty and the publicity value would start to erode. So I raised the possibility of doing a concert outside the United States. At first, some people thought the idea was very odd indeed. Our client, Philip Morris U.S.A., had the single job of selling cigarettes in the United States. (A separate company, Philip Morris International, sells worldwide.) But I felt the foreign concert would be justified if it could attract a lot of attention in the United States. China was my choice (before the Tiananmen Square crackdown). By bringing country music to China, we would have East meet West in a new and intriguing way.

Philip Morris bought the idea. In June 1987, I went to Beijing with Marlboro promotions manager Beth Kohl to arrange a concert for the following November that would star the hot groups Alabama and the Judds.

We were not able to swing it. Our difficulties in negotiating with the Chinese were monumental. I was sorry I had not brought Nixon and Kissinger along to open up the Forbidden City to country music. The China project was dead, at least for 1987. And we were staring disaster in the face. Philip Morris was committed by contract to do one more show in November 1987, starring Alabama and the Judds. Neither of these acts comes cheap. If we could not line up a concert, Philip Morris would be unhappy, to say the least. And our competitors would not try too hard to conceal their amusement at our discomfiture.

Out of this situation came a public relations coup. I could tell you it was all a result of consummate method and planning. But the reason we came up with the ultimate answer is that we had blown the China trip, and we were looking desperately for Plan B. Some of the great textbook strategies in business are the offspring of expediency and hindsight.

The Vietnam Veterans Memorial Needs Help

We began to work late into the night, looking for an appropriate location for a November concert. A map of the United States, marked with locations of previous Marlboro Country Music shows, did not bolster our morale. We seemed to have already performed in every major city. The idea was to have successful concerts with good crowds, but the goal was to garner substantial publicity, print, and broadcast.

We looked closer. While we had put on a concert in the Washington, D.C., area—at the Capital Center in suburban Maryland—we had never been to Washington proper. But when Charlie Brotman, a Marlboro consultant in Washington, looked at the calendar, he showed us that Washington might already be scheduled for at least one substantial public event. November 11, Veterans Day, would be the fifth anniversary of the Vietnam Veterans Memorial.

At first, we looked at this as a possible conflict. But then it started to look like an opportunity. We started to ask ourselves if there was some way we could tie in with the ceremonies at the memorial. Might it even be possible for us to become part of the ceremony? We might as well try.

When you are trying to arrange something like this, the magic words are "Can you use some money?" There is no cause so popular, no ceremony so sacrosanct, that the organizers cannot use cash. Why should this be an exception? Brotman called Jan Scruggs, chairman of the Vietnam Veterans Memorial Fund. Did the fund need money? Yes. They had to pay for the expensive process of inscribing additional names on the memorial wall. Fine. We offered to do a benefit concert to cover the expense. But we had certain conditions. Everyone associated with the event should talk about Marlboro as part of the fifth anniversary, and we wanted a presence at the ceremony—with Alabama and the Judds performing, and with Philip Morris president, Frank E. Resnik, as a speaker. The fifth anniversary would now become a two-day event, with the country music concert taking place the night before the ceremony.

The fund accepted the proposal. Money may not buy happiness, but it can usually open doors.

Making the Connection

Time was short. And we were still faced with the problem of building a strong bridge between the concert and the memorial's anniversary ceremony. If the participation of Philip Morris appeared to be dragged in from left field, the money we spent would be wasted, and there might even be a backlash of negative publicity for Philip Morris. The challenge was to make the tie-in stronger and more logical.

We decided to renew vivid impressions of the Vietnam War with a show of war photographs. We first talked with David Kennerly, the former White House photographer also known for his work in Vietnam. Kennerly was not available, but he recommended Eddie Adams, whose Vietnam pictures had won for him the Pulitzer Prize. Adams agreed to assist in developing the list of photos for a large-screen slide show, to attend the November 10 concert, to take part in the pre-concert press conference, and to participate in interviews on behalf of Marlboro. Philip Morris would pay him $3,500 plus expenses.

It was shaping up as a first-rate event. The content was right, the tone was right. But there was a great deal invested in the occasion. I wanted to do everything possible to make sure the events went off well and we got good coverage—a lot of it. The best way to do that would be to bring in a Very Big Name.

When in doubt, hire a star. There was one celebrity whose presence, above all others, would assure the right tone and maximum coverage for this event. Bob Hope. Hope's legendary record of entertaining American soldiers overseas could give the ceremonies a penetrating symbolism. And Hope's star quality and expertise at spokesmanship would assure that Marlboro was promoted effectively.

Or at least it seemed that way to me. I suggested Hope as the concert's master of ceremonies to Beth Kohl and Nancy Bogler of Marlboro. They liked the idea. We called Bob Hope. He was available. He would participate in a press conference, do the show, take part in Philip Morris hospitality after the show, and speak at the memorial the next day. He would not be the master of ceremonies for the concert; instead, he would do an opening monologue and perform in a finale with Alabama and the Judds. Hope wanted $70,000 for the two-day stint.

The Philip Morris people split on using Hope. Some thought it was a great idea. Others felt Bob Hope was too old, not funny anymore, and did not fit the brand image. And he was too expensive.

I responded that Hope was not old, but ageless. He was loved and respected, and nobody had a stronger tie-in to veterans. As for selling tickets, we were not hiring him to build up the gate but to escalate an ordinary country-music concert into a once-in-a-lifetime special event. As for Hope's being too expensive, I suggested we see if we could get the price down a little.

After some negotiation, Hope's asking price came down to $60,000. The Philip Morris people were having trouble saying yes or no. I was caught in what often goes on in corporations: indecisiveness. Risk taking is an endangered way of doing business. Finally, Beth

Kohl dropped it in my lap: "Call Len Saffir. If he thinks Hope is worth the money and will add to the story, let him OK it." It pushed me out on a limb, but I said, "Hire Bob Hope." And they did.

The machinery went into action: press kits, pins with the slogan "Marlboro Country Music honors Vietnam War Veterans," tote bags, notebooks, caps. Brotman's office and our office set up the media interviews and put out a series of releases.

The concert on November 10 was a sellout, with the audience, for the most part, in their twenties and thirties (perfect Marlboro demographics). The slide show was very moving. Hope got standing ovations when he walked on stage, after his monologue, and at the finale.

That night it snowed heavily. The next morning, Veterans Day, Washington was besieged by an unexpected driving snow. Linda Wallen, the skilled Philip Morris account supervisor of my office, ventured forth in one of the celebrity limousines to buy eighteen pairs of boots, gloves, and umbrellas. The snow caused us to move the morning interviews we had set up at the memorial into studios. When the ceremonies started, Hope put on rubber boots and a raincoat over his light California sports jacket and slacks, grabbed my arm, and we slowly mushed from the limo to the stage; his "snowmobile," he called me.

Hope's remarks onstage were appropriate and affecting. He was not doing one-liners now. He was summoning up more than forty years of looking out over the faces of young American servicemen and -women, in war and in times of danger, in every corner of the world.

One Little Tear

As Hope neared the end of his talk, he paused. A tear slowly made its way down his cheek.

As a person, I was touched. As a professional, I was jubilant. That tear of Hope's had escalated us into an odds-on bet to get an important play in the network news. The TV camera crews, always alert, zoomed in on Bob Hope's display of emotion. The cynical network pros would scoff at it. But they would run it. Sentiment outsells sophistication every time.

Was Bob Hope's tear planned? No. Was it totally spontaneous? Well, seven decades of performing have given him the instincts that deploy emotion to maximum effect. That is one of the things that make Hope worth the $60,000.

From our point of view, the rest of the event went perfectly. Or almost perfectly. We had gotten Philip Morris president, Frank Resnick, on the roster of speakers, and with his natural enthusiasm for his product, he got carried away and mentioned Philip Morris and its Marlboro brand many times. Too many for the nature of the occasion. Afterward, the event's master of ceremonies, Ted Koppel of *Nightline* fame, said to Linda Wallen, "If your president had mentioned Marlboro one more time, I would have kicked him." Sometime it's not good to get more than you pay for.

But, overall, the event was primarily a touching and appropriate ceremony. For ourselves, we were quite pleased that it incidentally did so much for Philip Morris, which received highly favorable publicity on the spot. We would be able to use the association in selling for a long time to come. Frank Resnick said afterward that it was one of the best events Philip Morris had done in years.

We had tailored the event for network television, and we received high and favorable visibility. But perhaps the most gratifying mention came in a November 10 feature story in the *New York Times,* which wrote of:

> . . . the ceremony, organized by the Vietnam Veterans Memorial Fund and sponsored by Marlboro Country Music, a country music tour promoted by Philip Morris, that is also paying to lodge the families [of the twenty-four veterans whose names were added to the memorial] during their stay in the capital. On Tuesday night, Marlboro Country Music will sponsor a benefit concert at Constitution Hall to raise money for the project.

Philip Morris was happy to receive a favorable mention in the *Times,* which is not usually kind to the tobacco industry. Overall, the coverage of the event justified the decision to use public relations as a marketing tool.

Nuts and Bolts of Event Marketing

You do not need to get a Bob Hope to use event marketing. It is a technique that, if worked right, can attract a lot of press attention in one fell swoop. It is the PR equivalent of working wholesale rather than retail.

Here are some principles:

- It is better to piggyback on an existing event than to create a new one purely for promotional purposes.

- Most event sponsors need money and are willing to consider letting a sponsor participate, if it is not too blatant.

- Choose an event that fits in with the image you're trying to project. If you have to explain why you are there, forget it.

- Patriotism and other honest emotions never go out of style with the vast majority of the American public.

- Hire show business professionals of a magnitude appropriate to the occasion. The disc jockey from a local radio station can add a lot to a local event. The media focus on names, not concepts. (That's why *People* magazine outsells the *Quarterly Review*.)

- Make sure you are mentioned generously in all the publicity regarding the event. In fact, it is best to handle the publicity yourself, if you can manage it.

- Be distinctly visible at the event, but do not turn it into an obvious sales pitch. You will alienate people and make yourself a target for the press.

Do everything possible to make the tour-stop look like a local event. Take Borden, for example. As the *Wall Street Journal* (October 30, 1991) pointed out, Borden's seventy-five-city Beach Boys tour is given the tailor-made touch: At every stop, the company involves local retailers, ad agencies, and consumers as the band rolls into town. Each concert is customized with special promotions and ticket giveaways at local stores. Grocers can qualify to receive show merchandise by building big displays. Many trade customers might get a backstage tour. Radio stations can climb aboard the bandwagon by airing special Beach Boys "anthology" shows.

Jeffrey Milgrom of Milgrom & Associates Event Marketing observes, "Sponsoring an event where you just put your name on some banners is over." Event marketing is a good way to take advantage of the insatiable hunger of the press, especially TV, for picturesque events. When you give them what they want, they will play along and give you what you want—favorable exposure that is not labeled as advertising. And since there is more mileage and greater credibility in becoming part of an event that is already established, look for one.

Here's how to start your search for the event that is right for you. Just about every city and town has a calendar of events, maintained by the community council or a similar organization. Look at it every month. When you see an event that might fit, find out more about it. Figure out ways you could get involved. Then approach the organizers about sharing the burden of sponsorship. Your contribution need not always be money. For example, if the United Way or another charity does a big annual telethon, let them use your offices and phones. Or contribute other administrative and logistic help.

The point is to get into the act, create a distinct and appropriate presence for yourself, and make sure it is adequately publicized. And let your image bask in the reflected glory.

Helping the Embattled Cigar

For me, the action in yet another arena of the tobacco wars has been particularly satisfying. This is my work on behalf of the cigar. Cigar advertising is not banned on television. The devastating statistics relating to cigarettes are not relevant to cigars. Furthermore, people were hissing at cigar smokers long before cigarettes were shown to cause cancer.

We determined to use public relations to give cigars a more positive image. In this case, PR is not altogether replacing advertising, but rather working alongside advertising.

Once cigar smoking was an OK American custom. Good guys smoked cigars. Successful men smoked expensive cigars, others smoked more modest brands, and certain members of the common people liked the long, thin, inexpensive cigars called "stogies." They weren't everybody's taste, but there was an aura of good humor about the smoke. The cigar was a celebration; the picture of the elated father passing out cigars to everyone became a part of folklore.

And the cigar seemed essentially American. In fact, the "stogie" is said to be so named because it was the favorite smoke of the Conestoga wagon drivers on the way west. Thomas Riley Marshall was vice president of the United States, but he would be utterly unknown to history except for his immortal remark, "What this country needs is a good five-cent cigar."

Then the tide turned. Cigar smokers found themselves in a painful position. When someone lit a cigar, people would act as if that person were lighting the fuse of a bomb. The aroma of a cigar, no matter how rich or delicate, was greeted as if it were mustard gas. And every time some new statistics were proclaimed by the Tobacco Institute or its opponents, things got worse for the small-cigar segment, which was caught in the middle. As Fletcher Knebel said in *Reader's Digest,* "It is now proved beyond doubt that smoking is one of the leading causes of statistics."

The Cigar Association of America became our client in 1984, at a truly desperate time for the industry. With a total budget of under a million dollars, with $400,000 devoted to public relations, the association was in no way able to mount the massive campaigns carried on by larger advocacy groups, such as the Tobacco Institute. As with cigarettes, cigar sales are declining—that is accepted as inevitable on all sides. But we've helped to ease the decline.

We've done this, not with gargantuan advertising, exhaustive reports, or huge expenditures, but with humor and appeals to fairness. My first instinct when I thought about this account was, "We can have some fun with this." My next thought was that having fun with the question was exactly the right approach.

Appealing for Fairness

Courtesy was one of the cornerstones of our campaign. While good manners do not seem as important as they once were, I felt that most Americans still have a basic inclination toward politeness. After all, we were not asking for much—just some decent consideration toward people who like to smoke an occasional cigar. Public relations works best when it appeals to the better human instinct.

Meanwhile, we were conducting research. Focus groups confirmed our feelings about the negative connotations of cigars. Cigar smoking was perceived as objectionable, particularly to women. There were negative images of the personalities and physical attributes of men who smoke cigars, and this negative image had rubbed off on cigar smokers. Many of them felt guilty about it. Moreover, people who thought they might enjoy cigars were deterred because they did not want to be offensive.

We had to modify perceptions among cigar smokers themselves as well as those who reached for the hatchet every time they saw someone light up. We had to somehow diminish the angry, heavy-breathing way in which questions relating to cigar smoking were being addressed. We had to inject courtesy, consideration, and good humor into the picture.

Sometimes you have to reduce the heat before increasing the illumination. I dreamed up a book, titled *101 Ways to Answer the Request: Would You Please Put Out the #(&*!\$ Cigar!* The strategy was twofold. First, we wanted to capitalize on the historic link between humor and the cigar. Groucho Marx's cigar was his trademark. George Burns's cigar was his constant companion onstage. W. C. Fields used cigars as an integral part of his unforgettable stage and screen personality. Contemporary comedians like Bill Cosby and David Letterman are well-known cigar smokers. We wanted to show that good guys smoke cigars, and that if you smile at them, they don't mind it; they are capable of laughing at themselves. Joking in the face of adversity is an admired act. It conveys good-humored courage and a commonsense approach, which can reduce supposedly calamitous occurrences to their proper size.

Second, we wanted to provide a gentle but definite defense of the cigar smoker's rights. Rather than make this confrontational, we determined to defuse the atmosphere by lightheartedness and under-standing.

The book, I felt, would be effective in itself. If we made it funny enough, people would enjoy it. And the book would also work for us in other ways, by intriguing the media enough that they would quote it and by providing a rallying point for those wanting to defend smok-ers' rights.

The ordinary gestation period for such a book might be six months or more. I hired six professional comedy writers, locked them in our conference room, and fed them pastrami sandwiches; at the end of a week, we had the text.

An artist provided the illustrations to go with the answers. These were presented in the form of a mock-serious instruction book. Among the "answers":

- The Andy Rooney: "Didja ever notice how the people who ask you to put out your cigar always wait till after you've lit it? Why do they do that? Or after you've put it out? Hey, where ya goin'? Wait, didja ever notice . . ."
- The Charles Bronson: "Any other last requests?"
- The White House Spokesman: "We believe it *is* out."
- The Executive Privilege: "I could do that, but it would be wrong."
- The Randy Newman: "Your growth is already stunted; don't worry about mine."

As you can see, these retorts were not intended for actual use, though I cannot guarantee that cigar smokers have not used them. In any event, the book turned out to be pretty funny. Simon & Schus-ter published it, and the results were gratifying. There was a lot of print publicity. Radio and TV talk shows found the topic sprightly. The bite-sized format of the book lended itself to quotation, enabling us to get a lot of broadcast mileage out of it.

And when people asked about the purpose of the book, we had an opportunity to call attention to the need for more tolerance and understanding between cigar smokers and nonsmokers. We referred the rear section of the book, "A Few Gentle Suggestions" to cigar smokers themselves, for ways to be considerate of others *and* enjoy their smokes.

The book struck just the right note. We elaborated our campaign along a number of tracks. For one thing, we underscored the idea that cigars are smoked by winners. (Basketball fans know of the "victory cigar" lit up by Red Auerbach when the Boston Celtics win, which is a good part of the time.) The research had shown that not all perceptions of cigar smokers were negative by any means. They were perceived as having favored status.

Tapping into Deeply Held Feelings

We capitalized on the cigar as part of the American grain. Looking through the perspective of history, we chose Mark Twain as the quintessential American—who also happened to smoke cigars. Mark Twain was courageous, brilliant, successful, shrewd, funny, and commonsensical. In 1985, the 150th anniversary of his birth, we helped to promote the festivities in Twain's hometown of Hannibal, Missouri. We retained Roger Durrett, a thirty-five-year-old actor who was already portraying Mark Twain in a one-man show, to use his interpretation of Twain while touring the country as ambassador-at-large for the Cigar Association of America. A news conference in New York, featuring the real mayor of Hannibal and Durrett as Twain, kicked off a twelve-city media tour, culminating in "An Evening with Mark Twain" at New York's Town Hall. Appearing as Twain, Durrett flourished a cigar and delivered Twain's funny and approving lines about cigars.

Another thrust of our campaign is encapsulated in the slogan "Relax. Enjoy a Cigar." We developed it for the Cigar Association. It is a great slogan, if I do say so myself, effective for advertising as well as public relations. We used it for PR by creating events keyed to the theme and having them covered by press and broadcast media. We ran a national songwriting contest on the theme. We created a special "taxpayers poll," inviting harried taxpayers, faced with an IRS deadline, to "Relax. Enjoy a Cigar." Smoke shops everywhere displayed point-of-sales materials related to the theme. Michael Talbott, the cigar-smoking actor who played Detective Switek on *Miami Vice*, was one of the judges of the songwriting contest and announced the results in New York. (Michael expressed his gratitude by getting me an extra's role in a *Miami Vice* TV episode, playing a customer in a South Beach bar tended by another extra, Pierre Mapes, president of NBC-TV.)

Ostensibly, the slogan is addressed to smokers, urging them to relax and indulge in the pleasure of a good smoke. This ties in with the idea of the cigar as something special—an extra-pleasant, even sumptuous interlude, a reward for accomplishment, or just a way to unwind during a busy day. But the slogan is aimed at nonsmokers as well, emphasizing the thought that cigars are a means of relaxation, that those who smoke them are not looking for trouble, and that it is a pretty good idea for all of us to relax and stop letting ourselves be driven up the wall by trivia.

Having Fun with the Idea

When you have a warm, relaxed theme, you can have fun with it. Taxpayers rushing to the post office on April 15 to beat the deadline are handed cigars by models clad in barrels that feature the "relax" slogan . . . as the TV cameras record the scene. Everybody knows this is a public relations tactic on behalf of the cigar business. The taxpayers are tense, maybe even a little embarrassed at first. And they are by no means all pro-cigar. But they smile, unwind, enjoy the moment. The cigar is no longer a cylinder of cultivated leaves. It is a symbol of relaxation.

When you don't take yourself too seriously, it's harder for opponents to attack you. When you are able to associate yourself with things that evoke a good feeling, people feel better about you. The association has to be logical, of course. It would be futile, for instance, to try to connect cigar smoking with high IQ, extraordinary physical prowess, beauty, or sainthood. The public would just not buy it.

But a cigar can be perceived as a reward, something special, something for a joyful occasion. Cigars do have a place in American social history, and they are associated with achievement. Above all, cigars can readily be hooked up with relaxation. How can you be tense when smoking a cigar? The very act of cigar smoking, the business of trimming and lighting, the long, slow puffs—this is the epitome of relaxation. To those who become hysterical at the sight of someone doing this, our campaign says, "Aw, come on. Is it really worth getting all worked up about? Why not relax and have a smile, even if you don't smoke cigars?"

Our success in associating cigars with congenial traditions led to the next moves. In 1988, we broke our Share Your Joy campaign. Our goal was to revive the custom of handing out cigars to celebrate the birth of a child. In recent years this custom has been more honored in the breach than in the observance. The antismoking movement cast a pall over the association of babies with tobacco.

But why? Customs are symbolic. Proud fathers have handed out millions of cigars to people who had no intention of smoking them. This did not make the gesture any less meaningful. Sure, today's new daddy might celebrate by handing out bouquets or gift certificates or chewing gum, but these would not have the same significance. Our position is that if you're going to give away something to celebrate a birth, it has to be a cigar. Otherwise, why bother?

We proposed that material from the National Committee for Prevention of Child Abuse be included in every box of "It's a Boy" and "It's a Girl" cigars. The purchasers could mail in a contribution to the committee and get some additional information about the mission and work of the group.

Our campaign for cigars could by no stretch of the imagination be described as aimed at youngsters. We concentrate on adults. Lighting up a cigar is a deliberate choice, not the frenzied act of an addict. We tell people to smoke cigars at special times, not continually. The cigar, as our campaign positions it, is an occasional treat or the symbol of something special.

The idea of the cigar as a special treat is the underpinning for another initiative, Cigar Lovers Day. The first Cigar Lovers Day, with Alan King, Red Auerbach, and Alan Thicke participating in a well-attended press conference, generated national publicity. Most of our effort was devoted to having local dealers sponsor special events, like a "Longest Ash Contest." Once again, we were just having fun.

There is one other major thrust in American social history that we are able to ride on: politics. Back more than 100 years ago, men bought cigars with pictures of their favorite candidates on the band. Long before the days of scientific polling, one way to measure the support of candidates—say, Grover Cleveland against Benjamin Harrison—was by the number of cigars sold.

A week before the 1988 election, we conducted a one-day cigar poll in New York's Grand Central Station. It attracted a lot of good-humored attention. While nobody, so far as I know, took the results with the utmost seriousness, there is a stubborn streak in many Americans that gives heed to such indications, perhaps in protest against the so-called certainties of Gallup and Harris.

All the proceeds from sales of the Bush and Dukakis cigars— which cost $1 apiece—were earmarked for the Vietnam Veterans of America. The media found the "cigar poll" results—Bush soundly defeating Dukakis—irresistible.

The Fruits of Our Work

I like the cigar campaign. As a professional, I am proud of what we accomplished on a limited budget for a small industry, which in the eighties and early nineties was caught between the opposing sides in a titanic struggle. Cigar smoking, of course, was on a gentle downward slope, a victim of cultural evolution. Cigar smokers were battling anti-tobacco legislation and the growing perception that cigars' trendiness had peaked.

We thought we did a good job, but we were forced to bow to the inevitable. Power Public Relations is strong but not miraculous.

But wait just a minute. A funny thing happened in the nineties soon after our years of toiling in the cigar vineyards: A cigar-smoking boom reversed a thirty-year decline in the business and left cigar makers, big and small, richer than they ever dreamed was possible while we were fighting the stogie wars. Retail sales of cigars in the United States rose to $1.4 billion in 1997 from $192 million in 1992. Americans in 1998 bought 4 billion machine-made cigars—a 33 percent increase in five years, according to my former client the Cigar Association of America. In terms of dollars, however, the pricier hand-rolled imports accounted for roughly half the revenue growth. Premium imports quadrupled to 400 million cigars between 1993 and 1998.

Could it all have happened because of Power Public Relations? After all, the folks at the Public Relations Society of America awarded the Cigar Association of America, along with my agency and myself, their coveted Silver Anvil award for our work.

By now maybe you are gritting your teeth in irritation about all our efforts. In that case, all I can say is, "Relax. Enjoy a Cigar."

9

Think Big (Sometimes)

Saving the Presidency

You can't write a book about Power Public Relations in the twentieth century without mentioning the Bill Clinton/Monica Lewinsky madness that gripped the country in 1998–1999. I'll do so—briefly—knowing I'm certainly not among the first to comment and, unfortunately, cannot be counted among the last.

With a background heavy in media, politics, and a life inside the Beltway, and being well grounded in PR, I couldn't resist the challenge I gave myself to see if I couldn't put Power Public Relations to work in order to bring early closure to the scandal that divided the country.

While I had absolutely no connections to the Clinton White House, that didn't stop me. I'll reveal my plans for you to ponder. Some readers might think them awful. Others will think differently.

On September 7, 1998, I presented my ideas to Erskine Bowles, then chief of staff to President Clinton. In a letter faxed and mailed to the White House, I suggested that President Clinton speak on national television directly to the youth of America. The speech should be crafted for schoolchildren, I wrote. I suggested that the speech should be delivered around dinnertime, and that all children, as well as their parents, be urged to tune in.

The subject matter, I offered, should be truth and lying. The president should tell his school-age viewing audience how people can mess up their future by telling untruths, using his own behavior as an example.

I believed then that the impact of such a speech would have gone a long way to bring closure to the mess. Lawmakers, even conservatives, would have concluded, from their own take on the speech, the media coverage, and America's reaction, that Clinton's mea culpa effectively did the job.

I told Bowles that I had once worked for Republican U.S. Senator James L. Buckley, and that I was writing my letter to him not as a partisan but as an American first, with the country and the office of the presidency in mind. On September 29, 1998, I received a handwritten response from the chief of staff on White House stationery, saying in part, "Your advice is genuine and constructive. I also believe it could be effective . . . and have sent it to the President so that he can personally respond. . . . I sincerely thank you."

A day later I received a second handwritten letter from Chief of Staff Bowles, bringing me up-to-date. He told me that he had showed my letter to the president, who had, in fact, taken some immediate action. Bowles enclosed a copy of the president's remarks of contrition delivered in the White House at the famous prayer breakfast of religious leaders on September 11. (My letter had been given to the president on September 9.)

In his remarks the president addressed "the children of this country" and said that they can learn in a profound way that integrity is important and selfishness is wrong. He cited an example of a little boy in Florida who came up to him during a recent trip and said he wanted to grow up and be president and to be just like him. He added, "I want the parents of all the children in America to be able to say that to their children."

From several more letters I received from Bowles, I knew that he had tried his best to get the president to do more. The president's remarks on children didn't accomplish what I had in mind, mainly because they were delivered in the wrong venue and didn't go far enough.

Bowles did tell me that Senator Buckley was most fortunate to have had my wise counsel. With that in mind, I would try something different. I would enlist the services of Judge Buckley. I turned to my former boss, who after he left the Senate, became a justice on the U.S. Court of Appeals in Washington.

On October 9, 1998, I wrote Jim Buckley and asked him if he would consider calling a meeting of all the players: the House and Senate leadership of both parties, the House Judiciary Committee leadership, the relevant federal judges in Washington and Little Rock, Judge Starr and Clinton's counsel, and maybe even some clergy and former presidents Carter, Ford, and Bush. I suggested they be kept locked up in a room, as at a Middle East peace summit or labor negotiation until they came to some agreement that would be acceptable to all. I felt that when the American public knew what was going on, the assembled parties would have no choice but to come to a settlement. I felt that Buckley had the right credentials, as a Republican, a distinguished jurist, and the first Republican senator to call for President Nixon's resignation, to succeed at the undertaking.

Buckley replied, "I can't think of a greater compliment than the one that is inherent in your 'bold suggestion'—and typically bold it is. Given its source, I have given it careful thought." He declined, however, though he said I made a very good case and went on to suggest others who could "fill the role better than he would."

I gave up my Power Public Relations attempts to make a difference in Washington from my home in Florida.

Monica, Inc.

After a Greta Garbo–like year during the Clinton/Lewinsky scandal in 1998, Monica Lewinsky and her handlers decided on a Power Public Relations campaign. Nothing small.

She retained a retinue of PR practitioners, media consultants, television coaches, and makeover artists, as if she were launching a major political campaign. John Scanlon, the PR practitioner whose clients have ranged from CBS and Brown Williamson to Ivana Trump during her divorce from Donald, was among the many professionals retained by the Lewinsky family.

Finally, on televisions screens and retail book shelves around the world, there was Monica Lewinsky, well rehearsed and skillfully managed.

According to a *New York Times* editorial of March 5, 1999, Lewinsky "is at last benefiting from high-priced coaching in the fields of public relations."

Think Saving the Children

As cited above, big ideas don't always cost a lot of money, but if they do, they may be worth it. A former client of mine at the Michelin Tire Company told a group that I was among the most creative persons he had ever met—but then added that my ideas always cost too much.

For Philip Morris, it was different. A longtime client, the giant company never let expense be a roadblock to big ideas.

On the morning of June 4, 1989, the second day of the Chinese military assault on the mass student demonstrations in Beijing's Tiananmen Square, I was in my office, talking to a friend on the telephone. She told me that her son was among about 250 American students attending Beijing University. Power Public Relations bells went off in my head.

I quickly called my friend Peter Jennings at ABC and alerted him to the news of the American students who might have been in danger when the six weeks of protest came to a bloody breaking point the day before. (Give tips to the media even when you're not selling something; it will eventually pay off.) He immediately interviewed my friend by telephone about her son and then broke into regular programming to broadcast the news.

I then called my client Tom Ricke, the head of corporate information at Philip Morris Companies. I suggested to Tom that Philip Morris should lease a jumbo jet and fly into Beijing to pick up all the American students who might have been in the way of the tanks and machine guns of 200,000 army troops ordered to reclaim Beijing from the students. He loved the idea and said he would call me right back.

In less than a half hour, Tom called me and said that he had talked to John Murphy, then the president of the company, who told him to "do it" but to make certain we had the blessings of the State Department.

I gathered some of our people and told them to find a plane big enough for the task. Within an hour, they had arranged to charter a jet based in Indianapolis. I told Tom, who said we would take one of Philip Morris's smaller jets from Teterboro, New Jersey, to Indianapolis later that day. He added that we didn't have time even to go home for an overnight bag.

Meanwhile, I called the State Department, not to ask permission but simply to tell them what we intended to do and get their "blessings" as requested by Philip Morris president Murphy. Thirty-six hours later and after enlisting additional help from Senator Edward Kennedy, we were still waiting to break through the federal bureaucracy. No one would comment one way or the other. After two days, we aborted the project.

Power Public Relations for George Washington?

Spinning in the White House seemed to have caught on for even those with the responsibility of preserving the image of the first president of the United States.

In February 1999, Power Public Relations troops were called upon to brighten up the image of George Washington. It seemed to the folks at Mount Vernon, Virginia, the capital of George Washington's legacy, that the father of our country was on a "downward slide" and needed a makeover.

Thus began a year-long $3 million public relations campaign to reposition George Washington as a national figure with a "lot of sizzle." According to Michael Quinn, the deputy director of programs at Mount Vernon, "Washington had great name recognition but not a real high quotient of excitement." "Dull" and "boring" were words Quinn used to describe our first president in an interview with the *New York Times* on February 8, 1999. "He was the first president, of course . . . but so what?"

Thousands of press kits were sent to thousands of communities throughout the country to encourage festivities at Mount Vernon. Two Web sites, three books, and a series of videos were planned to establish George Washington as the "first guy." Robert Redford wants to make the movie.

Thinking big doesn't always work, but failure to do so from time to time would be a sin if you want to practice real Power Public Relations.

10

The Secrets of Crisis Management

Preparing for Disaster

At 8:00 A.M. on November 12, 1989, the telephone rang at the headquarters of Porsche Cars North America (PCNA) in Reno, Nevada. The caller was a local TV reporter. She had just learned about an accident from local police. A sports car had hit a school bus carrying forty children. Many children were injured; a yet-undetermined number were dead. The car was a Porsche 944. The driver, who had been taken to the hospital, was a Porsche executive. The preliminary police report stated that the car had been going at a speed in excess of ninety miles per hour.

Porsche was in the middle of a major advertising blitz featuring the high-performance aspects of the cars. Porsche Cars North America is the marketing operation of the German maker of luxury sports cars. That night Porsche had a two-minute commercial scheduled to run on *Monday Night Football* on ABC. One week after that, Porsche Cars North America was to open a vital Dealer Council meeting in Los Angeles.

At 8:05 A.M., a newspaper reporter called PCNA headquarters, asking for comment on the story. For several hours, calls from various reporters poured in. The questions asked by the media were getting increasingly sharp and difficult. Reporters were focusing on the manufacturer's emphasis on power and performance. Did Porsche stand behind the driver? How much evidence did they have of mechanical failure? Had the driver been on a training run for an upcoming road race? Why was he driving at ninety miles per hour? What could Porsche say to the parents of the dead and injured children? When would company officials meet with the media to answer questions? How did Porsche intend to defend itself and its automobiles? Were Porsche cars built to exceed speed limits?

At 9:30 A.M., an AP radio reporter called from Los Angeles: Would PCNA comment on a statement that had just been made by a national consumer organization associated with Ralph Nader? The gist of the statement was that Porsche cars are unsafe, and that the company promotes reckless, high-speed driving.

Five minutes later, news came from the hospital: Eight children were confirmed dead; twelve were in intensive care. Now the besieging media calls intensified, with the questions growing more pointed and the atmosphere more charged with tension.

At 10:00 A.M., PCNA received a phone call of a different kind: Tony Mayo, a Porsche dealer in New York, was so upset that he could hardly talk. He had just heard a bulletin about the accident, quoting a consumer organization as saying that Porsche cars are unsafe. "What the hell is going on there?" he asked.

Feverish meetings were going on at Porsche headquarters, but they were continually interrupted by phone calls, faxes, and bulletins. At 10:15 A.M., Clarence Ditlow of the Center for Auto Safety issued a statement to the effect that while all the facts were not known, the accident had raised serious questions about Porsche cars and policies. Reaction to the statement began to mount.

Then at 10:45 A.M., there came a phone call from the mother of one of the hospitalized children. Her son had suffered burns over more than 50 percent of his body. He had to be flown immediately to a burn center in Los Angeles. There were no commercial flights available. Would Porsche charter a plane?

While the Porsche people were still trying to deal with this agonizing call, the hospital called. The driver of the Porsche in the accident had escaped serious injury. The hospital was swarming with media people who wanted to talk to him. Television and print media were calling PCNA headquarters, asking for photographs of the driver and of the Porsche model he was driving—preferably both together. They wanted copies of Porsche print advertising, and they wanted Porsche TV commercials.

Now a new concern emerged. Porsche headquarters learned from Washington that the chairpersons of three key subcommittees of the Congress were preparing to issue statements on the accident. And the chairperson of the oversight and investigations subcommittee of the House of Representatives had scheduled a press conference. The rumor was that he would launch a probe. The chairman was Representative John Dingell of Michigan, a staunch supporter of American car manufacturers.

At 11:10 A.M., the producer of *Nightline* called. Ted Koppel would be doing a show that night on sports cars and car manufacturers who promote high speed. The show would, of course, be tied in with the accident and would no doubt show footage of the accident. Koppel would like to have Brian Bowler, president and CEO of Porsche Cars North America, on the show, or if Bowler was not available, another high-level executive. They would do a remote from Reno.

Soon after the *Nightline* call, at 11:30 A.M., Porsche's vice president of sales took a call from a Porsche dealer in Arlington, Virginia. The dealer had just gotten a call from *Nightline*. The show wanted to interview him and shoot footage of the dealership. The dealer wanted to know what to do.

While headquarters was still debating this aspect of the situation, another call came in at 11:35 A.M. It was from Ted Koppel personally, saying that it was in the company's own best interests to come on the show and answer questions fully and candidly. After all, they did not have anything to hide, did they?

And so the morning went on, with dozens of media calls and other phone messages pouring in. Staff were dealing with one critical question after another about Porsche, its cars, and its policies. Feverish efforts were made to balance the shocking tragedy of the accident with plans and decisions aimed at protecting the company.

It was a dramatic story, with tremendous media appeal and serious national implications. Yet very few readers of this book have ever heard anything about it. The reason? *The accident that triggered these events never happened.* The bulletins, the phone calls, the telecommunications exchanges, the meetings—all these things happened. They were part of Project Ambush, a crisis management "fire drill" for

Porsche Cars North America that I conceived and executed with my group at Porter Novelli.

Porter Novelli had built a crisis action plan for Porsche. The plan was based on a set of general principles. Types of potential crises were identified and analyzed. Key audiences, including adversaries, were enumerated and described. Company resources were marshalled, to be ready when needed. A crisis action team was designated and trained.

To determine how well Porsche could handle an emergency, we created a realistic crisis drill, incorporating potential problems involving management, local and national media, company philosophy and practice, dealer relations, government regulatory agencies—the works. The drill, called Project Ambush, was prepared in secrecy. Key people at Porsche knew that there might be a Project Ambush in the works, but they did not know when it might come or what form it might take.

The 8:00 A.M. call on that fictional, fateful morning started with the line, "This is a Project Ambush call." The Porsche people knew it was a drill. This did not diminish the seriousness with which they took it or the intensity with which they considered their actions. They were, after all, being called upon to demonstrate their coolness and effectiveness under fire. In that sense, it was a true emergency for everyone concerned.

The Project Ambush team from Porter Novelli monitored the entire exercise, which ran from 8:00 A.M. to 1:00 P.M. The agency team was ready to respond to whatever decisions the Porsche crisis team made. For example, Porsche decided to hold a press conference, and agency people were ready in Reno to act as the media, firing the toughest possible questions and showing maximum skepticism at the answers.

Following Project Ambush, there were thorough debriefing sessions, discussions, and critiques, with extensive input from Porsche people. Porter Novelli analyzed reports from its "moles" at client headquarters, who reported on how the Porsche group reacted and how decisions were reached. The end result was some revision of the crisis plan. The biggest benefit, probably, was that Porsche's key personnel got their baptism of fire in handling a major emergency and emerged better prepared to handle the real thing. CEO Brian Bowler said he had never been under as much stress in his life as he was during the drill. All in all, Porsche did well because they had a plan to follow.

While the "crisis" did not actually happen, it was steeped in reality. It was the kind of thing that could have happened. To some extent, it was drawn from a tragedy in Kentucky in 1988, in which a pickup truck hit a school bus, killing twenty-four children and three adults. Among the factors considered in the trial of the driver, eighteen months later, was the design and safety of the bus, built by Ford Motor Company and the Sheller-Globe Corporation.

The Critical First Few Minutes

It is essential to have well-trained crisis action teams who know what to do right away in an emergency. The opening moments are critical. Word and actions under that instant pressure cannot be recalled. If they are unwise, they can seriously damage or doom any subsequent effort to recoup.

Inaction can be equally disastrous. It is natural for unprepared individuals to resort to "No comment." These days—whether it is fair or not—the response to "No comment" is likely to be, "They're trying to cover up something!" So the most important things you do in handling a crisis are the things you do in the first few minutes—at least from a public relations point of view.

And, make no mistake about it, crisis planning is a public relations matter. Obviously, other company departments are deeply involved in the aftermath of an emergency—getting plants or equipment back on line, making up for lost inventory, replacing key people, finding out what went wrong to prevent a recurrence. But if the image of the company and product are so compromised that business drops to a trickle—and stays that way—then what these other departments do will not matter all that much. Public relations is the lead function in crisis, and the key to crisis management is preparation—including, perhaps, the kind of drill I have just described.

On January 29, 1992, the *New York Times* reported that Dow-Corning's handling of the controversy that led to the Food and Drug Administration's call for a moratorium on breast implants could be compared to the Exxon Corporation's response to the *Exxon Valdez* oil spill. Critics said that Dow-Corning's mistakes included a lack of public action by its chief executive, too little sympathy and compassion for women who said they were harmed, and the failure to get the news out quickly. "It's a textbook case of crisis mismanagement," said Gerald C. Meyers, a consultant on such matters. He told the *Times:*

> It looks like the lawyers are in charge trying to limit their liability. But the damage is much worse to the corporation if they lose in the court of public opinion than if they lose in the court of law.

The Vital Importance of Prethinking

In a paper written for the International Public Relations Association, Amelia Lobsenz, chairman and CEO of Lobsenz-Stevens Inc., wrote, "One thing is evident: it is a mistake for a corporation not to prethink a policy on how to handle the strictly 'news' aspects of bad news." She urges that companies designate spokespersons for emergencies, make sure those spokespersons are available, establish information centers close to, but not at, the crisis scene, and respond to all media inquiries: "If you tell a reporter you will get back to them with information, do so. Nothing fuels media hostility more than unfulfilled promises."

Lobsenz points to one example among many of the consequences of ignoring these precautions. One day a fire started in the factory of a company making, among other items, infant cribs. Power was shut off and workers evacuated. Some employees suffered minor smoke inhalation and injuries. Fire engines and ambulances showed up— and also reporters.

Journalists could not find any company spokesperson, so they turned to others on the scene. Evening TV news stressed the spectacular flames, billowing smoke, people hospitalized with injuries. Employees told tales of confusion and chaos. One man speculated, on the basis of no particular expertise, that it could have started in a faulty electrical box. On-camera reporters stressed that there were no company officials on the scene, and that one executive, reached by phone, had "no comment" when asked if all employees were accounted for.

This was bad enough, but worse was to come. The company kept to its basic "no comment" posture. Then an article appeared, speculating on the question of whether vapors from the fire had contaminated thousands of cribs that were in production and seemed to have come out undamaged.

Company officials were furious at this "blowing things out of proportion." They knew the undamaged cribs were perfectly safe. But the damage was done. Who wants to buy a crib that may poison a baby? Sales plummeted and stayed down for a disastrously long time.

If the media had been given factual responses right from the start, and if well-informed company spokespersons had been available to discuss all aspects of the situation, including rumors about contamination, the story would never have reached such wide and catastrophic proportions.

"There Ain't No Secrets"

Having a crisis plan—and holding drills to test the plan—helps to dispel one of the most persistent notions among some corporate types: If you ignore it, it will go away. Ronald Thody, senior vice president–corporate communications for Bank of America, addressed that myth in a speech to the Public Relations Round Table in 1990:

> It seems to me there are only two schools of press relations. . . . One is the "take charge" school. The other is the "sit on it" school. The former is characterized by openness, candor, accessibility. . . . The latter school of thought operates on the basic assumption that it's none of their business and doesn't feel compelled to reveal anything, unless forced by circumstances or law.

Back in 1882, William H. Vanderbilt could say, "The public be damned," and get away with it. Not today. Ronald Thody says, "The 'sit on it' school is merely arrogant and almost always succeeds only in delaying the day of reckoning." He declares, "In the 'take charge' mode, you have the best chance of getting the story told right, because you tell it right and you tell it first. . . . You define the problem, you set the context, and in many cases, you preempt criticism." Thody winds up by warning against ignoring a basic truth of corporate America: *"There ain't no secrets."*

General Principles for Crisis Management

Richard Weiner has outlined the basic response to a crisis: "In general, crisis response programs feature three phases: identify the problem; develop the solution; communicate the action to all of the publics." When you are in the middle of a fast-breaking emergency, you may have to do all of these things almost simultaneously and under tremendous pressure. That is why it is vital to have a specific, detailed plan, and to make sure everybody knows how to work the plan.

Here are more detailed steps for handling the basics of crisis management:

1. *Isolate a crisis team from daily business concerns to focus on the problem.*
   Centralize and control the flow of information through the crisis team. Have designated spokespersons. Only designated and well-prepared spokespersons should talk to the media. Train spokespersons in advance on the company's posture and its message strategy.
2. *Develop a strategy based on a worst-case scenario.*
   Think of the worst things that could happen, then gear your strategy to those eventualities.
3. *Aim at containment, not suppression.*
   Amelia Lobsenz observes, "The reason why local crises become national and even international problems is usually because of a failure to handle communications effectively at

the local level." Put the problem into proper perspective for the media. Try to contain it geographically or to one kind of incident.

4. *Know potential allies in advance and call on them.*
   Identify public and private groups whose interests may overlap yours in time of crisis. Line up third-party support.

5. *Have a long-term crisis plan ready.*
   Most crises, even if severe, break fast and are over fast. In a few cases, the crisis lingers over a substantial period. Be ready. If spokespersons have to get back to their regular duties, have trained replacements ready to step in. Assess, in advance, the resources that would have to be devoted to a long-term crisis, and make sure they will be available. Set up provisions to review marketing, communications, and other company plans in the light of a continuing crisis. To the extent possible, clear the way for most functions to move forward without having everyone periodically sidetracked by the emergency.

6. *Draw up a comprehensive crisis action plan.*
   Distribute this document to all appropriate staff. When new people come in, make sure they get briefed on the crisis plan. Well-prepared plans can go wrong because personnel changed in key spots and nobody briefed the new employees. The action plan should contain:
   - A statement of the principles to apply in dealing with a crisis
   - A comprehensive listing of the kinds of crises that may occur
   - A listing of key audiences and an assessment of each, with particular attention to adversaries
   - An analysis of resources for the crisis plan
   - A list of the members of the crisis team (and backups for each post), with titles, locations, phone and fax numbers.

7. *Rehearse the crisis team.*
   Hold periodic workouts. Occasionally test the system with a "fire drill." There are usually four reasons for crises being handled badly:

- A lack of openness, honesty, or availability at the very beginning
- Failure to prepare for the worst case
- Failure to communicate honest, human emotion and concern by the company
- Refusal to put the company's long-term goals before short-term needs

Sometimes, complete openness means taking a hit in the short run, but it is worth it in the long run.

One other point should be made about the crisis plan. You cannot have a good communications plan for crises and a bad one for normal times. *PR Newswire* advises, "Good crisis communications is an outgrowth of good communications. If it doesn't work well normally, it's not going to work well during a time of stress." Clumsy work during an emergency can destroy credibility, but if the credibility isn't there to start with, it can't be created when things go wrong.

Be Quick with the Facts, Slow with the Blame

Scapegoating is a common reaction in time of trouble. Companies facing a crisis naturally ask, "Who's responsible for this?" The search for a culprit is a high-priority item—*if* it will help to end the crisis more quickly, or if the company is being blamed for something that can be proved to be somebody else's responsibility. If neither of these conditions exists, it's best not to make the assessment of blame one of the early goals.

It can be dangerous to finger a culprit prematurely. Peter Hannaford, chairman and CEO of The Hannaford Company, points to the experience of Hygrade, manufacturer of Ball Park frankfurters. Detroit consumers began finding foreign objects in Ball Park franks. It started when a homemaker said she had found a razor blade in one of the franks.

At first Hygrade people thought a chip from plant machinery might have found its way into the product. The company made two good decisions, according to Hannaford: "They decided to be open with the media and they decided Hygrade would have a single spokesperson."

But Hygrade also made a mistake. When they saw the foreign substance, they knew it was not there by accident. It was a fragment of a razor blade. This led to the conclusion that the hot dog had been sabotaged by "a misguided employee." This premature announcement turned out to be dead wrong. Employee morale had been high at the plant, but employees were hurt when management seemed so quick to blame them. Other objects began to turn up in Ball Park franks. The media gave the story a big play. Hygrade had to recall 350,000 pounds of franks. And, ultimately, the company had to eat its "disgruntled employee" theory. The Hygrade executive who was handling the crisis called the employees together and apologized. Now the company began to suspect a series of hoaxes, some of them copycatted after the initial story. But this time, the company did not rush to the media with its new theory.

Hygrade was able to substantiate the second theory. In one case, for example, a person—not an employee—who had reported a razor blade in a frank failed a lie-detector test and then admitted she had put it there herself. The company worked hard to get the media to give as much coverage to the exposure of the hoaxes as they had given to the discovery of the objects. The media played it this way. There were no more reports of foreign objects in the company's franks. The community in which the main plant is located banded together for "Livonia Loves Hygrade" week, during which the citizens consumed 148,000 pounds of Ball Park franks.

The company did not sue the hoaxers. It would have gotten very little money out of them, and the suits would have kept the story going after it had come to a successful conclusion from Hygrade's point of view.

With the exception of the premature—and wrong—assignment of blame to a disgruntled employee, Hygrade did a good job of being open with the media, having one credible spokesperson, and, especially, in making sure the "good news" ending of the story received adequate play.

The Tylenol Crisis Was "Easy"

Most writing on crisis management starts with two celebrated cases: Tylenol and Union Carbide. I think the cases I've cited earlier shed more light on the problem, and I have some heretical ideas about the famous episodes.

Followers of the public relations scene are fond of applauding Johnson & Johnson's handling of its 1982 Tylenol crisis as a model for handling a major emergency. Johnson & Johnson did a wonderful job. Almost a product headed for oblivion in the eighties, Tylenol regained its lead throughout the nineties. The company pulled the product off the shelves quickly and did not return it until a tamper-proof package had been designed. A tough, articulate CEO, James Burke, clearly presented management's commitment to fighting for the company's rights and its reputation. The company was open to the media, responding to questions and requests for interviews throughout the crisis. The company gave itself the vital advantage of daily public opinion research to help shape communications. And, when Tylenol was ready to make a comeback, Johnson & Johnson made it a major media event, with the first thirty-city teleconference.

Guiding its tactics was the company's strategic decision to sacrifice short-term results for long-term survival and recovery. This meant clearing $100 million worth of product off the shelves in one day, in order to regain the product's 70 percent market share a year later.

All in all, Johnson & Johnson and its communications department, headed by Larry Foster, did a fine job. Their performance is often compared favorably to that of Union Carbide, when, in December 1984, poisonous gas from the Union Carbide insecticide plant in Bhopal, India, killed 2,000 and injured 150,000.

Yet I tend to agree with Gerald E. Murray, executive vice president of Ruder & Finn, when he questions the conventional wisdom:

> So-called experts are often quick to cite Tylenol as the perfect crisis case history. Fact is, Tylenol was "easy"! Certainly not easy relative to the seven deaths or the huge financial losses. . . . But "easy" because Tylenol was "on the side of the

angels." Tylenol was attacked. Tylenol didn't initiate any harm. Tylenol did, however, suffer a total loss of market share overnight. So the business recovery was no mean feat.

Union Carbide faced a much tougher situation, beginning with the sheer magnitude of the casualties. Under the circumstances, though some will disagree, Union Carbide did a creditable job, especially considering the difficulties of dealing with a disaster so far away, and the fact that the Indian government—which owned 49 percent of the plant—was the company's principal accuser. Union Carbide was coping with an awful tragedy and an international incident. The company gathered intelligence rapidly and demonstrated its concern through CEO Warren Anderson's dramatic—and dangerous—flight to India to deal with the issue firsthand.

Murray points out something else in connection with the Bhopal disaster. The Chemical Manufacturer's Association gave tremendous help to Union Carbide. The association handled some 3,500 media inquiries in the five days following the news. This kind of outside support, especially when it is high-caliber professional support, is very valuable. Companies should find out whether their industry associations are set up to help in a crisis; if not, it makes sense for companies within an industry to help equip the industry association to be a resource in times of trouble.

The Use of an "Enemies List"

Richard Nixon got into deeper trouble when it was disclosed that his White House staff maintained an "enemies list." While this device might be unwise for a politician, a form of it is a useful part of a crisis plan.

The plan that we developed for Porsche contained, along with a listing of key audiences, a breakdown of potential adversaries. The list included consumer advocate groups, groups concerned with auto safety, and frequently quoted experts in the field. Other possibilities for a potential adversaries list might be competitive companies, industry associations, labor groups, prominent columnists—people or organizations whose positions, inclinations, and self-interest may tend to make them critical in a crisis.

We must face the fact that when crisis strikes, the company is a target. The company that seems to be at fault in a bad situation will be attacked, not only for that situation, but sometimes for other things having little connection with the immediate problem. It is a good idea to anticipate the attacks, the nature of them, and who may deliver them.

Sometimes, criticism by adversaries may be muted or even forestalled by direct communication. For example, a company coping with an emergency might want to get in touch immediately with congressional representatives and consumer advocates. This may not prevent the attacks, but at least the company's position will be reflected.

Preemptive Public Relations

Preemptive public relations is rarely necessary, but when it becomes necessary, it is urgent. When a company or an industry knows something bad is going to happen, it can deploy a PR team to soften the blow. That is what the food industry did late in 1991. The threat on the horizon was that ogre of TV land, the *60 Minutes* show.

A mention on *60 Minutes* can turn a product into an overnight success. But a negative segment on *60 Minutes* can create an instant depression in significant segments of the economy. So, when it became known that *60 Minutes* was going to do a show on monosodium glutamate (MSG), the shock waves spread rapidly, since MSG (as the *Wall Street Journal* of October 17, 1991, said) "is used in everything from chicken chow mein to corn chips." The industry launched one of the largest preemptive campaigns in history.

Part of the preemptive public relations in this case was anticipatory. The food industry was lining up authorities to contradict damaging claims on the *60 Minutes* segment, when and if it ran. Part of it involved moves that were made before the fact, to cushion the blow. And, of course, a lot of it was directly aimed at the show itself. The *60*

Minutes producer, Don Hewitt, was besieged with facts, figures, arguments, and pleas. But not threats.

It is hard to say how well this worked. The MSG people were probably well advised to do it.

Anticipating Disasters

A useful tool for production managers is the "walk-through." It simply means that the executive periodically walks through the plant, looks at what is going on, and listens to what is being said—and not being said. You can learn more that way than you can from looking at printouts.

Communications and PR professionals should have walk-throughs of their operations to get a sense of what could go wrong. Robert Slater, vice president of Manning, Selvage & Lee, told the New York chapter of the Public Relations Society of America how to spot potential trouble areas:

> Begin at the plant level. Check the plant, its processes, its potentially hazardous raw materials. The plant manager may say, "Ridiculous. Here's PR coming around, sticking its nose in my responsibility again. If—and when—a disaster happens, I'll take care of it." You *know* something's going to happen in his plant.

Apart from the walk-through of plants, warehouses, and other operations areas, PR practitioners should learn all about the company's shipping and its products. Ask worst-case questions:

- Is it conceivable—not likely, but conceivable—that people could be badly hurt by one of our products?
- If I were a saboteur, how would I sabotage the company?
- What is the worst thing that could happen in the plant, en route, and at the customer's end?

There are all kinds of reasons why public relations practitioners should get close to the nitty-gritty and become thoroughly familiar with everything that is going on. One important reason is that it helps in envisioning the kinds of emergencies that could come up.

Have Someone on the Scene in Emergencies

Let us say a company has its headquarters in Chicago and its plants in several locations around the country. There is an explosion in the Little Rock plant. The company has followed the rule of establishing one authorized spokesperson. The trouble is that the spokesperson is in Chicago.

When a story is breaking, local media cannot be asked to wait while an authorized spokesperson flies in from hundreds or thousands of miles away, or issues a statement by phone or fax. Reporters will be frustrated and annoyed. The company's story will be treated with great skepticism. The dreaded word *cover-up* will lurk behind every news item.

Credibility as a spokesperson depends on more than rank. The spokesperson has to be someone who can be viewed as knowing what actually happened. So there should be a well-prepared spokesperson at—or near—every place where a major emergency might occur.

The spokesperson does not have to be prepared to issue broad-scale corporate pronouncements. But that person should be prepared to do two things:

1. Give the press factual answers
2. Keep these factual answers within the guidelines of the company's communications policy

Airco, Inc., of Montvale, New Jersey, tells its people:

Uncooperative dealings with the press in an emergency situation or disaster at your plant or laboratory can be very costly to the company—in terms of reputation, credibility, and community relations—*for a long period of time.* It is vital that you be prepared to deal with the press in emergencies, such as on-the-job fatalities and serious injuries, explosions and fires, natural disasters (storms, floods), environmental incidents (spills, pollution), or major accidents involving company vehicles.

Here are some of the big questions that an on-the-spot spokesperson should be ready to handle.

- *What happened?*
  Give the essentials without going into highly technical detail. Was there an explosion? How many explosions? Fire? Floor or wall collapse? (Give the facts without speculation: "There was an explosion in the plating department." Do not add, "It was probably caused by . . .")

- *Was anybody killed or hurt?*
  In the first minutes after the emergency, it may be evident that people were hurt, but not how many. It is enough to say, "We have had some injuries." Low estimates that keep mounting are not helpful, nor are high estimates that make a lurid impact. In cases of serious injury or fatality, victims' families must be notified first, but it is best not to say that this is being done. Also, the spokesperson should volunteer information about people who were *not* injured and who reacted quickly or helped in rescue attempts.

- *When did it happen?*
  Pinpoint the timetable as accurately as possible, in as much detail as possible.

- *Where did it happen?*
  Locate and describe the areas involved. Stick to function. You could say, "That's where they paint the frames," but do not say, "We store inflammable liquids there."

- *How much damage was there?*
  The spokesperson should not get into dollar estimates, discussion of how long the facility will be shut down, or other

specifics. Media can be assured that they will be allowed to see for themselves as soon as it is safe.

- *What caused it?*
  Speculation about the cause could be very harmful. In most situations, the spokesperson should just say that a thorough investigation has already been started, and should perhaps describe the measures that will be taken to determine the cause.

Reporters covering an accident or other emergency know that the spokesperson is limited in what can be said. The media will demand those facts which ought to be available and will respond negatively to excessive vagueness or delay. With few exceptions, they will accept the fact that speculation about causes or premature information about injuries is out. However, they will be alert and ready to jump on any unwary statement that is made.

Obviously, the company wants all media contacts to be handled by the spokesperson. Some companies have tried to issue ironclad orders. For example, a public relations plan for disasters and emergencies, issued by Marriott Hotels in the 1980s, said, "The property's employees are *strictly prohibited* from making any statement, providing information, commenting on the situation, or talking with the media. All inquiries should be directed to the Midwest public relations manager."

Gag orders are usually impractical. You have a dazed, smoke-stained employee standing outside a burning building. A TV reporter sticks a mike in his face. It is impossible to predict what the employee may say, but he or she is unlikely to say, "All inquiries should be directed to the Midwest public relations manager."

This brings up another point. Should the designated spokesperson be a public relations practitioner? Probably not. First of all, in the case of factories and other such places where accidents may occur, there are probably no PR practitioners in attendance. Second, the media want to talk with a professional, a line manager, or some other *primary* source. Disaster stories that say, for example, "The company statement was read by the vice president for public relations, Joe Doe, . . ." do not always inspire a lot of confidence.

If possible, it is good to have a public relations pro supporting and assisting the spokesperson and providing background information to the press. But the story of what happened should come from somebody who can tell it authoritatively.

Be Quick, Be Sure, Be Ready, Be Truthful

The essence of handling emergencies, for the short and long term, is to have a workable plan and to drill key people on implementing that plan if disaster strikes. The plan must provide for an authoritative spokesperson, openness and truthfulness with the media, and quick response to the unpredictable twists and turns of the situation.

11

Gentrifying the National Enquirer

The Art of Image Revision

The word *corporation* stems from *corpus,* Latin for "body," and, indeed, the concept of the corporation is that of a legal body with certain privileges, responsibilities, and protections. But these days, people form definite ideas of what big corporations are like, as if the thousands and thousands of people in the company all fused into one gigantic creature.

It is important that the giant be viewed as a nice giant. When a corporation gets a bad image, that image casts a shadow over the company's products, no matter how good they are. Dow Chemical's image as a manufacturer of napalm was not helpful to the sale of bathroom cleaners. It took years for the unfortunate image to wear off. General Electric, once viewed as a rather cold company, has put a lot of money and effort into a well-conceived campaign to give the corporation a warm and caring image: "We bring good things to life."

The right image is important, not only in selling products but in raising capital and dealing with government bodies. It is vital when the time comes to sell the company, and it helps in raising morale within the company.

One of the tasks of modern public relations is to modify corporate images—which is harder than creating them from scratch. The image that was perfect at one time may no longer suit the company's new plans or the new realities of the marketplace.

Tabloid Seeks Transformation

Take the case of the *National Enquirer*. Changing the image of this well-known tabloid was one of the most delightful challenges I ever worked on.

Everybody knows the tabloids, if only from reading the shrieking headlines while waiting at the checkout line: "Grandad Turns Gay After Female Heart Transplant!" . . . "Liz to Be Teddy's First Lady!" . . . "UFO Alien Eats 80-Pound Labrador!" . . . "Elvis Sires Sextuplets from Beyond Grave!" The *National Enquirer* is the granddaddy of all the tabloids, beginning in 1926 as the *New York Enquirer*, a broadsheet with horse-racing entries and results. In 1952, the paper was bought by Generoso Pope Jr. At the age of twenty-five, Pope was an MIT graduate, an alumnus of the CIA, and editor and publisher of his father's Italian-language *Il Progresso*. Under young Pope's guidance, the *Enquirer*—whose circulation had sunk to 17,000—was transformed into a sensational phantasmagoria of the bizarre, the titillating, and the unthinkable.

Sales took off like a rocket. People grabbed the *Enquirer* off the racks at newsstands and corner stores. But, around the midsixties, Pope looked ahead and saw great promise and a potential problem. The promise was the supermarket. The problem was that the *Enquirer's* mixture of sex and occultism—now being emulated by several rivals—would be too spicy for supermarket managers, who wanted to entice their customers but not shock them into a dead faint.

Seeking Respectability

The *Enquirer* began a shift toward emphasizing traditional American values and more strongly presenting service features—diet, health, beauty, money. The earlier mixture was not totally discarded, either. The *Enquirer* still entertained its readers with out-of-this-world sensations. But much of the gore was gone. While three-headed martians from UFOs still made astounding suggestions to dumbfounded maidens, the paper was not so likely to scream forth the depredations of "Tots Who Slay Family of Six and Eat Them!"

When we undertook the further changing of the *Enquirer*'s image in 1986, we were not talking about turning the publication into the *Christian Science Monitor* or the *Financial Times*. The *Enquirer* was—and remains—a big success, with a circulation of about 2 million.

Our approach to repositioning the *Enquirer* was to emphasize the differences between it and its competition. Gossip is one thing; squalor is another. The *Enquirer* is a journal of celebrity gossip, more pungent than *People* magazine or the TV show *Lifestyles of the Rich and Famous*. One of our thrusts, then, is to underscore that the paper's gossip is accurate gossip. Let's face it: back in 1981, when the *Enquirer* settled Carol Burnett's libel suit for $800,000 (Burnett had sued for $10 million), the time had come to make radical changes. In the 1970s, more than $75 million worth of lawsuits had been filed by, among others, Redd Foxx, Hedy Lamarr, Larry Hagman, Richard Pryor, and Raquel Welsh. The carefree days when the facts did not get in the way of a good story were clearly gone.

Of necessity, the *Enquirer* had installed elaborate procedures to ensure accuracy. We decided to publicize them by placing stories about the *Enquirer*'s research department, run by a former *Time* magazine staffer. We placed stories about the fact that celebrity items must be tape-recorded or corroborated by two sources; about the paper's checking of medical stories in advance with such organizations as the American Heart Association; and, overall, about the safeguards that enabled us to state, "The *Enquirer* ranks as one of the most error-proof publications in the country." The fact that this accuracy is devoted to whether or not Madonna is pregnant is beside the point.

Values, Not Sleaze

To dispel the aura of sleaze, we focused on the celebration of traditional American values. The *Enquirer* gives three kinds of awards. The Hero Award is given to those who risk their lives to save another. The Honest Person Award goes to those who find large sums of money or valuables and return them. The Good Samaritan Award is bestowed on those who help the less fortunate by feeding the hungry and housing and clothing the poor.

We recommended that the *Enquirer* bring all these honorees together for a special awards ceremony. The place was to be Washington, D.C. The budget would be $100,000, with most of the money going to fly the winners—with spouses or friends—to Washington for two days. The amount involved in the award itself is only a modest $150 and a Certificate of Honor.

The initial plan called for everyone to stay at the Mayflower Hotel, where an awards lunch would be held. But, as we reviewed this, it seemed too ordinary and not calculated to attract press and government officials.

So, why not hold the ceremony in the U.S. Capitol itself? Although many people are not aware of it, getting the use of a room in the Capitol is relatively simple. I like to hold functions there when it is at all appropriate. The location confers dignity and importance, and perhaps even a suggestion of government sponsorship or, at least, official sanction.

The appearance of official sanction can add solidity to a lightweight event. Because the *Enquirer* is based in Lantana, Florida, we got in touch with Senator Lawton Chiles, then the senior senator from Florida, and later its governor. (He was succeeded by Jeb Bush in 1998, and died shortly thereafter.) We were assigned the Mansfield Room, just across the hall from the entrance to the Senate Chamber. We had taken an important step in building credibility. Now it was time to line up an eminent speaker. And a funny thing happened. We could get none of the well-known politicians we approached. They did not seem to want to be associated with the *National Enquirer.*

So we took a different tack. Inasmuch as we were honoring heroes, why not honor one of the nation's outstanding heroes? It happened that the year (1987) marked the twenty-fifth anniversary of America's first orbital space flight. That flight had been taken by John Glenn, a Democratic senator from Ohio, former presidential candidate—a bona fide hero then and certainly since his 1998 space flight. We called Senator Glenn's press secretary. Would Glenn accept our award?

Officeholders almost always accept awards. The donor of the award would have to be infamous indeed for the recipient to refuse it. And, after all, *Enquirer* readers vote, too. So we got a positive response, but the big question remained. Would he be available to receive the award in person? We had made it convenient by rescheduling the event as a breakfast, so it would require just a moment of his time. Glenn's office was not sure they wanted the senator to get that involved.

We needed someone else in case Glenn did not show up. However, now we had going for us the fact that Senator Glenn had agreed to accept the award. We approached Representative Bob Michel, Republican from Peoria, Illinois, and the House Minority Leader. We asked Representative Michel to make a brief keynote speech, and we offered $2,500 for his favorite charity. Representative Michel accepted.

Now we rolled out the releases. Michel would be the keynote speaker, and Glenn would get a special American Hero award. In addition to the sung hero, unsung heroes from across the country would get awards. All would join for a breakfast in the Mansfield Room in the Capitol, sponsored by Senator Lawton Chiles.

Pretty impressive. The ceremony garnered a great deal of publicity in the national and major-market media. Segments of the ceremony appeared on several dozen television stations nationwide. We targeted special efforts to the hometowns of the award winners. Later, a special video was developed to reach potential advertisers.

Not only did Senator Glenn show up to accept the award, he spoke to the assemblage and stayed for the entire event, doing interviews for the media at its conclusion. The message of the event was clear. The *National Enquirer* stands for positive American values, honoring ordinary Americans who have shown their commitment to honesty, charity, and valor. The participation of important national figures, like Glenn and Michel, bestowed stature and credibility on the *Enquirer.* We had taken an important step in enhancing the image of the publication, and it turned out to be a relatively inexpensive PR jackpot compared to Senator Glenn's 1998 billion-dollar Power Public Relations flight into space.

The Thrill Is Not Gone

Image change is tricky. We did not want to promulgate the idea that the *Enquirer* had become stuffy. The publication had achieved its success with thrills—and it was important to demonstrate that the thrills were still there in ample measure. The best image change retains the useful qualities of the old image. The episode of the Gary Hart photographs in the *Enquirer* took care of that concern.

On May 19, 1987, we got a phone call from Iain Calder, the editor of the *Enquirer*. The paper had some interesting photos that would run in the next issue, dated June 2. These were photos of some folks having fun on vacation. The folks happened to be Gary Hart, at that time the leading contender for the Democratic nomination for president, and Donna Rice, at play on a yachting trip. The key picture, which would run on page one, showed Rice sitting on Hart's lap, in a close embrace. Each was holding a drink. The presidential candidate wore a T-shirt bearing the name of the yacht: *Monkey Business*.

We wanted maximum publicity. But we wanted people to buy the paper, too. We went into emergency session to decide how to exploit the story. We discussed a press conference, either in New York or Lantana. We discussed releasing copies of the photographs. This was big national news, and there was no question that we would get major play. The Hart/Rice story was hot, but confused—full of claims, charges, countercharges, and denials. We had hard evidence. Release of the evidence would make page one of the papers and lead the TV news.

But if we released too much information, we would destroy the motivation to buy the paper. So we decided to give exclusive interviews with editor Calder to the three major TV networks. To intensify the drama of the story, we had a member of Edward Bennett Williams's Washington law firm call the key network people. Williams, whose firm represented the *Enquirer*, was renowned as the consummate Washington insider. When he talked, editors listened.

The *Enquirer* would be partly distributed to supermarkets and newstands on the following Monday, May 25, with distribution being completed on Tuesday. We scheduled Calder's interviews for Sunday,

May 24. However, the paper was by now being printed in *Enquirer* plants around the country, and word leaked out. We learned that UPI was planning to run a story. So we moved our plan up one day. Calder broke the news by conducting three separate interviews in his suite at the Jefferson Hotel in Washington on Saturday, May 23. At the same time, we were calling wire services and major newspapers across the country.

Results were satisfactory, to say the least. The story about the *Enquirer* having the pictures was tops on television, page one in the newspapers. The *Enquirer*'s average circulation of 4.5 million climbed beyond 5 million for that issue. The photographs, with credit to the *Enquirer,* would eventually run more times than Pulitzer Prize–winning photos from World War II and subsequent wars.

And interest in the story continued beyond the breaking of the photographs. There was the collateral story revolving around the burning question: How had the *Enquirer* obtained the photographs? (The pictures were, in fact, taken with Rice's camera by her friend Lynn Armandt, who was also along on the now famous—or infamous—cruise of the *Monkey Business* to Bimini, and sold to the *Enquirer* for a low five-figure sum.) Speculation began to firm up around the proposition that it was the ambitious Rice herself who first broke the news of the relationship. This speculation was not, perhaps, ill founded.

The Deep Six for Gary Hart

The *Enquirer* story accompanying the photos was in the grand old tradition, starting with the news that "Gary Hart's secret girl-friend, Donna Rice, was confiding to friends that Hart was plan-ning to divorce his wife after he was elected President—then marry Donna and bring her to the White House as his new First Lady." The story ended on a touching note, disclosing that Rice is "getting show-business offers. But she says no success as an actress or model can make up for the heartbreak of losing Gary Hart and the chance to live in the White House." Despite sentiments like these, many in the public came to suspect that Hart had been set up and used by his sailing companion. The perception did not help Hart.

Another continuing topic was the ethics of the news coverage. *Newsweek* observed, "The images give fresh life to the questions about Hart's judgment and self-destructive psychology." *Time* delivered profundities about "two kinds of news, the important and the interesting. . . . Like every big news story, Gary Hart's downfall happily combined both." But, *Time* went on, "Importance did not require a competition to see who could get the sexiest picture of Donna Rice with Hart, which the scandal-tabloid *National Enquirer* won." Along with these high-level considerations, both *Time* and *Newsweek* found space to run the photo of Rice on Hart's lap. Apart from a high regard for journalistic integrity, it also helps to have a healthy ability to run with the hare and hunt with the hounds.

In July 1987, we compiled a report on the Donna Rice/Gary Hart article. Publicity had resulted in more than 700 print articles with combined circulation of more than 65 million. There had been comparable, extensive TV coverage. This coverage talked about the *Enquirer* as well as the two principals. We had helped to see to that by sending out background materials to print media and videocassettes to TV stations, right after the story broke.

Nor was this the end. When former Senator Hart made his astonishing reentry into the presidential race, the whole thing surfaced again.

Image changing rarely calls for the adoption of a completely new look. You have to keep the winning features of the old image while altering losing parts. That was our job with the *National Enquirer*. We made the *Enquirer* look more like traditional, American home cooking—but we retained all the old spice. With the O. J. Simpson trial and Monica madness in the nineties, the *Enquirer* lifted itself to the role of fierce competitor to the major print and broadcast media.

12

From Lawsuits to Murder Trials

PR and the Scales of Justice

Justice is blind, they say, and, indeed, the traditional statue of Justice shows her robed and blindfolded, holding a scale. But it seems that Justice can see through that blindfold to watch television and read the papers and newsmagazines.

That is why public relations has become an influential factor in civil and criminal trials. Defense attorneys (and often prosecutors) stand on the courthouse steps and plead their cases for the TV cameras. Well-coached parties to lawsuits give shrewdly calculated interviews designed to pressure the opposition into a more favorable settlement.

Today, many individuals and organizations involved in court cases hire public relations counsel along with legal counsel—to good effect.

PR Rescues a Legal Case

Here is a case in which PR pressure helped to bring about a favorable settlement for the plaintiff in a David-and-Goliath legal battle against a huge and powerful opponent. The case weaves together a number of threads: "lender liability," the legal concept under which borrowers are successfully suing lenders on the grounds of unfair treatment; Texas, and its boom-and-bust economy; the tremendous proliferation of luxury hotels; and the American dream of entrepreneurial success.

The case was a suit for $7 billion brought against Metropolitan Life Insurance Company by Patrick J. Kennedy, a Texas hotel entrepreneur. Pat Kennedy is a man with a big idea. The idea to build a hotel came to him while looking out the window of Nix Medical Center in downtown San Antonio more than three decades ago.

San Antonio was getting ready for the HemisFair 1968 World's Fair. Kennedy was at the hospital for the birth of his eighth child. As Kennedy gazed out at the soon-to-be-vacated grounds of his law school alma mater, St. Mary's University, he thought about the city's lack of first-class facilities to house visitors. Kennedy's imaginative eye saw a luxury hotel rising on the St. Mary's site.

Pat Kennedy is a lawyer and former army officer. Once his dream took hold, he devoted himself to it wholeheartedly. His idea was to build a hotel combining the opulence of Texas prosperity with the heritage of San Antonio. Kennedy got the financing and pushed through the project. La Mansion del Rio, a luxury hotel with Colonial Spanish architecture, opened on San Antonio's famed River Walk in time for the world's fair. It gained rapid success.

Building on the success of his first hotel, Kennedy opened La Mansion del Norte on the north side of San Antonio in 1978. Metropolitan Life Insurance Company loaned Kennedy $8.1 million to finance the expansion. La Mansion del Norte became profitable during its first year.

In 1979 La Mansion del Rio was expanded to nearly double the hotel's original size. Kennedy was now working very closely with Metropolitan Life. The relationship went well beyond that of a borrower and lender. Kennedy took his next step, buying a five-acre site in Austin for construction of a new La Mansion hotel in the state capital. The Texas economy was rolling, his hotels were prospering, and Metropolitan Life was a staunch ally.

Metropolitan Life Becomes a Player

But, unknown to Kennedy, Metropolitan Life had decided to become a player, not just a lender, in the hotel industry. In 1981, Metropolitan Life acquired an interest in Doubletree Hotels, an aggressive, competitive Arizona-based hotel chain.

With Metropolitan Life's help, Doubletree planned an explosive expansion. According to internal Doubletree documents, a key to the expansion was Metropolitan Life's ability to squeeze hotel companies to which it had loaned money to the point where they were ripe for takeover by Doubletree, following foreclosure or forced sale.

The world energy situation deteriorated, and the Texas economy met hard times. With business activity down, the hotel industry ran into tough going. Jim Schmidt, president of Doubletree, called Kennedy to talk about an acquisition. Kennedy declined. By this time, however, Metropolitan Life had informed Doubletree that La Mansion was under financial pressure because of the Texas economy. Pat Kennedy's La Mansion hotels were targeted for a takeover.

Peter Bidstrup, Doubletree's chairman, called Kennedy, who again declined to talk about a deal. Bidstrup said, "Pat will now ruminate about the future while feeling more pain." Metropolitan Life, which had moved to foreclose other Texas hotels that were targets for Doubletree, allegedly gave Doubletree confidential information on La Mansion and indicated the possibility of foreclosure.

Now the squeeze play began. On December 19, 1986, Metropolitan Life announced that it had bought the remaining 80 percent of Doubletree stock. At about the same date, Metropolitan Life suddenly told Kennedy his request of refinancing had been turned down. Kennedy and his team flew to Houston. They demanded to see Fred Arnholt, southwestern regional vice president of Metropolitan Life. Arnholt refused. Kennedy and his advisers camped in the Metropolitan Life offices until Arnholt agreed to see them. At the meeting, the insurance company threatened foreclosure, adding that it would pursue Kennedy on his personal guarantee. Metropolitan Life said it would take over La Mansion del Norte to begin with, installing Doubletree as manager. Kennedy fought back hard, and Metropolitan Life reluctantly agreed to consider a ninety-day extension.

Rumor of a takeover of La Mansion circulated through the industry. Morale deteriorated; people started leaving La Mansion.

In October 1987, Pat Kennedy found a Texas investor who was willing to put up the money needed to bring the Metropolitan Life loan current and to provide for a permanent workout agreement. A junior Metropolitan Life lending officer complimented Kennedy on the quality of the proposal and promised to give it consideration.

A meeting was called for December 2, 1987. Metropolitan Life turned down Kennedy's proposal, refused to accept payments, and suddenly declared the loan on La Mansion del Norte to be in default.

As soon as the meeting was over, Doubletree was notified that Metropolitan Life intended to foreclose. Foreclosure was proceeding when, on February 1, 1988, La Mansion filed suit and obtained a temporary restraining order. Kennedy and La Mansion charged Metropolitan Life and Doubletree with fraud, breach of faith, interference, duress, breach of confidential relationship and fiduciary duties, and deceptive trade practices.

Trial was set for May 1988. Metropolitan obtained two postponements. At this point, the case suddenly achieved widespread prominence.

Bad Ink for Metropolitan Life

Business Week's issue of August 22, 1988, carried a three-page article about the case. The headline— "Did Met Put the Squeeze on Hotel Debtors?"—suggests the tone of the piece. While the facts are laid out fairly and accurately, the overall effect is damaging to Metropolitan Life. A lot of the story is told from Pat Kennedy's point of view:

> Patrick J. Kennedy had every reason to feel confident as he walked into Metropolitan Life Insurance Co.'s Houston office early one morning. . . . Within minutes after entering Arnholt's office, Kennedy knew he was in trouble. . . . Kennedy was startled. This didn't seem to be the usual case of a creditor who has lost confidence in a borrower's ability to pay. . . . He wondered whether Met really wanted him to get through his cash crunch. Maybe it wanted him to default.

While the *Business Week* article does not draw any conclusions, its presentation of the issues, along with quotes from people in business and academia, is not a strong boost for Metropolitan Life.

Furthermore, that same issue of *Business Week* carried an editorial headed, "Is Met Life Setting a Bad Example?" The editorial says, "It seems indisputable that Met has been using its influence as one of the hotel industry's biggest lenders and equity owners to help Doubletree get management contracts." Metropolitan Life came under fire from two directions: "Other hotel managers say they will shun loans from Met due to its divided loyalties, and other lenders criticize Met, saying they avoid ventures that compete with their customers." *Business Week* declares that diversification by financial institutions has been healthy and has spurred competition, but adds that the managers of these institutions "should heed the warning of the Met episode. In their urge to offer a wider array of services, they need to be ever-sensitive to the problem of conflicts between their financial and nonfinancial activities."

Maybe Metropolitan Life had not been keenly sensitive to the problem of conflicts, but its executives were certainly sensitive to the *Business Week* article. They were stung by just about everything in the piece, right down to the concluding sentence: "Worst of all, Met's ownership of Doubletree may have tarnished a conservative, caring image that took the Old Lady of One Madison Avenue 120 years to create."

How It Happened

Around the middle of 1988, Kennedy and his lawyer, Larry Macon, decided they needed public relations help. Metropolitan Life did not blink at the lawsuit, even with its billion-dollar numbers. Maybe PR pressure would cause the company to take pause. They went to a local firm, which talked about putting out some press releases. Macon and Kennedy had something a little more robust in mind. They wound up retaining my firm at the time, Porter Novelli. I personally took on the assignment, and I saw a chance to project a sympathetic image for Pat Kennedy through the mass media as well as the business press. To me, the perfect place to start was *60 Minutes*. The story was the kind of conflict that *60 Minutes* loves: a little guy battling against gigantic forces that threaten to crush him.

I talked to Sandy Socolow, a *60 Minutes* producer. Sandy and I, at one time, worked for the same news agency, INS. I replaced him in INS's Tokyo bureau. Socolow agreed that the idea had promise. After talking with Pat Kennedy, Socolow seemed even more convinced. He scheduled a trip to San Antonio. And then, on the eve of his departure, the project was suddenly derailed. The *60 Minutes* producers each work up stories for particular stars. Socolow's star at this time was Harry Reasoner, and Reasoner, when he heard about the idea, informed Socolow that he, Reasoner, was getting married to the head nurse at the Metropolitan Life executive suite.

Talk about conflict! You certainly could not have a story about Metropolitan Life anchored by the husband of CEO John Creedon's nurse. I tried to interest other *60 Minutes* producers in the idea, but they showed an understandable lack of enthusiasm for taking on a project that had been dropped by a colleague.

That was the end of the *60 Minutes* strategy. I looked around for another way to get the campaign going on a high note. A story in an influential business publication would not reach the huge audience commanded by *60 Minutes*, but it would be read by people whose opinions mattered to Metropolitan Life. I broached the idea of such a story to Chris Welles of *Business Week*. Welles is *Business Week*'s number one investigative reporter. He was interested but cautious. He would not touch it if it were just a dispute between Kennedy and his lender. I insisted that the case had wider implications. Welles began to check it out, concluded that the story was important, and wrote it. In all, he spent six full weeks working on the story.

The major reason that the *Business Week* article is short on quotes from Metropolitan Life people and lacks a strong reflection of their point of view is that the huge insurance company was exceedingly wary about dealing with the press. In fact, Metropolitan Life would not talk with Welles in person, but asked him to submit written questions.

Mishandling the Press

Metropolitan Life had made several miscalculations. Like it or not, public relations is a considerable factor today in building reputations, marketing products, influencing stockholders—and in conducting lawsuits. It is not that the judge or jury will be so influenced by stories planted in the media that they will give one side a break, but that what appears in print and on television helps to shape the environment of opinion within which attitudes are adopted and judgments are formed. Obviously, the influence is subtle and difficult to measure. In selecting juries, lawyers focus on the degree to which jurors have been exposed to publicity and the ways in which they have been affected.

But in the case of *Kennedy vs. Metropolitan Life,* there was more to it than that. Kennedy and Macon knew that if the case went to a jury, there would probably be a clear-cut outcome. Kennedy would win his suit or he would lose it (although the Kennedy camp worried that they could win a Pyrrhic victory, with the jury agreeing to Kennedy's allegations but awarding him so little in damages that he would come out a financial loser).

If, however, the case were to be settled, there might not be a clear-cut winner. Macon and Kennedy knew that in such settlements, the amount of money paid to the plaintiff is sometimes kept secret. But Pat Kennedy wanted there to be no doubt that he was the winner. For one thing, Kennedy was a proud man, who felt that he had been scorned and mistreated. There was also a practical aspect. If Kennedy were to stay in business and resume his dream of a ring of La Mansion hotels in Texas and other states, he would need to also look like a winner. Good people do not come to work for losers. Lenders do not lend money to losers. A clear winning image would be more than just gratifying for Pat Kennedy. He saw it as a business necessity.

So he determined to pursue a winning strategy in the arena of public opinion as well as in court. He is a quiet, conservative man, but he has a keen appreciation for the importance of adroit public relations to his case. It came as an unwelcome surprise to some executives of Metropolitan Life that their adversary was using publicity against them. This did not conform with their image of Kennedy.

In keeping Chris Welles at arm's length, Metropolitan Life made the kind of mistake about the media that sometimes plagues very large organizations (and highly successful people), especially when they have enjoyed wide admiration. Media people are not willing to settle for the kind of regal approach that requires submitting questions in writing. In this case, Welles was not about to drop the story when Metropolitan Life would not talk to him. Big companies occasionally still cherish the notion that unwillingness to cooperate can keep something from being printed or aired. Usually, it works the other way. The reporters sense that there is something there, and they go after it more energetically.

Since *Business Week*'s reporter had ample access to Kennedy and the Kennedy team, the story reflected the Kennedy viewpoint. Metropolitan Life and its public relations professionals, if in fact they were even brought in, had miscalculated the reaction of the media.

During the legal skirmishing that followed, Metropolitan Life's lawyers often mentioned the fact that Kennedy had hired a New York PR firm, usually adding with a kind of disapproving intonation that this was the same company that represented the *National Enquirer.* Metropolitan Life's questions on this issue sought to discover whether Kennedy might be spending hotel operating funds on PR for his own case. Kennedy's people were able to point out that Metropolitan Life itself spent a pretty penny on public relations, as well as on its massive advertising campaigns.

Is It a Sin to Use Public Relations?

Metropolitan Life's lawyers evidently felt that Pat Kennedy was vulnerable because he had hired a public relations firm. Not just any PR firm, but a big, New York outfit. One tactic was to emphasize the fact that these publicists had "unsavory" clients. How would it look to a Texas jury when this supposed straight arrow, Patrick J. Kennedy, was exposed as having brought in these sharp New York press agents to hype his case?

The claims were true. Kennedy was represented by Porter Novelli, which had at one time worked for the *National Enquirer*—the supermarket tabloid that had run the notorious picture of Gary Hart cavorting with Donna Rice aboard the yacht *Monkey Business.* Chapter 11 chronicles that story in detail.

Metropolitan Life cried foul. The idea seemed to be that using public relations was somehow out of bounds. The Kennedy forces dismissed this contention, citing the fact that Metropolitan Life had PR professionals on its staff, spent a lot of money on public relations, and, in addition, had spent hundreds of millions to project a winsome, innocent image of Metropolitan Life throughout the tremendous advertising campaign featuring the moppets from the comic strip "Peanuts." ("Get Met. It Pays.")

PR's Growing Presence in Court

What Kennedy did in hiring a PR consultant was realistic. For better or for worse, public relations has, in recent years, become a far more important player in the business game than was once the case. Once, public relations was pretty much confined to sending out news releases when a new product came out or somebody got promoted. A few companies still seem to operate that way. Public relations is a low-level activity, grinding out puff pieces, until something goes wrong. Then the CEO demands that the company's director of public relations keep the bad news out of the papers.

Public relations is potentially more complex and more effective than that. It can't live up to the exaggerated claims made by its most zealous advocates, but it is true that if you can influence the way people think, you can make money. Public relations is better at influencing the way people think than it used to be. So many businesspeople today consider the engineering of public perception as a standard element of any success plan. (Ask Donald Trump whether public relations is just sending out news releases.)

Kennedy figured he needed the best legal counsel he could get. Larry Macon was the best. And he figured he needed good PR counsel as well, since public perception might be pretty important in the case.

The court skirmish continued, with Metropolitan Life seeking delays and Kennedy pressing for trial. After the *Business Week* article, the case began to be covered substantially in the media, including the *Wall Street Journal* and the important hotel and real estate trade press. Metropolitan Life continued to show itself to be highly sensitive to negative publicity. And why not? The company's campaign of TV spots, featuring Charlie Brown, Snoopy, Lucy, and the rest of the "Peanuts" gang, presents an image of simple, winsome straightforwardness. The Kennedy version, which depicted Metropolitan Life as a ruthless practitioner of squeeze tactics, was definitely at odds with this idyllic vision. People would be shocked to learn that Snoopy mercilessly hounds people out of business in order to seize the fruits of their enterprise.

Pat Kennedy was hanging on by his fingernails through the delays. But as the trial date was nearing, Metropolitan Life was now paying a big price as well, with a great deal of negative publicity in the media. (After the case was settled, a Metropolitan Life lawyer in its New York City headquarters told a *Wall Street Journal* reporter that Metropolitan Life was getting clobbered in the media by some small hotel in Texas. To prove his point, he pointed to a stack of clippings on his desk from publications throughout the country.)

The End of the Fight

Then suddenly, almost on the eve of the trial, it ended. Late on the night of Tuesday, March 14, 1989, the lawyers representing both sides met in the home of presiding judge Peter Michael Curry and signed off on a settlement that had been agreed to earlier in the day.

Kennedy's four-star La Mansion del Rio hotel would not be lost. It would go on to rank as the premier hotel in San Antonio in the late 1990s. Rick Lyman, writing in the *New York Times* (November 29, 1998), said the 337-room La Mansion del Rio is "so popular that it is difficult to get a room."

Both parties agreed that the terms and conditions of the settlement be kept secret. This concerned Pat Kennedy. Without breaking an agreement, how could we communicate to the San Antonio media and business community that Kennedy was not a loser? The day after the settlement, hundreds of guests, hastily invited (by plan), gathered in the hotel's Iberian Ballroom to drink champagne amid festive balloons. The winner was obvious, and no details had to be released.

Some three years later, perhaps mindful of *Business Week*'s stinging criticism that ownership of Doubletree Hotels may have "tarnished the old lady," Metropolitan Life sold the Doubletree chain and went out of the hotel ownership business.

When the conservative businessman Pat Kennedy hired a public relations counsel along with his legal counsel, some felt that he had made a very odd move indeed. But Kennedy had read the trends correctly. Public relations is now an influential factor in legal maneuvering. In this case, Metropolitan Life's increasing uneasiness about publicity contributed substantially to their willingness to settle. The final evidence of that is the battle waged by their lawyers to have the settlement include a gag order that would prohibit all parties from saying anything about the case.

Public opinion is now a weighty presence in court. Those who have to go to court are strengthening their cases by bringing public opinion to their side.

Using Public Relations to Win Without a Lawsuit

Potential litigants will increasingly use public relations to win without going to court. *The Patriarch: The Rise and Fall of the Bingham Dynasty,* by Susan E. Tifft and Alex S. Jones (Summit Books, 1991), tells the story of the intrigues and battles among the members of the family that owned the *Louisville Courier-Journal,* once one of the country's great newspapers. Sallie Bingham, a daughter of the clan, wanted to force the other members of the family to give her what she considered her rightful due, even if it meant selling the paper. She hired lawyers, of course; she also hired Jackie Markham, a public relations specialist, who got news organizations to run stories favorable to her client, and who created a "wave of inevitability" that would persuade the other Binghams of the futility of opposing Sallie's demands.

The paper was ultimately sold.

Public Relations in a Murder Case

These days, even murder suspects have PR counsel. In August 1990, five students at the University of Florida were murdered and horribly mutilated. Within days of the discovery of the bodies, Edward Lewis Humphrey, eighteen, a former student at the university, was arrested for assaulting his seventy-nine-year-old grandmother.

While serving a prison sentence for this crime, Humphrey became a suspect in the killings. The state's attorney revealed that he would seek indictments for the murders against Humphrey and Danny Rolling, a Louisiana drifter.

In August 1991, as the state was putting together its case, Florida TV stations received a seven-minute video, taped in prison, on which Humphrey is interviewed by his brother George and by Marti MacKenzie, a public relations consultant for Humphrey's lawyer, who was present at the taping. The tape shows Humphrey talking and looking quite different from the way he was in the courtroom after his conviction for assaulting his grandmother. Then, the scar-faced Humphrey, shackled and wearing a red jail suit, had made faces at people in the courtroom and, in general, presented a thoroughly frightening image.

On the prison tape, Ed Humphrey appeared at ease. He explained that he had not been taking his medication for manic depression at the time he scared people in the courtroom. Humphrey was not asked directly if he had committed the murders, but he said he was "horrified." He went on, "I thought it was terrible that they could actually think I could have anything to do with something like that. It made me feel really terrible inside. It really hurt me. . . . I haven't done anything wrong."

The suspect told about his "great relationship" with his grandmother, who visited him nearly every week; his hopes to put his life together after getting out; and his gratitude to the doctors, nurses, and guards at his prison psychiatric unit.

Humphrey, who walks with a limp because of a metal rod inserted in his leg after a 1989 car accident that also left his face badly scarred, said, "The first thing I'm going to do is get my hair cut by a regular barber." Then, "I'm going to have my scars taken care of and have the rod removed from my leg. I'm going to spend a lot of time with my family, and I'm going to get with them to make up for the time that we missed when I was in prison. I hope eventually to go back to school."

This prison interview video was the idea of Marti MacKenzie, president of Professional Profile, Inc., an Orlando firm specializing in public relations for attorneys. She handles corporate law, criminal law, personal injury, and other legal cases. MacKenzie and Humphrey's lawyer had felt that Humphrey was not being presented fairly on television. They wanted to create a visual impression of him as he was a year after his conviction, in a controlled environment.

The venture was successful. Television stations carried significant portions of the tape—and that was the whole idea. Even a fleeting image on television has a powerful and lasting impression. MacKenzie wanted people to see a soft-spoken, rational Humphrey, to replace the picture of the menacing figure in prison chains.

Newspapers carrying the story of the prison videotape called it a "carefully orchestrated" event—but they reported what Humphrey said. MacKenzie had felt the newspaper coverage of the case was not damaging. It was the TV stations that she and the Humphrey defense team were worried about, and getting television to run the interview was a plus.

The first thing that MacKenzie cooked up for Humphrey, hours after his release from jail in September 1991, was a news conference. MacKenzie and Humphrey's lawyer picked up Humphrey at the prison and headed for a pancake house, where MacKenzie briefed her client. She then took him shopping in Orlando, where he bought a blue blazer, red tie, and striped white shirt for the press conference. In between, they stopped at MacKenzie's hair salon, where he had a haircut and shampoo.

Then, hours after his release from jail, Humphrey faced a pack of television cameras and reporters called together by MacKenzie. Humphrey was calm, spoke softly, and expressed his thanks for being able to tell the public about what he called his injustice.

Marti MacKenzie is among those out ahead in a field that will become more crowded: PR consultants only handling work for attorneys and taking on all kinds of cases, including criminal cases. Perhaps the major element in creating the need for this kind of public relations is television. The concept that a jury leaves all its preconceptions at the courtroom door has always been something of a fiction, but the power of television has destroyed it utterly. Jurors cannot banish vivid images from their heads. Even the most cogent and articulate courtroom advocate has a lot of trouble changing the minds of juries that have been conditioned by the media.

So—whatever the outcome of the Humphrey case—public relations for lawyers is becoming a necessity. Marti MacKenzie now has a seminar for lawyers, in which she teaches them about the media.

Posttrial Public Relations

Public relations efforts do not end when the jury brings in its verdict.

In one of the most lurid cases of recent years, Pamela Smart was convicted of murder in 1991. The jury found that Smart, as a staff member of a New Hampshire high school, had lured three students into killing her husband. Soon after Smart began to serve a life sentence, her new lawyer said that part of her appeal process would be devoted to reclaiming her reputation from a wave of negative press. One feature of the campaign is the *Friends of Pam Smart Newsletter,* which carries poems; pleas for contributions; testimonials to her innocence; criticism of the judge, the prosecutors, and the trial; and messages from Smart herself, like (as quoted by John Larrabee in *USA Today*), "When I lay down at night, the last thing I see is the shadow of the bars reflected on my wall. It is a constant reminder that I cannot go home."

Unfortunately for Smart, many of her supporters seem to be gentlemen who are enamored of the twenty-four-year-old woman. They desire some of the bikini photos for which she used to pose. But the PR effort goes on, with Smart's lawyer furnishing the press with provocative tidbits about possible bombshells that will clear his client.

Pamela Smart brings a public relations background to the campaign. Though she was frequently referred to as a teacher, she was actually doing PR-related work at the school's media center. She continues to be a big celebrity, getting more than fifty letters a day in prison.

The Use of Public Relations on Appeal

When Michael Milken was the junk-bond king of the world, he was not overly given to publicity. However, after he pleaded guilty to six securities-related felonies and was sentenced to ten years in federal prison, his appeal process included not only the services of such illustrious lawyers as Alan Dershowitz, but a considerable public relations effort.

As part of the campaign, Dershowitz—never a behind-the-scenes attorney, as evidenced by his endless television appearances during the O. J. Simpson trial and Clinton/Lewinsky days—was prominently represented on op-ed pages, denouncing the injustice done to his client. Also, as the *Wall Street Journal* reported on October 10, 1991, Milken's mother wrote a series of letters imploring the judge, Kimba Wood, to reconsider the sentence. Somehow the letters became known to the press. Kenneth Lerer, described by the *Journal* as being with the public relations firm representing Milken, said, "I wasn't even aware that the letters existed." The letters contained such appeals as, "Keeping him at Pleasanton [prison] mopping floors is making a difference to absolutely no one."

Pleading Cases in the Public Mind

Legal public relations, already a thriving branch of the discipline, will grow in sophistication and power. It works. Juries do not deliberate in a vacuum. Their memories are not wiped clean when they enter the jury box. Even judges have been known to read the papers and watch TV. So if you can skew the perception of jurors and judges in your favor, your chances of a favorable outcome are enhanced. Your legal counsel handles legal matters and courtroom advocacy. Your public relations counsel engineers the perceptions of those who will decide your case.

At no time in history was this more evident than in the years of 1998–1999, an era where the catchall names of Whitewater and Monica monopolized page one and prime time.

13

New Ways That PR Serves Clients

A Wide-Ranging Discipline

This chapter talks about client-agency relationships. "Agency" in this context can mean an in-house public relations department. These days more and more PR departments—like those at Bristol Myers (now Bristol Myers Squibb) and the Smithsonian, for example—function like outside agencies, with account teams assigned to their "clients," who are other divisions or brand groups in the company. The PR department's "fees" are allocated like those of an outside firm.

When a client has a good relationship with its public relations firm (or consultant), the company reaps benefits beyond the contracted services of the agency. The PR firm acts as a kind of antenna, sensing moods and shifts in public opinion, warning about the downsides of projected policies, giving the client and its people a substance and flair.

When the relationship is bad, the work goes badly. Good rapport between client and agency is more important in public relations than in advertising. For one thing, it is important for the PR practitioners to know all the ins and outs of the client company, so they can spot new PR possibilities. A bad relationship restricts contacts to a chilly formality that helps to close the valve of creativity.

Misunderstanding is one of the biggest enemies of a good working relationship. Some clients do not know what public relations is—and is not. They think public relations practitioners grind out releases and get tickets for shows. They assume that public relations is just like advertising, so they wonder why the agency cannot say exactly when and where a story will run. They skimp on cooperation and ask for miracles.

The agency people can be equally at fault. They resent what they see as pointless delays and lack of cooperation. They stop thinking big because they are tired of having their ideas shot down. They say and do things designed to keep the account, rather than to do a good job.

We will look at several key points about agency-client relations in this chapter.

Contributors, Not Chameleons

"How's your new PR agency working out?" A CEO, asked this question by a lunch companion, beams with satisfaction: "Great! They've only been on the job a month, but they've adapted so well they seem like old hands in the organization."

This is not a plus. The public relations consultant—particularly in the first days of the association—should not adapt so readily as to become part of the wallpaper. Public relations practitioners with something on the ball are bound to have some differing opinions and new ideas when they start working on an account. However, if the client's top management does not seem to welcome this fresh thinking, some PR consultants will play it safe. Instead of speaking up, they become so much a part of the team that they stifle or even misrepresent their opinions.

When this happens, clients get less than they pay for. One of the major benefits of a new PR agency should be the opportunity to get a fresh slant on the company from an expert point of view. Too many clients encourage conformity rather than individuality. This is not because top management is autocratic or egocentric. Very few bosses require that their advisers, as well as their employees, be toadies and yes-men. More often than not, this kind of thing happens because the client has a mistaken notion of what public relations is supposed to do. The client is looking for the perfect spokespersons, people who can sell the status quo, as if they are sales reps.

Smart clients encourage off-the-wall thinking from their PR teams just as they do with their advertising teams. When they see their advisers acting too docile, they worry. Good clients want PR pros to look around with a fresh, critical eye and make suggestions. "What if . . . ?" should be heard often.

Sometimes, new PR practitioners try to provide new thinking, but they keep getting shot down. Every time they talk about a different approach, they are told, "We tried that once, and it didn't work." The CEO of the client company should set the example by encouraging creative thinking and different solutions.

The arrival of fresh talent with novel viewpoints and experience is a great chance to experiment with new approaches. Clients ought to make it clear that they don't want chameleon-like conformity. The idea is to demand creativity and to welcome it when it comes.

How Many Ideas Did You Reject?

Senior managers in client companies are rightly concerned about scheduling their time. They tend to want proposals to be presented in finished form, so they can make swift decisions without getting involved in the nuts and bolts. Obviously, there are, at any given time, a number of higher priorities than the current PR campaign. So the PR professionals will sift through ideas, hone them down, and present a "turnkey" proposition.

Every now and then, the chief client should ask, "How many ideas went into the hopper before they decided on this plan?" Jean L. Farinelli, onetime chairman and CEO of Creamer Dickson Basford, Inc., a PR firm, says, "I personally believe that the best creativity seldom occurs in the first dozen ideas presented. Rather, these only start the creative process."

The client assumes that bushels of ideas have been distilled into the final plan. But assuming is not the same as knowing. Every now and then, the CEO should check the flow of ideas upstream: read over the preliminary memos, read the minutes of a planning meeting, even sit in on a meeting. The purpose is not to direct the flow, but to make sure it is abundant.

Some top executives shy away from this, feeling that they might inhibit creativity. Wrong! If the presence of the boss inhibits creativity at any level in any department, then the boss needs an internal image overhaul. (Bosses could do worse than ask their PR counsel about this.) It is important that clients make sure their PR agency is generating a lot of ideas.

Encourage Risk Taking

Play-it-safe PR accomplishes little. Risk taking is universally accepted as something managers have to do. But all too often, a public relations plan is shot down because it carries even a slight amount of risk. "Couldn't this make some people mad?" asks the president. The PR professional says, "Sure, but look at the pluses." But line management magnifies the risk and shoots down the proposal.

One reason this happens is that line management does not really believe in the benefits of public relations. They are intangible. They cannot be quantified. You cannot directly attribute sales to public relations—at least, not usually. So even the smallest risk feels big, like a speck of dust in the eye.

Good clients encourage their PR teams to consider and propose risk-taking strategies, just as risk is fostered in other areas of the enterprise. Public relations advisers should not feel that they are risking their jobs when they talk about bold programs that involve large risks for large returns. The company does not have to buy the proposal—but the PR practitioners should be praised for making it, and encouraged to keep on thinking creatively.

Expose New People to the Public Relations Agency

It is a good idea to build public relations awareness in senior managers throughout the organization. One way to do this is by sending these managers to courses. Another, and potentially better, way is to have managers from disparate departments—production, research and development, finance—sit in on meetings with the PR professionals.

Put together varied mixtures. Jean Farinelli says, "Some of the most creatively productive brainstorming sessions I have ever seen mixed secretaries, lawyers, mail clerks, janitors, accountants, and communications people all together."

Rotate managers and key persons from different parts of the company into the PR meetings. Bring people in from branches. This will give everybody a better feel for the company's image and PR efforts, and how they tie in with departmental efforts. And visitors can contribute new viewpoints and ideas.

Hit the Ground Running

Using a cliché that remains popular in public relations as well as in advertising, agencies making a pitch often promise to "hit the ground running." This sounds good to the client. Clients figure they will be getting their money's worth from day one. And, perhaps more to the point, the people in the client organization who selected a particular agency will be able to point to a flurry of activity at the outset of the relationship. This will be used to justify the choice.

But this can be a trap, explains David Finn:

> Public relations is not something that can be turned on like a spigot or scheduled like an ad or commercial. It is an exploratory process in which one must establish goals, seek and, sometimes, even create opportunities, evaluate options, anticipate obstacles and ways of overcoming them, and assign

the most qualified professionals to initiate the activity which
is most likely to achieve the best results.

This is a sound view. But it is not exciting. It suggests that instead of hitting the ground running, the PR agency should hit the ground walking, in obedience to the adage that you have to learn to walk before you can run. And the new agency should hit the ground thinking, not talking.

As soon as the relationship is signed, the PR agency should begin doing homework. Some clients do not buy this. They say, "These people ought to have known all about us before we hired them. In fact, that is one of the reasons we hired them. They were very knowledgeable about our company and our industry."

We have to be clear about this. The homework a PR firm does to make an impressive presentation is not as deep or as broad as the homework required to do the best possible job. When there is pressure for immediate results, the agency's "homework" will be directed toward getting something out as fast as possible. There are three things wrong with this. The hastily done project is apt to be misdirected and mediocre. In focusing on a specific task too fast, the agency may be missing better ideas in other areas of the company. And worst of all, client and agency blow the chance to build a foundation for a really productive program.

Public relations practitioners who have not had a chance to do their homework are less likely to say no to bad ideas. The client wants to break a story on a new product development. The new PR agency has a hunch that this may be a bad idea. But the agency people have not been around long enough to point to specific reasons why it is a bad idea. They could say, "While there is nothing definite, we have an uneasy feeling about this, and we think you should wait." It takes a lot of guts to say this, especially when everybody is looking for quick action. Not every agency has that kind of guts. So the story gets broken. A reporter from a leading trade magazine is granted an interview. The reporter does her own homework, talks to competitors, spots a flaw in the plan, and runs a devastatingly negative story.

Make sure the new agency has enough time to do in-depth homework on the company.

Getting Acquainted with the Media

"We'd like you to sit down with some of the media people," says the new PR adviser to the CEO.

"You mean we're going to have a press conference already? Great! This is quicker action than I expected. What am I going to announce?"

"Well, we're not talking about a press conference exactly. Just a get-together with the key media."

"Why? What's the agenda?"

"To let them get to know you, to let you get to know them, to build a relationship. The idea is to provide them with some background, so when we are ready to give them something substantive, they'll know what it's about—and be sympathetic to our viewpoint, we hope."

"I'm afraid my plate is too full in the next few weeks. You go ahead and meet with these people and brief me later."

When Jim Buckley was elected U.S. Senator from New York, I went to Washington with him as his press secretary. The first thing I did for Buckley was to start a weekly press breakfast (the media brought the doughnuts, we supplied the coffee) in the senator's office. Every Tuesday morning, without fail, except for holidays and when the senator might have been traveling, he met with the New York press. Oftentimes, national press members would drop by.

No senator from New York had ever made himself this accessible to the media. Alan Emory, of the *Watertown Times,* the dean of the New York press corps, hailed Buckley for his openness. The press got to know Buckley, where he stood on every issue, what kind of person he was, and that he was not a bomb thrower. The Tuesday-morning crowd talked to their colleagues in the press galleries throughout Washington. It would cause David Broder, probably the top political reporter in the country and, certainly, not a conservative Republican, to say that Buckley was one of the nicest and smartest men ever to serve in the Senate. Long after his Senate days, when Buckley served as a justice on the U.S. Court of Appeals in Washington, Broder still had the same to say about the former senator.

Action-oriented clients tend to be impatient with PR agencies—especially newly hired ones—that want "time-wasting" meetings with media or just between the PR professionals and senior members of management. "All they're doing is spinning their wheels and wasting our time," said one client of such meetings, "and then they send us a bill."

It is important to build foundations. Client people should get to know agency people. And the agency should have a chance to establish rapport between client and media. This will help subsequent campaigns work better, because the earth has been cultivated in preparation to receive the seeds.

When clients balk at get-together meetings, a lot of the fault may be laid at the door of the agency. In the pitch for the business, the agency does not stress the fact that it is going to conduct thorough preliminary meetings. Instead, the emphasis is on velocity and impact. The agency's professionals give the impression that they are a bullet already in the chamber, and all it takes is a pull of the trigger to send the shot into the bull's-eye.

During the agency's pitch, before the hiring, astute clients will give the agency team a chance to talk about the preliminaries: "How do you plan to get to know all about us, and have us get to know the media? And how long will that take?" If the prospective agency says or implies that the preliminaries are unimportant, the client should press the point. Maybe the preliminaries can be telescoped or dispensed with, but the agency should be able to explain why.

The first stages of agency-client relationships should provide for low-key, foundation-building meetings.

Assume Media Skepticism

The first time a client says, "We have a great message, and the media should be very receptive to it" (or words to that effect), a responsible public relations professional should reply, "What makes you think so?" Then, the PR adviser should proceed to dispel illusions about how the world is panting to learn all about the company and its products.

We all tend to think the sun rises and sets on our own children. We magnify the virtues, minimize the flaws. That is only natural. Why should parents be objective? But objectivity is healthy in anticipating media reaction to a PR campaign. Editors, writers, reporters, program directors—they are hard-boiled and skeptical. It is built in. They would think of themselves as patsies if they seemed to buy a PR-generated story too easily.

Sometimes it is hard for public relations professionals to explain this to clients, who think of it as an alibi in advance for poor performance. So, the PR professionals should not just sit around trying to explain it. They should give the client early, unpressured exposure to media people. This gives the client a better feel for the real world of public relations. After all, "know your market" is basic in selling, and the media are the initial market in PR work.

It is all right for clients to be enthusiastic about their stories. But do not expect the PR team to share in the euphoria. It is best for them to operate on a worst-case basis and make the basic assumption that there is considerable resistance to overcome. That is as sound an approach in public relations as it is in selling.

Think of the media as a very hard-to-convince customer.

Put Follow-Up in Place

The new public relations program gets off on a high note—a major press conference, an article in an influential magazine, a segment on a network TV show. But nothing much seems to happen after that. Some interest is generated, but it dwindles out.

Everybody—client and PR adviser alike—can get so caught up in the planning and execution of a big event that there is not much follow-up planning. This is particularly likely to happen when the agency is new. The agency wants the first big happening to go just right. Every resource goes into getting off to a fast start. There is not much planning for the long haul.

Clients can help to keep this from happening by asking, "What happens after that?" For example, require the agency to have a step-by-step program to follow up a big announcement. This program could include stories in other media, comments from influentials, and exploitation of new developments.

Just about any major public relations development should have a follow-up plan attached to it.

Look for Feedback

Everybody feels wonderful when the first fruits of a new public relations program begin to appear. A big story ran, the CEO gave a major speech, there was an impressive appearance on a TV show. Folks are exultant: "It's working!"

It is not working until it translates into the necessary next steps. David Finn remarks that once the first results emerge, "One may wonder whether anybody important noticed." The kickoff may have been great, but there is "very little feedback from key audiences."

On-the-ball management will not sit around wondering whether the right people saw the story. They will make sure—through e-mail, faxes, reprints, mailings, telemarketing, and any other means. The "key people" can be major customers, suppliers, prospects, and any other influentials within the industry. The big PR occurrence should be handled like a big break in the market for the company's products. Set time lines. Establish benchmarks. Apply criteria. Make sure the thing is merchandised to the hilt.

The merchandising plan for the event should be thoroughly in place before the event. As Finn comments, "Any form of media coverage is transitory, by definition. Another feature soon will be highlighted and old ones forgotten." The client can help a lot by asking the right questions and making pertinent suggestions. The PR agency, especially if new on the job, may be very good at placing a big story but may not know all of the ways in which the story should be merchandised. Should there be television news clips to show at sales meetings around the country? Immediate calls on big customers? Tie-in advertising?

Working by itself, the public relations agency will usually not be able to get every ounce of value out of the event, because the agency's practitioners do not know the business intimately enough. The merchandising of public relations is a joint effort, and it is an effort that must be worked out in advance. All too often, people are sitting around a few days after the appearance of a laudatory article when somebody says, "Do you think we should have gotten quotes from our U.K. affiliates to run in the piece?"

Assuming good results from the PR campaign, be fully ready to cash in.

Selling Blue Sky

The public relations agency has been given the job of promoting a new product. The agency has gone to work with enthusiasm and ingenuity to get some prominent TV coverage of the new product in a novel setting, with magnetic celebrities involved. The story breaks. It should stimulate immediate demand for the product.

It does stimulate the demand—but the product is unavailable in many areas. The PR agency had sat in on meetings in which production, advertising, promotion, and delivery schedules were coordinated. The PR agency, knowing the futility of gaining attention for a product that is not yet available, has been careful to stay within the time frame. And this took some doing, because it is very hard to predict, let alone control, when certain kinds of media coverage will break. Nevertheless, with some skill and some luck, the agency succeeded, or so it thought.

But, at some point, there had been a production glitch on the product. The rollout had been interrupted. Nobody told the public relations agency. So the big PR break, which could not be duplicated, was of limited use to marketing. Afterward, there was finger-pointing, agonizing, and recrimination.

Often the agency can do little about something like this, because of the long lead time. But in this case, the glitch was visible early. The public relations effort could have been delayed.

The PR agency must be kept informed at every stage about anything that could affect the success of the program.

Process Is Controllable; Results Are Not

A sound public relations program will achieve good results and, sometimes, unexpectedly great results. Big breakthroughs are very hard to predict, because the openings that make them possible happen so fast. Client and agency should work together to make sure they have a program with the strength and flexibility to exploit such openings. Agencies that miss clear openings should be held accountable. However, clients who invariably demand jackpot results are not only very unrealistic, they are self-defeating. If jackpots were an everyday occurrence, they would no longer be jackpots.

Talented, dedicated people in a good working relationship will usually hit targets of opportunity when they appear. Smart clients do not demand unreasonable results. They demand top performance.

When a creative, professional PR agency is working with a good client, then the results are likely to be optimal. But they cannot be forced.

Contacts Are Overrated

"It's not what you know, it's who you know."

There is a persistent myth that top-notch public relations pros achieve their effects through contacts. The illusion has it that these PR aces are constantly having lunch and drinks with the producer of *60 Minutes* and the editorial board of the *New York Times,* and that getting good publicity is simply a matter of "placement."

Placement in public relations can be a misleading word. The advertiser can choose where and when an ad appears, because the advertiser is paying for it. The essence of publicity is that you do not pay for it. Therefore, public relations practitioners try to persuade the media to run stories, but they have no power to place the stories.

As to the notion that the greatest value of a PR agency is contact, this is a myth—and a destructive myth at that. Agencies that try to impress prospects by boasting of contacts are suspect. After all, contacts change; what clients should be looking for is the *brains and skill to come up with programs that the media will find irresistible.*

Keep Advertising and Public Relations Untangled

It is inevitable that people in the client organization will persistently act as if public relations is identical to advertising. They will insist that releases and articles be written as if they were ad copy; they will expect that public relations can be tested by the same tests applied to advertising.

Public relations can work closely with advertising, supplement it, augment it, even replace it in certain cases. But public relations is *not* advertising. For example, we can look at the concept of testing. Advertisements carry repeat messages in select media. Useful yardsticks have been developed to test the impact and retention of ads. Public relations must be held up against altogether different yardsticks.

The thing clients should remember is that public relations has power because it is *not* paid for, at least in the terms that advertising is paid for. Material that appears in the news columns has more credibility than ads.

So public relations cannot be judged by the size of the story or the number of minutes of broadcast time. Clients should understand the principles of public relations, at least to the extent of avoiding confusion with advertising.

Hold public relations accountable—but accountable to realistic standards.

Image Is a Function of Reality

Some PR professionals deplore the word *image* because it is so often misused. They complain that too many clients think of PR practitioners as super manipulators who can create images that bedazzle the public into buying weak stories or inferior products. Image building is a legitimate topic for a discussion of public relations. It is, to a considerable extent, what PR practitioners do. The trouble comes when PR professionals and clients alike misunderstand the term. "Imaging" may involve sharpening perceptions, broadening them, or in some cases changing them. Imaging is not the building of illusions or the blurring of minds so that the truth cannot be perceived.

In thinking about image, clients and professionals should talk about skillful projection or real qualities, not the construction of something imaginary. The best approach is to take it as a given that the substance is there before anybody goes to work on bringing out the image.

Image building is portrait painting, not manipulation.

Assuming the Integrity of the Agency

Some companies retain public relations agencies and then treat them as if they were fly-by-night suppliers that have to be watched every second to keep them from cheating the client. This is a sure way to diminish the contribution of the agency.

Public relations agencies do not usually deal in precisely quantifiable commodities. If your paper cup supplier bills you for sixty cases and knowingly delivers fifty-nine, you have every right to nail the business. Furthermore, you will be well advised to get another paper cup supplier. Life is too short, and there are too many other claims on management's attention, to warrant doing business with anyone you do not trust.

But the relationship with the PR firm may *begin* with lack of trust, at least among some members of management. From day one, the agency's work is eyed askance. Maybe this goes back to the old days of the press agents, who were considered necessary evils but rogues who would take everything that was not nailed down.

Public relations people are professionals. Their stock-in-trade is their knowledge and expertise. They should be treated like professionals, as long as they continue to merit the right to that treatment. This does not mean a client should take everything the PR agency says on faith or pay all of its bills, no matter how steep, without asking questions. It does mean that—as with advertising agencies, lawyers, and other service providers—a lot of what the PR agency deals with is intangible. If a client equates "intangible" with "blue sky," then the client might be better off without a PR agency.

The best way to start is to assume that the agency is professional and trustworthy, and to act on that assumption. If there is good reason to question the basic assumption, then the problem should be thrashed out and, if necessary, the relationship should be terminated. If the agency continues to act with professionalism, then it deserves to be treated professionally.

An opening assumption of professionalism can always be reversed; an opening assumption of untrustworthiness may be irreversible.

Asking the Impossible Guarantees Trouble

The client says, "I want this story to run on the front page of the *Wall Street Journal.*"

"The *Journal* is our primary target," says the account executive. "We are tailoring it to the *Journal,* and we will do everything we can . . ."

"You'll have to do better than that. I want your assurance that it will run there, and within the next two months."

The client is demanding an assurance that cannot be given. The account executive should point that out clearly. In a perfect world, all PR practitioners would do so. However, under heavy pressure from insistent clients, some PR practitioners permit themselves to be pushed too far in the direction of giving a guarantee: "It will run there. You can bet on it."

The story doesn't run in the *Wall Street Journal*. The client rips into the agency for making promises on which it cannot deliver. The agency deserves a lot of what it gets; the promises should not have been made.

But the client is at fault as well. By pushing the agency too hard for assurance, the client helped to cause what is now seen as a failure. If the agency remains on board, it will be inclined to cut back on the scope of its efforts, aiming stories at only those media which are sure of attainment. Everybody loses; the agency does less than it is capable of, and the client gets less than it might have.

Some clients continually act as if they really expected the impossible. They demand guarantees on placement; they demand that the PR agency keep unfavorable news from being covered; they even demand that the agency keep competitive products from being covered. Often such clients are not really so ignorant of the limitations on the agency. They know there cannot be guarantees, but they push for them anyway, on the assumption that it will make the PR practitioners work harder.

Painting the PR agency into a corner does not enable it to grow wings.

A Conditional "Yes" Is Better than a Premature "No"

"Yes" is, of course, far more welcome than "no" to the PR firm. And "yes"—even when there are doubts—can give clients more for their money. Here is a typical situation. The agency comes in with an ambitious plan to do something different. As is frequently the case with something new, there is a lot of opposition in client management. Some of that opposition, moreover, may be quite justified.

Some clients would just say no, reasoning that letting the agency go on might be a waste of time. But this kind of quickness on the trigger might not be the best course. The client will probably do better by uttering a conditional yes, while pointing out the reservations and making it clear that the plan must meet certain criteria that it does not now seem to meet. The PR practitioners can then dispel misconceptions, modify the plan, or decide that it will not fly.

Saying no too early and too often puts the damper on creativity. *When a plan has potential, astute clients tend to give qualified approval. It makes the relationship more productive, and it may result in a great plan.*

Quick Response Sparks Good Work

A lot of good public relations work calls for fast action to take advantage of opportunities. The agency learns that a TV show is planning a segment or a publication is planning an article, and there is very little time to do something about it. The client should respond fast with a definite and authoritative answer and with the necessary help.

This can mean that the ordinary approval route is telescoped or bypassed. The client and the agency should set up machinery in advance to take advantage of such contingencies. Specific members of management should be designated as having the availability and authority to move fast. Or, even better, the client should trust the agency well enough to give it the authority to act.

Approval routines can be cumbersome and slow. Often, more people are involved than necessary. There are political reasons for this. Public relations agencies understand the realities, and they are, ordinarily, eager to get the participation of as many client representatives as possible. This includes people who cannot really say yes or no, but whose cooperation is important. These considerations go by the boards when quick action is required.

Clients should respond quickly to everything as a matter of course; it keeps the agency on its toes. But there should be special and definite plans to enable the agency to move fast to take advantage of opportunities.

Good Chemistry Means a Lot

You can despise your paper cup supplier, but as long as paper cups are delivered at a good price, it does not matter what you think. That is not the case with agency-client relationships. As David Finn says, "The client and agency should like each other, . . . and that good chemistry should remain operative throughout the relationship if good results are to be achieved."

For example, the client may like the agency's work but not be too fond of the account executive. It is best to be frank about it and ask for a change. That works both ways. Public relations practitioners should not work with clients they do not like. Liking the other person does not mean agreeing with everything, but it does mean mutual understanding and respect. *In public relations, good personal chemistry is important.*

Clashes Between Disciplines

Specialists know more about their specialties than does the general public. This is not exactly news. But it is a fact that can cause problems between client and PR agency.

Robert J. Wood (in his *Confessions of a PR Man,* with Max Gunther, NAL, 1988) tells about working with the University of Chicago. One day Wood heard the eminent physicist Willard Libby describe two discoveries. Dr. Libby (who would go on to win a Nobel prize) was most excited about his discovery that the level of cosmic radiation reaching the Earth had remained constant for at least 25,000 years. Dr. Libby had made another discovery as well. He could use carbon 14 to fix the age of fossils, bones, and other archaeological finds.

Wood was not all that excited by the cosmic radiation data—but his sense of what was newsworthy was stimulated by the carbon-dating discovery. Wood wrote a story featuring what he called the "atomic clock." Dr. Libby objected, saying the story was upside-down—that the radiation-level find was more significant.

Wood rewrote the story Dr. Libby's way but warned that he had no control over how editors would play it. The story got broad coverage. In almost every case, the "atomic clock" received the major attention. Later, Dr. Libby told Wood, "From now on, I'll take care of the lab, and you take care of the public relations."

Professionals are often offended at what PR practitioners do with their specialties. They think the material is oversimplified, even sensationalized. They resist the translation of scientific jargon into everyday language. They want stories written like articles for professional journals.

Client management should see to it that these concerns do not impinge on the PR team's ability to do its job. *Let PR professionals call the shots in their specialty.*

Letting the PR Agency In on All Relevant Information

A company wants to build a chemical plant in a town. They anticipate opposition, so top management decides to buy up properties at the targeted site under a cloak of great secrecy. They even keep it secret from their public relations firm. The operation proceeds—until one day a local reporter gets wind of what is going on. All hell breaks loose. The firestorm is so intense that the company is finally forced to back off.

All companies make plans that should be kept secret. However, hiding the plans from the PR professionals is bad policy. Public relations practitioners are used to keeping secrets. If there is a public relations dimension to the plan, they need time to plan for it. Even more to the point, public relations may well be able to offer some useful guidance on how to proceed. That would certainly have been the case in the covert buying of property. The PR team would have been able to gauge the likelihood of discovery. They would surely have prepared a plan to try to handle the backlash.

PR involvement does not automatically mean publicity. *Sometimes the secret plan is the most important one for PR input.*

Dramatizing the Downside

The senior managers of an organization sit in a conference room, watching a presentation. Up front is the public relations director, who is talking about headlines projected on a screen. The headlines are hypothetical; they refer to stories that might be written about the company—if certain things happen.

So far, this looks like an unremarkable event—a PR professional discussing a projected campaign. But these are *not* the kinds of headlines the company would like to see. In fact, they are negative and are harmful to the company's image:

- Acme Accused of Squeezing Small Competitors
- Gouging Attributed to Manufacturer
- Fair or Foul? Acme Fights for Domination
- How Acme Drove Me Out of Business

Moving on from the headlines, the PR director will present fictitious excerpts from exposé shows of the *60 Minutes* variety, along with negative sound bites from news programs. Is public relations not concerned with the brighter side? Why is the PR director wallowing around in all this made-up bad news, and why are these executives listening to it?

What is happening is that the PR director is fulfilling a role that will become prominent in more companies as the full value of the new public relations comes into play. Through the experience and imagination of the PR function, corporate policy makers are being alerted to the public relations downside of a projected course of action.

It is vital for a company to be able to foresee as many important consequences as possible before launching a program of any kind. In the past, such deliberations have slighted media and public reaction.

Executives, focused on their own disciplines and concerns, brush aside PR concerns as unimportant. "So what if we increase effluents into the river? Who is going to find out about it?"

Years ago, it was less important for companies to worry about such matters. The press did not pursue them doggedly. Media tended to be gentler with stories harmful to the interests of businesses. The reactions of the world in general—and of particular publics, like legislative bodies and the financial markets—were, perhaps, not of great significance.

Now it is different. It is as important to anticipate a public relations disaster as a product failure, in many instances. The discipline best able to look at these matters is public relations. The role of the new public relations is to make policy-level executives aware of what can happen if they pursue a certain course of action. The company may still take the contemplated actions, but at least the top brass is aware of the negative PR possibilities. And often the plan can be modified to stave off the worst possible PR consequences.

The Procter & Gamble Public Relations Disaster

The front page of the *Wall Street Journal* of August 12, 1991, carried a story headlined "Procter & Gamble Calls In the Law to Track News Leak: Phone Files Are Subpoenaed and Police Check Who Called *Wall Street Journal*." A couple of months earlier, the *Journal* had run a few stories about the company's "troubled" food and beverage division, saying that the head of the division had resigned under pressure and that parts of the division might be sold. The series of earlier stories quoted "current and former Procter & Gamble managers."

To Procter & Gamble, this spelled L-E-A-K. And the company went all out to discover the sources of the leak. Among the measures taken was a complaint to the police. The authorities obtained a grand-jury subpoena to get phone records of calls made between Cincinnati and the home of a *Journal* reporter. A former Procter & Gamble manager "said he had been questioned for an hour by the Cincinnati fraud squad."

No one who is familiar with the towering importance of Procter & Gamble in Cincinnati would be surprised by the news that the company has a lot of clout—although it might be a little surprising that Procter and Gamble's power could still mobilize the Hamilton County prosecutor's office on such an errand. (The prosecutor, according to the *Wall Street Journal,* said "he was unfamiliar with the subpoena issued out of his office. Efforts to reach him yesterday were unavailing.")

The real surprise is that the company would do such a thing. Granted, Procter & Gamble is an old, established concern, renowned for maintaining traditional attitudes in this modern day. But it is also a giant corporation making its way in today's corporate battlefield, which is dotted with media mines. After all, Procter & Gamble had long since learned the hard way about unwelcome publicity—when zealots declared the company's age-old logo was a symbol of devil worship. The real surprise is that the company made its problem a criminal justice case—incurring the damaging media coverage that was sure to follow.

Not all senior managers would assume that there would be unwelcome publicity. They might have cherished the naive notion that the enlistment of the prosecutor's office and the police could be kept secret, even though the cops would be out questioning former Procter & Gamble people about their contacts with the newspaper. More likely, if senior managers thought about it, they might dismiss the possible negative publicity as of little consequence. For one thing, they might reason that not all that many consumers of Procter & Gamble products read the *Wall Street Journal.*

Such reasoning would be dead wrong. The *Journal* is an instant seedbed of TV news. If a story in the *Journal* has sensational or exploitable potential, you will see the story on the evening news and perhaps, a few days later on the syndicated tabloid shows like *Hard Copy* and *A Current Affair.* The *New York Times* and the *Wall Street Journal* are the basic research laboratories for the TV hot-story specialists.

Other media did pick up the story. For days, it made television and radio news. It came out that the sweep of telephone records was exceptionally broad in scope. The *Journal* of August 15 reported, "Cincinnati law-enforcement authorities had access to the phone records of hundreds of thousands of Ohio residents." Procter & Gamble was made to look as if it were ruthlessly rummaging through the phone records of everybody with a 513 area code.

It became a First Amendment case, with all sorts of organizations protesting. Procter & Gamble tried to deflect questions by saying, "This investigation is being conducted by the Cincinnati police department. You need to contact the police department about the subpoena." Nobody in the office of the Hamilton County prosecutor—which issued the subpoena—would comment. The police fraud squad was unavailable.

Procter & Gamble said it had only gone to the police when its own investigation of the leaks failed—as if this made everything all right. The *Wall Street Journal* would not buy this: "But the subpoena was issued just four working days after the second article appeared, raising questions about the thoroughness of Procter & Gamble's investigation."

The *Wall Street Journal* did not fail to note who would pay for all this: "Cincinnati Bell said it bore the cost of complying with the court order. State utility officials noted that the expense, while 'negligible,' would ultimately be charged to customers."

Conceivably, some Procter & Gamble officials were surprised at the ferocity with which the *Journal* went after the company. And not just in the news columns. There is often a dichotomy between the *Wall Street Journal*'s news stories and its editorials. The news staff does mercilessly objective, muckraking stories on business; the editorial writers have a tendency to temper the wind toward the shorn corporate lamb, sometimes giving the impression that they feel there is no such thing as business wrongdoing. But this is a question of whose ox is gored. The *Journal* lambasted Procter & Gamble in its editorial columns.

All in all, the affair was turning out to be a fiasco for Procter & Gamble and for Cincinnati. The company was portrayed as a bloated ogre, invading the privacy of millions of people, not just its own employees. Cincinnati looked like an old-time company town in the worst sense, where the mayor, the sheriff, and everybody else is in the pocket of the big, ruthless company. Employee loyalty, by which Procter & Gamble sets great store, was not likely to be enhanced. And the very scope of the investigation probably insulated the culprits whom

Procter & Gamble was seeking. Anyone who got fired or penalized as a result of this could be expected to become an instant media martyr and, also, be expected to retain a lawyer who would start a mammoth and well-publicized lawsuit against the company. It was hard to see any pluses at all for Procter & Gamble. For a firm that has always sold its name as representing quality and customer sensitivity, this was truly not a good move.

Preventing Public Relations Disasters

It is possible to imagine the meeting at which this ill-starred venture was launched. A number of senior Procter & Gamble officials are seething with fury at the insolence of employees—or ex-employees—who would dare to talk to the press about a story the company would rather not see printed. This was not a matter of disclosing market strategies or secret formulas; it was a story about a Procter & Gamble division being in trouble and the head of the division being pressured to resign. Such stories are not unusual, but evidently it was intolerable to the Procter & Gamble brass to be the subject of such reportage.

The internal investigation of the leak seems doomed—and, anyway, there is a suspicion that outsiders had a hand in it. So somebody comes up with the bright idea of tapping the resources of the prosecutor's office, the police department, and the telephone company. Why not? After all, what are they there for?

So the move is made—and the roof falls in.

This episode is a vivid example of the need to *have the public relations function involved in all policy decisions,* not just to figure out the public relations angles, but to issue an early warning of the possible dangers. We doubt that public relations was part of the team that decided on this course of action. Any competent PR professional would have forcefully pointed out what might take place and, indeed, what probably would take place. If a responsible PR voice was raised, it was ignored.

Today it is practically mandatory that companies use their public relations advisers this way. The first thing the PR professional can do is emphasize that it is very hard to keep the lid on unwelcome news. The discussion should be based on the *assumption* that a proposed action will become widely known. This is not a worst-case scenario—it is a *probable*-case scenario. The first job of the PR professional in dramatizing the downside is to dispel the comforting notion that things can be kept quiet if the company wants them kept quiet.

Next, the PR professional will present the question, What will the media do with the story? Here is where the PR professional can use showmanship—bring home with a jolt what can be expected. We can imagine the impact if the Procter & Gamble brass had been able to see, in advance, headlines like this: "Procter & Gamble Calls in the Law to Track News Leak"; "P&G Violates First Amendment"; "Cincy Cops Probe P&G 'Enemies.'" Would the company have been quite so eager to go ahead?

Public relations still tends to get left out of the takeoffs but called in at the crash landings. No doubt Procter & Gamble's public relations counselors were called upon when the negative stories broke, as they were summoned when the man-in-the-moon logo was accused of satanism. As organizations get more sophisticated about public relations, they will value more highly the *preventive* function of the discipline. Public relations practitioners may not be able to "keep it out of the papers"—but they can make recommendations, in advance, that will keep the question from coming up.

14

How to Stage-Manage the Interview

The Public Relations Professional as Star Maker

Media professionals respond to good interviewees. They give good interviewees more attention and greater credence. So it is vital that interview subjects handle the give-and-take with coolness, authority, and ease. An interview is like a show: it can be a hit or a bomb. The public relations professional is the impresario.

The interview is a trade-off. The interviewee wants something: personal publicity, attention to a cause, promotion for a product, service, or business. The interviewer wants something as well: an entertaining broadcast segment, facts for a story, confirmation of rumors, conflict with other points of view. This chapter will tell you the tactics public relations pros use to produce "hit" interviews.

When an interview is slated, interviewee and PR professional should prepare thoroughly. Obviously, the time and place must be pinned down. If it is television, the interviewee should know how—and how not—to dress. There are no strict rules. At one time, people going on television avoided wearing white, because it tended to glare on the screen, but today's improved equipment eliminates that as a concern. In most cases, dress is pretty much a matter of taste. It is not an audience with the Pope: the interviewee need not dress with excessive sobriety. However, busy patterns do not usually work well except in small doses, as in a tie or scarf. Dark suits—gray or navy blue—usually look better than light ones. Dresses of one predominant color, offset by contrasting touches, are often better bets than garments of many colors.

If visual materials—charts, graphs, products, photos—are important to the interview, they must be furnished to the interviewer beforehand, so they can be integrated with the interview.

Getting Ready for the Interview

Many interviewees have supreme confidence in their ability to think on their feet and handle tough questions. Nevertheless, it is important that there be a briefing session with the PR professional.

Defining the Objectives

The idea of the interview is to convey a certain message or messages. Write them down:

- This is an important new development.
- Our new product is the best on the market.
- The company is carrying out its responsibilities.
- We are succeeding and growing.

Once the objectives have been identified, you can prepare to work them into the answers.

Anticipate the Questions

The public relations pro should come up with a list of the questions that are likely to be asked—starting with the toughest. The interviewee may protest, "That is not a fair question. . . . They are not going to ask that. . . . I am not going to get into that . . ." Interviewee and PR practitioners need to be in complete agreement: nothing legitimate in the way of a question can be ruled out. And there is no way to control what will be asked.

Certain executives think the PR practitioners can rule unwelcome questions out of bounds: "I am not prepared to answer, so tell them not to ask that one." If certain questions are really tricky, or if the interviewee is unwilling to deal with them, then the interview should be scrubbed.

"No comment" is not a satisfactory response. Nor is "I will have my people get back to you later." Corporate leaders are used to dealing in the broad strokes while having subordinates work out details. In a press interview, particularly a TV interview, the interviewee does not have this luxury. Interviewers will understand that the other party does not have command of every tiny bit of nitty-gritty, but he or she must be able to talk about significant details.

Do Not Set Ground Rules

Some interviewees want strict ground rules. Interviewers do not like to be fenced in by ground rules. Furthermore, if ground rules are forced on an interviewer, that person may be somewhat antagonistic. An antagonistic interviewer has many ways to make the subject look bad. It is far better to work hard to get the interviewee ready to handle hard questions.

Obviously, an interview that is broadcast live is the most risky. But the subject should not develop a false sense of security because an interview is being taped. Tape costs money; editing is expensive; the broadcast people are in control of the editing. They may not take out parts just because the subject wants them taken out. In fact, if the subject is made to look bad, that is exactly the part that may be left in. The plus side to the live interview is that you can get your point across with no fear of it being edited out.

When the subject is accompanied on the interview by the public relations professional, the PR professional can be of some help. But not all that much. Media professionals do not usually like it when PR practitioners come along with the subject as "keepers." Take your PR practitioner along, but that person should speak only when spoken to.

Rehearse, Rehearse, Rehearse

It is hard to get busy, important people to rehearse an interview. They are likely to say, "Give me a list of the questions, and I will go over them." That is not good enough. On television and radio, how interviewees comport themselves can be as significant as what they say. And, while the circumstances are different, the same goes for a newspaper or magazine interview.

So, there should be a pull-no-punches rehearsal, at which questions are asked and are answered. The best kind of rehearsal for a TV interview may be one in which a mock interview is videotaped and played back. Many people have thought they were answering questions cogently and interestingly, only to find, to their chagrin, that they actually come across as incomprehensible, wooden, long-winded, and evasive.

The interviewee ought to jot down likely questions on index cards and rehearse alone in front of a mirror. A tape recorder is handy; by listening to the answers, the subject can refine the answers to make them crisper and more persuasive.

Find Out What the Interviewer Is Like

Watch or listen to the person who will conduct the interview. Get an impression of how quickly the interview moves along, how sharply vague answers are followed up, how short answers should be.

If it is a print interview, read things the writer has written. Form an impression of the style. Thoughtful? Colorful? Staccato? Funny?

Knowing what the interviewer is like does not mean that the subject should go to great lengths to change his or her own style. But, for example, if the show calls for very short answers, that should be the keynote. In a broadcast interview, it is important to remember that both parties are cooperating to put on a piece of entertainment.

Practice Positive Mental Posture

Subjects should go into the interview with a positive frame of mind. Interviewees ought to be given tips like the following:

- You are being interviewed because you are the expert. You know more about the subject than your interviewer. In a meeting around a conference table, you would give your views and be listened to with interest. The situation is no different in the media interview.

- Aggressiveness, even hostility, from the questioner should not be a problem. You are used to handling tough questions without blowing your cool. If the interviewer seems tough, that person is only doing a job, making a better show, getting a better story. You can participate, rather than resist, by answering crisply and with good humor.

- The TV audience does not expect you to be as slick as the professional interviewer. If you appear honest and well informed, the audience will want to hear what you have to say. If you seem confident and good-natured, the audience will like you. If the interviewer gets tough, you will win the sympathy of the audience by being calm and unshaken. Audiences side with the underdog; they do not like to see professionals use professional tricks to make guests look bad.

- Stage fright is a natural phenomenon. Sir Laurence Olivier, for one, never got over it. Veteran actors and TV personalities have it. Your interviewer may have it. Your stage fright will disappear as you become intent on the give-and-take of the interview. Listening and thinking about your answers are the best cure for the butterflies.

- If you have done your homework and know your objectives, you will succeed.

- The interview is a forum and an opportunity. Do not worry about not being asked the right question. Give the answer you have prepared to a question that is somewhat in the ballpark. Good interviewees are adept at answering the questions they like, rather than the questions they were asked.

Looking Alive on Television

Television is a medium of movement. One of the most common problems with people who are being interviewed is that they *do not move*. Their bodies are immobile. Their faces are stolid. They speak clearly, but the lips are about the only thing moving.

When the speaker is immobile, even though relaxed, the tube conveys a picture of rigidity and uptightness. Interviewees should usually be encouraged to loosen up. Lean forward; sit back. Moving the hands, arms, and shoulders—as is usually the case in ordinary speech—gives a feeling of naturalness to the subject.

The face should move along with the hands. A close-up of an unmoving face is peculiar and somewhat forbidding. The interviewee ought to show facial animation, not just when speaking, but to a certain degree, when listening. The best way to do this is to really *listen* to the interviewer. Lean forward. Look at the other person. Listen and think.

When talking, the interviewee should move the head, purse the lips, smile, or look serious, if it feels natural. Usually, when subjects talk with animation, they can be all the more impressive when, for effect, they let their faces "freeze"—to show disapproval or to convey a sense of deep seriousness.

The subject should look, on the TV screen, to be at ease. Nobody expects the professional demeanor of a Jay Leno or Oprah Winfrey, but audiences do want someone who does not seem uptight. The nervousness depletes authority and credibility, it arouses suspicion ("What is he so nervous about?"), and it tends to make the audience more conscious of the person than the message.

Make It Short and Taut

When responding to a question at a boardroom meeting, an executive may feel justified in taking all the time in the world. On television, that is a self-destructive luxury.

The key advice: Talk in headlines and keep the answer under twenty seconds. The "headline" is a pithy instant answer to the question. It does not have to be a complete sentence; a phrase will do, as in this example:

QUESTION: After a history of concentrating on the domestic market, why is your company breaking the tradition to open branches overseas?

ANSWER: Rising opportunity and a changing world. People in at least half a dozen countries now need [name products] and have what it takes to use them. We see an opportunity, and we are moving aggressively to take it.

That is a capsule, headline answer. It is broad. It does not cover all the small details and subtle shadings.

This makes many interviewees uncomfortable. They feel compelled to elaborate, lest somebody, someplace, be lacking the last bit of information or not understand all the nuances.

The TV interview is not the place to explore the nuances. If there is a danger that brief answers will cause trouble, then the interview should not take place.

If the headline answer is interesting and provocative, the interviewer may signal a willingness to hear more, at which time the subject can elaborate. In elaboration, the answer should still be crisp and short—not a speech. But PR professionals should warn subjects that interviewers usually do not ask for elaboration. Intent on their own agendas and their needs for a good snappy show, they move on to the next question.

Body Language

On television, the picture is often more important than the words. The interviewee should master the "executive pose" for use in the informal, around-the-coffee-table situation that is the format of so many interviews. Here are the basics of the executive pose:

- Legs crossed at the knee
- One hand folded over the other on the lap
- Hands not clasped, but free for natural gestures

- Elbows on chair armrests
- Jacket unbuttoned
- Body ready to lean forward from the waist in answering questions

Note that this is a basic posture, to be adapted depending on whether the interviewee is male or female, short or tall, thin or stout, and any other combinations. It is not a rigid pose, but rather the configuration toward which the body should move when at rest.

Some interviewees tend to look trim and alert while talking, then let themselves slump. When the camera catches the subjects in a slump, the snap into good posture on cue looks phony. It is important to listen with attention and poise.

The subject should usually look at the other speaker rather than trying to play to the camera. Efforts to spot the camera with the red light will result in shots that show the subject looking bewildered or inattentive. Interviewees should ignore any monitors that may be in sight on the set during the interview. Check dress and posture in the monitor before the show starts, then forget about it.

What If They Do Not Ask the Right Question?

If the interviewer does not ask the right questions, how does the interviewee get in all those good points that were rehearsed? This takes some preparation, but it can be done. One way is to give a brief answer to a question in the same general area and then to "bridge" to the desired bit: "In that connection, I might add that, along with its speed, [name product] has three safety features that are brand-new in the industry." The interviewer will probably have to ask for an elaboration of that one.

Another way to cover points that need to be covered is to volunteer the material. Responding to a question, the subject says, "There are two answers to that. Before I get to them, there is something I forgot to mention before . . . " Give the volunteered answer quickly, then answer the original question.

Television is often referred to in terms of sound bites. Actually, a thirty-second sound bite is pretty long in this medium. The best interviewees talk in "bites."

Helping Out a Print Interviewer

The interviewee does not have to talk in short bursts to a newspaper or magazine interviewer. But it is still a good idea to preface the answer with a "headline" that encapsulates the point, then to elaborate. The elaboration should contain quotable facts and figures. Even more important, it should contain, if possible, usable anecdotes. Anecdotes are meat and drink to journalists. Have a store of them and sprinkle them through the interview.

If there is a possibility of using pictures to illustrate the story, they should be given to the newspaper or magazine. Black-and-white glossies are preferred, except in exceptional circumstances. The shots usually should include people, even in product photos. Only design engineers drool with delight over unadorned pictures of machines. The interviewer might be given a selection of shots of the interviewee. Candid, informal shots are usually better than formal portraits. The size of the photos can vary—they will be cropped and changed in size. It is best to provide pictures that are larger than necessary. Small ones get grainy when they are blown up. Among the most popular sizes are $4'' \times 5''$ and $5'' \times 7''$.

Sometimes, though not often, the interview may be enhanced by charts or graphs. These will be most welcome if they are provided "camera-ready"—pasted-up mechanicals that need only to be shot and printed. Unlike the broadcast interview, it is possible to get back to the print interviewer with additional material. But you must do it fast.

Should You Refuse to Face the Media?

As a general rule, you should not be afraid of the media. They are not the enemy, and if they are, you may be able to neutralize them. Of course, if you have been involved in unscrupulous practices and *60 Minutes* is after you, you might as well hide (or get the best PR counsel money can buy to help soften the blows).

There are many who look upon the media as the enemy and refuse to see them. They are the losers. When I first went to Washington in 1971, as newly elected Senator Jim Buckley's press secretary, I started immediately battling many of Buckley's Washington-based conservative supporters. For the most part, they were antimedia. They still are. They are the ones who coined the phrase "the Eastern liberal establishment" in referring to the *New York Times, Washington Post,* and others.

I had met Les Whitten, Jack Anderson's top investigative assistant, at a cocktail party. Les thought it would be great if "Jim and Jack" had lunch. While I certainly knew that Anderson was not a supporter of conservative causes, I was still more than pleased to get the two together. Lunch was scheduled about one week in advance at a popular downtown Washington restaurant. It was written in on Buckley's schedule. The word got around.

Pretty soon, we were flooded with calls from the senator's conservative friends. "Call the luncheon off," they all urged, referring to Anderson as the enemy. "He will bug the luncheon and then use it against Buckley," several warned.

Buckley and Anderson—I joined them as well—met for lunch. It lasted a delightful two hours. Conversation went from world issues to the environment to bird-watching. Anderson saw Buckley for what he was—a caring, thoughtful, intelligent person, a far cry from the perception many had of him. For his six-year term in office, Anderson wrote glowingly of Buckley, several dozen times.

Handling Hostility

Sometimes, an interviewer may be hostile because it is the interviewer's style. Mike Wallace, Sam Donaldson, and similar personalities have made aggressive questioning a high-rated TV art form, and in the hands of certain interviewers, it is a short step from aggressiveness to hostility.

Sometimes the interviewer may be aggressive and confrontational because the situation calls for it. There have been negative developments; the interviewer is trying to explain bad news; the interviewee is not prepared to comment on something that the interviewer wants to hear about.

Occasionally, an interviewer seems—at least to the subject—to become aggressive and hostile for no reason at all. This can happen because the subject mishandles the process and makes the interviewer angry. An angry interviewer can, with a smile, make an amateurish subject look very bad.

Here are some elements of a survival kit for interviewees when the atmosphere is stormy.

Remain Detached and Unemotional

The host of the show zaps in an unexpected zinger. The target, a corporate executive who is rarely challenged, responds with sarcastic acidity. The executive thinks she has scored a point; in actuality, she comes across on the screen looking very bad.

By far the best thing to do, when confronted with hostility, is to pause, breathe in slowly, and answer unemotionally. When subjects blow their cool, they puts themselves in the hands of the interviewer. Television hosts are professionals at keeping their cool. They can needle a hotheaded subject into making unwise statements and acting with unbecoming rudeness.

Avoid Head-On Confrontation

Having remained cool, the next challenge for the interviewee is to respond to a hostile question without showing anger or making the interview into a shootout. Answers to avoid:

- "You've got that all wrong."
- "I must strongly disagree with you!"
- "You haven't got your facts straight."
- "That's all wrong, and I'm going to tell you why."
- "Where did you get that idea?"

The trick is to avoid addressing the host as "you" in a negative or confrontational sense. It is much better to make it positive:

- "You raise an interesting point. Let's look at it."
- "You put the problem very well. I'd like to tell you how it's being solved."
- "You've identified an issue that many people have raised. In part they're correct; in part they're incorrect. Let's look at the issue."

Then give a calm answer—the answer that has been rehearsed—addressed to the broad TV audience, not to the interviewer. The interviewee's posture should be that the hostility of the questioner is irrelevant; the important thing is to talk to the people who are watching, and talk to them on the assumption that they are fair and rational. Such a posture may rile the interviewer a little, but that is all right; the subject should continue talking to the audience, without rising to the bait of further provocative jabs.

Restate the Case

There is one advantage to a skeptical, aggressive interview. The subject gets a chance to restate the desired message, with appropriate variations. A well-delivered message, in the context of hostile questions, gains credibility. The idea is for the subject to calmly insist on his or her points, without restating the critic's position. To restate the oppositional point of view just gives it more credibility and attention.

An interviewer may become impatient with the subject covering the same ground. The subject, refusing to be flustered, can just say, "Since we seem to have some misunderstanding here, don't you want me to try to clear it up?"

Changing the Subject

When a questioner keeps harping on a topic, the subject can say, "Since we've covered that, maybe you'd like to move on to talk about the next step." The interviewer may not like it, but the tactic puts the ball in his or her court. The interviewer must justify returning to a topic that has been discussed or else look as if he or she is picking on the subject.

Peter Hannaford urges interviewees to remember that they have rights. Ground rules on time and topics can be set beforehand. (But, as we have said, the privilege of declaring unwanted topics taboo must be used very sparingly, if at all.) And if a taped interview gets too heated, confusing, or rough, you can say, "Can we stop and take that again?" There is no guarantee that a previous, unwanted answer will not be used, but they will stop the tape and take it again.

Beware of Humor

Snappy interjections and flip remarks are dangerous. They may go well at a meeting or in a speech before a friendly and familiar audience. In an interview by a broadcast or print reporter, however, leave humor alone. It can backfire. The interviewee can look calloused or frivolous. Worse (and this happens with dismaying frequency), what is meant as a joke is taken seriously.

Hannaford mentions the senior executive of a big Washington PR firm who told a *Washington Post* reporter during the Cold War days that the firm might take, as a client, "a Communist government, if one of those Eastern European ones [asks]. It's a business. We're mercenaries." Casual asides like "We're mercenaries" can be suicidal.

They may be quoted widely, and the lame explanation "I was kidding" does not help.

Some people will argue that U.S. Senator Al D'Amato of New York lost his reelection bid in 1998 because of all his gaffes in the years prior to the election.

Trick Questions

Savvy interviewers can use tricky questions to make it tough on interviewees. One form of trick question is the front-loaded type:

QUESTION: Your business is declining; you're being investigated for illegal practices; some of your key people are about to leave you. How are you going to turn the situation around?

Here, the questioner loads the question with negative assumptions. The right answer rejects the assumptions first, then answers the question:

ANSWER: I don't agree with your statements. We will continue to grow, and we will increase our profitability, because we have good people making good products, which we sell at a good price.

Then there is the doomed-alternative question. The interviewer poses an either/or question, but whichever answer the interviewee gives, he or she is in trouble:

QUESTION: Your product hasn't performed as planned. Is it because of bad design or faulty manufacture?

The subject should be emphatic in rejecting the two alternatives offered:

ANSWER: Neither. The product works very well when it's used properly. We have now modified and simplified our product instructions, and you will find that the public acceptance is reaching the point we had aimed at.

Another ploy used by experienced interviewers is not a question. It is nothing at all—a pregnant pause. The subject gives a short, effective answer to a tough question. The interviewer does not say anything. The subject begins to sweat. The dead air is oppressive. Finally, the subject begins to blurt out some additional explanations, which usually seem weak and apologetic.

When a TV interviewer pauses, the interviewee should simply sit there, thinking about questions that are likely to come up next. The dead air is the host's responsibility, not the subject's. The subject should look at the host with a calm, expectant smile. The camera should show a cool, confident face.

Another technique used by experienced questioners—lawyers in cross-examination, psychiatrists, TV hosts—is the echo. The questioner simply repeats the last few words of the previous answer:

SUBJECT: We expect the plant to be in full operation before the end of the year.

INTERVIEWER: *(with a trailing-off, questioning inflection)* . . . before the end of the year . . .

This ploy can prod many people to elaborate on the answer—or to qualify or modify it:

SUBJECT: Yes, well, by the end of the year, if all goes well. If we have problems with the site, or availability of supplies, there could, of course, be some delay. But not much beyond the spring of next year . . .

Now the guest has blown the advantage of the crisp, firm answer and has opened a door through which the questioner can storm with harassing questions that imply something is likely to go wrong, and long delays can probably be expected.

One way to counter this tactic is to repeat, firmly, the words the questioner has echoed:

SUBJECT: Yes, exactly, *before the end of the year.*

Such calm, deliberate reiteration makes the interviewee look firm and credible. The important thing is to be aware that interviewers will use these tricks, not out of malice, but because they may make for a better show.

Types of Hostile Interviewers—and How to Deal with Them

Tough interviewers fall into certain patterns. Here are some of the principal ones. The interviewee and PR counsel should watch the TV interviewer in action before the interview takes place, to see which approaches this particular host favors.

The Multiquestioner

Some interviewers fire two or three questions in a row:

INTERVIEWER: How much damage was done? How did it start? Who is responsible?

The way to handle a multiquestioner is to pause, take a breath, then answer one question—choosing the one you want to answer:

SUBJECT: Preliminary investigation shows the fire started in the boiler room. The investigation is continuing. Now, what was the next question?

By calmly dealing with one question at a time, the subject can relieve the pressure of rapid-fire questions.

The Interrupter

Another type of interviewer constantly interrupts, seeming rarely to let the subject complete a sentence or a thought. Frequently, this sort of behavior is seen in hosts who are—or feel they are—local or national celebrities whose aggressive style precludes courtesy.

One good way to handle the interrupter is to stop talking, listen with patience and good humor to the interruption, and then go on: "As I was saying . . . " The idea is not to show anger or nervousness at the interruptions, but to take them as a matter of course, an obstacle that has to be overcome.

If the interrupter is too insistent and too rude, the subject can say, with cool good humor, "I'd like to answer that question. May I?" This is polite. It does not reply in kind with rudeness. It is a mistake to say, "You keep interrupting me," or, "I'll answer that if you just give me a chance."

The Restater

Sometimes an interviewer repeats what the subject says but repeats it incorrectly. Usually the incorrectness makes the subject look bad:

SUBJECT: We are rescheduling the opening for June 1.

INTERVIEWER: You're delaying the opening until June 1.

The prescribed treatment here is to repeat your own, correct answer and then to clarify politely:

SUBJECT: We are *rescheduling* for June 1. This is not a matter of delay. It is to conform with the wishes of the mayor, who wants to be present at the ceremony.

The Labeler

Another tactic of a hostile interviewer is to start off by hanging a label around the subject's neck. It is rarely a positive label:

INTERVIEWER: Here's the spokesperson for an industry that's laying off thousands of people in our city.

The subject cannot meekly accept the label. It must be corrected, politely but firmly. The best way to do this is by turning the negative into a positive:

SUBJECT: Thank you. I'd like to make a slight change in your introduction. While I'm not the spokesperson for a whole industry, I welcome the chance to talk about the industry, which has given jobs to thousands for many years and is fighting to save jobs and get our city back to economic health. Could I briefly describe three ways in which that is happening?

Follow-up

After the interview ends, the PR practitioner's work continues. The first step in follow-up is to find out when the interview (if taped) will run. Alert employees, customers, prospects, suppliers, industry bigwigs, and everyone else you know. Use the TV interview as a learning experience: analyze, discuss, and figure out how to do even better next time.

15

Getting on Radio and Television

How to Interest the Gatekeepers

"Too basic."

That is what I thought after first sketching out this chapter. True, effectiveness through the broadcast media is tremendously important. But, after all, this is a book full of heretical dissents, radical proposals, and futuristic speculation. Why include the nuts and bolts of getting on TV and radio? Doesn't everyone in the business know it already?

After checking around, I found that everyone in the business does *not* know it already. And I found that a lot of people outside public relations are interested in what lies behind so much of what they see on the TV screen.

So here is the approach I use and try to pass along to others. Television and radio are penetration media. They slice through the clutter to affect the viewer (and, to an extent, the listener). Whether your organization is big or small, you can build sales by having your product or service discussed on the air in a nonadvertising context.

By and large, television is the best place to be. By using some tested approaches (and avoiding certain pitfalls), you can make the reach and power of television work for you.

Delivering What Television Wants

Television is always looking for interesting people who have something interesting to say and who say it well. The great proliferation of news shows and talk shows gives organizations of all kinds a chance to project an image and tell a story on the most effective of all media.

What Do You Want from Television?

Television exposure can promote a particular product or service, or present a company in a favorable light. You want television to get more people to know about you and what you are selling or advocating.

The Trade-Off

TV talk shows and news programs have a symbiotic relationship with PR practitioners. Television is willing to allow itself to be used to promote products, books, movies—whatever. Television requires that the sell not be too blatant, that the performer be entertaining and instructive, and that the information and opinion presented by the performer be valid.

I use the word *performer* advisedly. When you appear on a TV talk or news show, you are there to help the show attract an audience and sell advertising. The spokesperson may be CEO of a superpowerful, multinational corporation, but if that spokesperson is long-winded, boring, or unhelpful, television is not interested.

What Do You Have That Is Media-Worthy?

If you want TV exposure to promote a particular product, look for the things about the product that might be most interesting or amusing to the TV audience. What is new and different about it? Does it tie in to some current trend? What differences can it make in people's lives? How was the product or service developed? What needs is it intended to meet? Can you think of any interesting anecdotes about the product, its users, or those who produce it?

Maybe you are not promoting a particular product but, rather, your whole company. What is interesting about the company to the casual TV viewer? (This question must be answered objectively. The people whose hearts and souls are involved with the organization think that every little detail is of great interest. Alas, the world at large could not care less about the nuts and bolts of the organization.)

Maybe the company, through its TV representative, can provide something of real use to the audience—something above and beyond the utility implicit in what the company sells. A manufacturer might have helpful things to say about how to use and care for household tools and appliances. A bank might offer tips on keeping the domestic books. A company in the food industry could provide information on nutrition, diet, and preservation. The key to media-worthiness is objective information that entertains and helps the audience.

What Makes a Good Television Spokesperson?

The spokesperson must be someone with authority and credibility—the chairman, the president, a senior executive. If the subject is special or technical, the spokesperson should be the company's leading expert.

The spokesperson should be attractive and articulate. Visual impact is more than 80 percent of television's effect. A person who speaks well but looks shifty or insignificant will not make a good impression. It is better to pick someone who looks good. People can be taught to talk effectively on television.

Brevity is essential. The standard format is Q&A. The TV host or anchorperson asks a question. The guest should answer with a short, punchy statement, thirty seconds or less, then add detail as it seems appropriate. Long, detailed explanations do not go well on the tube.

Mobility is another essential. When nonprofessionals appear on television, they tend to become rigid. Only their lips move. Television is a visual medium; it requires movement. Television spokespersons should move around in their chairs (although the head should always be absolutely vertical, not on a slant). Smile. Nod the head. Move the hands. Lean forward and *listen* carefully.

Coolness is the third requirement. The spokesperson is there to put on a show that projects the desired impression. The TV host asking the questions will not be familiar with—or interested in—the particular details of the message. Typically, the host comes into the studio with thirty to sixty seconds to go, glances at the release or backgrounder, and starts to ask questions. The guest should be ready with punch responses (not jokes), anecdotes (the more anecdotes, especially about people, the better), and plausible answers to all the questions that might reasonably be asked.

It is all right for the spokesperson to mention the company and its products, as long as the mentions are not blatantly dragged in and not too frequent. Visual demonstrations are better than mentions. Show the product in operation. Show photos or film. Show graphs and charts.

Making the Pitch to the Television Program

Getting on a local TV station can be initiated through personal contacts. Get to know the station executives, who usually belong to civic organizations and often show up at various local functions. If the company advertises on television, so much the better, but do not assume that buying advertising gives you an automatic inside track for getting on shows.

Find out what the station wants. Watch all the relevant programs. Look for the areas in which your organization could provide information or expertise.

Once you have decided on the show, make the approach *in writing*. Do not call up the program director and say, "Hey, you ought to have us on your news show." Local TV executives are very good at turning down such advances in the nicest possible way.

Prepare a press kit. The press kit should contain, at a minimum, a pitch letter; the biography of the spokesperson; a 5″ × 7″ glossy black-and-white or color photo with caption; a release or backgrounder; and a fact sheet.

Using Celebrities

The spokesperson is the embodiment of your company on the air. That person should project the qualities you want projected—innovation, reliability, integrity.

For local promotions, it is usually best to use someone from your own organization—someone who does well on television and radio and can speak authoritatively about your product. For national promotions, it is probably best to select a "name"—someone who is a known quantity to program directors. Otherwise you must spend time and money establishing the spokesperson before you even start the campaign.

Experience and Expertise

Public relations spokespersons must have experience, if not expertise, in the products or services they are promoting. Here public relations differs sharply from advertising. Skillful producers of commercials used Joe DiMaggio's grace and stature in a carefully crafted commercial for a coffeemaker. DiMaggio did not have to know anything about the product. Nobody was going to ask him questions to which he had to ad-lib answers.

The PR spokesperson goes into the Q&A, where you have to be able to do more than just say, "Very good—twenty-five cents a box" with sincerity. Since the spokesperson is on the show, ostensibly, to give the audience something useful, familiarity with the subject is a must. At Porter Novelli, we used former New York Yankee Mickey Mantle as a spokesperson for the U.S. launch of Voltaren, a Ciba-Geigy arthritis drug.

Mickey was a perfect spokesperson. He was known to the world, and he suffered from arthritis. Mickey praised Voltaren. The drug helped him play golf again, he told a *Today* show audience. He also said that it helped him cure a hangover. This ad-lib was not greeted with enthusiasm by the folks at Ciba-Geigy.

Mickey was so successful in promoting the drug on television that the competitors started crying foul to the FDA. Ciba-Geigy was forced to pull back on the work we were doing with Mickey, but not before Voltaren became number one in the country.

Divided Loyalties

Beware the spokesperson with divided loyalties. Broadcast producers do not like a lot of plugs. They understand that the plug is the quid pro quo of the guest appearance, but they do not want the editorial content of their shows to deteriorate into a lot of name-brand mentions.

An experienced spokesperson knows this and will keep the plug content at an acceptable level. However, if the spokesperson represents more than one client, you may face a dismaying experience. You go to the trouble of arranging the appearance, and your representative adds a plug for someone else, adulterating your message and, perhaps, alienating the show.

This can happen to the best of them. Judy Twersky, who heads up her own PR firm, was arranging appearances for Bob Vila, the home improvement expert, representing Sears Roebuck. Twersky managed to get Vila, formerly the host of PBS's *This Old House,* on the *Letterman* show, where Vila would build a bookcase with David.

Everything went fine. The bookcase, put together with Sears Roebuck tools, grew before the audience's eyes. Then came the problem. In addition to his work for Sears, Vila also represented Time-Life Books. When the bookcase was finished, he said, "This bookcase will be perfect for your Time-Life Books." Letterman and his producers (who are particularly cautious about plugs) were livid. Sears was not very happy, either.

Overdoing It

While you are in a live television situation, do not overdo your attempts to get credit. You may antagonize your interviewer and make it harder to get on the air again. Here is a good case in point that took place on *Good Morning America,* during a discussion about loan guarantees to Israel for Soviet Jewish immigrants.

Michael Lerner, editor of the liberal *Tikkun* magazine, was a guest. He appeared holding a copy of his magazine directly in front of him, so that viewers could read its name. It crowded the frame and distracted the viewer from the conversation between Lerner and the host. The usually mild-mannered host, Charlie Gibson, uncharacteristically peeved, said to his guest, "Just a point of personal privilege. I've mentioned your magazine's name. Now please take it down."

Media Tours

Media tours work particularly well when you are introducing a product, creating or enhancing an image, or trying to boost lagging sales. The staple of the media tour is television. The objective is to get your message on the right TV shows at the right time. Some messages work well on radio, particularly drive-time radio. And media stopovers in a market can be fleshed out with newspaper interviews. But, basically, television is the name of the game.

It is a mistake to think that public relations in general, and TV appearances in particular, can be a substitute for advertising. In certain areas, public relations has to fill the breach because advertising is forbidden or restricted. As I described in Chapter 8, cigarette manufacturers have devised a wide assortment of ploys for getting on television to make up for the banishment of their advertising. A few professionals—lawyers, physicians, accountants—advertise on television, but most do not. Nevertheless, creative public relations will place sales pitches in advantageous television contexts.

You cannot assume that placing spokespersons on TV shows will enable you to cut back on advertising, although the notion does have a certain surface plausibility, especially when the economy is soft. A lot of people cherish the idea that, since you do not pay directly for the TV time when a guest appears, it is free, or at least very cheap.

True, having spokespeople appear on television can give you a tremendous bang for the buck. *CBS Evening News* carries a brief feature on an unknown plastic toy, and 17 million orders flood in within two weeks, making a young entrepreneur into a millionaire. Television's power works best when it is used in a coordinated advertising and PR campaign. One vital ingredient of the plan can be a media tour.

You'll need to pick the right spots. Everybody wants to get on the big network shows—*Today, Good Morning America, CBS Morning News, 60 Minutes*. The bigger the show, the harder it is to get on it. If you think you have a story hot enough for one of these shows, you should talk with a PR professional who can advise you realistically on your chances, and who can, if it is justified, handle the negotiations.

Video News Releases

Television is a voracious consumer of material. Television news is a highly competitive business. Program directors welcome interesting, well-produced features or news stories, especially when they are provided free.

These circumstances have led to the creation of the video news release (VNR), a carefully constructed ninety-second to two-minute videotape that meets television standards for usability. It projects the message of the VNR's producer within the framework of a standard TV news story. The VNR promotes your product or tells your story in a way that makes it seem like a legitimate news item, not a plug. Video news releases will become a lot more important. News programs that cannot afford to do their own stories will run many VNRs. In fact, shows of the twenty-first century may be largely VNRs.

Here are some of the questions to ask in determining whether to invest in a VNR:

- Does the topic have a news angle? Is it about a technological breakthrough? Does it make life easier? Does it demonstrate an emerging trend? Is there something humorous or touching?

- Can the story be told in two minutes or less? Does it have interesting visual elements?

- Is the topic sufficiently different from other TV fare to appeal to a producer?

- Will exposure on TV news shows help to sell the product?
- What sales promotions can be tied in with the exposure?
- Is the VNR important enough to warrant the cost ($20,000 to $40,000)?

Producing the VNR

Look for independent video producers who have worked in TV news. The VNR is not for inexperienced people. Making good VNRs is a specialized art that fits promotional needs with broadcast news ground rules. The producer has to have the experience and "feel" to put in enough objective meat to induce the show to run the piece.

Get itemized price estimates. Find out how much of the job the producer will farm out. The producer's markup of subcontractor charges will inflate the cost.

Pick a producer with whom you feel comfortable talking. The producer has to understand your needs and the audience you want to reach. Beware the producer who tends to fit everything into the same mold.

You will be presented with a concept and working script (with shooting descriptions) for approval. Once you sign off, the producer goes to work. You should have a knowledgeable representative at all shooting sessions, not to second-guess the producer, but to make sure the proper focus is maintained.

Your VNR may use a voice-over. Have the producer let you listen to announcers' voices before selecting one. You want a voice that feels right as an expression of your organization. (The producer may record the audio portion of the VNR on a different channel, so the news director has the option of using station reporters for commentary while the visual part is rolling.)

Distributing the VNR

You will want to get the VNR to TV stations in all the areas where you want the message to air. (If your list is not very big, you should rethink the expense of the VNR.) There are two ways of distributing the VNR—satellite feed or hard copy.

Hard copy—mailing a videocassette to all the target outlets—is preferred. It gives news directors flexibility in airing the piece. If the VNR carries a hard news or breaking story, or is keyed to quickly changing current developments, it must be distributed by satellite. If the budget allows, the best plan may be to supplement hard copy with satellite.

Your producer will work with you in selecting a distribution house. The distribution house should furnish interim and final reports on which outlets aired the piece and when it was aired.

Radio

Radio interviews can reach a specific audience with in-depth motivational messages. Most all-news and all-talk stations are AM. If you are trying to reach a businessperson audience, morning and evening drive time are primary targets. If your audience consists of people who are likely to be home during the day, you may find it easier to arrange an interview, because more PR practitioners are vying for drive time. FM stations tend to have all-music formats, appealing to a younger audience. Some FM stations do interviews.

If your message is compatible with the station's profile, go for it. Otherwise, concentrate on the network-affiliated and independent stations with the biggest wattage and the highest listenership.

Late-night radio has become a good place for placing spokespersons for interviews. Listen to the show. Be sure your spokesperson and message will be treated courteously. Make sure the atmosphere of the show is one you are comfortable with. Some radio talk shows go to extremes to find an audience. A spokesperson might be treated all right on such a show, but the message is heard in a context of fervent political partisanship.

"Insult" hosts like Bob Grant, a New York radio fixture, may treat guests courteously but berate those who call in. John Tarrant did an interview segment with Grant while promoting a book. Grant conversed knowledgeably about the book. Then he took calls from listeners. But whenever a caller asked a question, the "host" would bellow, "Idiot! Get off the phone!" Finally the guest pleaded, "Mr. Grant, I'd like to answer some of the questions." Grant said, "All right, Mr. Tarrant, but you're very nice to waste your time talking to these jerks!"

Make certain the atmosphere of the show provides a reasonable setting for your spokesperson and your message.

Making Cost-Effective Pitches for Broadcast Time

Some PR practitioners send releases to all radio and TV stations. This is a waste of time and money, and it erodes credibility with the stations. Radio and television stations are as diverse as sections in a newspaper.

Build compartmentalized lists of broadcast outlets, or keep your list culled to those stations whose formats suit you. There are thousands of radio stations—big band/nostalgia, adult contemporary, easy listening, rhythm and blues. Your likely market is news/talk or all-news stations. Focus on them. Tailor your pitch letter to the particular radio station. Keep it short; it should be no more than one page.

With advertising, you have a guarantee that your commercial will run. There are no guarantees in public relations. Many stations do not book until the actual day of the event. Chicago, one of the toughest radio/TV markets, usually makes decisions in the morning, depending on what is going on that day.

When making your follow-up call, ask the program director how much time you have. Ordinarily it is two minutes, tops. Be ready to make your pitch in that time. At the outset, you might ask, "Can I have two minutes of your time?"

You have a better chance when you pitch for spots that the stations find difficult to fill. Sundays are slowest for broadcast. July and August are the easiest times of the year to get spokespersons on, as stations are scrambling for guests.

16

Running Effective News Conferences

Is It News?

The news conference is a staple item of public relations. When used well, it gets stories used and wins friends in the media.

It is also a production, aimed at a tough audience. To get the desired response from this audience, PR professionals must ensure that the production is well managed. This means the stars should be well rehearsed, the props should be ready, and the production should run smoothly.

Deciding to Hold a News Conference

The first question about a news conference is whether to have one. Some nonprofessionals think the answer is simple. Since a news conference implies more importance than merely sending out a release, they feel that their PR professionals should always arrange conferences whenever there is anything the client wants to get into print or on the air.

Wrong. The tool is a *news* conference, not a "*con*" conference. The worst use of the device is to call reporters together and then try to con them into running a nonstory that is simply a puff for the client's point of view. Those who see these occasions as just opportunities for manipulation often refer to them as "press conferences." We should stick to the term *news* conference as a semantic reminder that solid meat must be served to the media.

Newsworthiness

What constitutes news? When an organization is involved in a big, ongoing story, almost any statement of substance by a top officer is news. Unfortunately, such ongoing stories are usually negative; there is a problem, scandal, or disaster.

If the logic of the news conference is not dictated by a general situation, then somebody has to decide whether the desired message adds up to something substantial enough to warrant a full-blown news conference. Perhaps it should be disseminated via some other means. This decision should be made by a PR professional and no one else. Public relations professionals can—and should—put themselves in the shoes of reporters, editors, and program directors and ask, "What's in this for me?" If a cold-blooded, objective answer turns out to be that the story lacks sufficient appeal or will be seen just as a plug, then the decision should be *no conference*.

Holding a news conference is not a "can't lose" situation. Some think that, even if the story does not get picked up by the media, the worst that can happen is that the company spent some money to hold the meeting. That is not so. A dud conference puts you in the position of the boy who cried "Wolf!" Media people will not show up the next time, even if there really *is* something to say. Furthermore, reporters will tell their colleagues. The organization will become something of a media joke.

New developments constitute news. A new product or service is news. It is big news to the organization and, probably, pretty big news to the industry. Whether it is news beyond those confines is a key consideration in deciding on whether to have the news conference.

Sometimes the material is too complex for the press to absorb at a news conference. For example, Virginia Slims wanted to hold a lavish press presentation for the release of the findings of its American Women's Poll. I fought to persuade them not to have the traditional conference at the Hotel Pierre, with all the trimmings. It was the fifth

Slims' survey over a fifteen-year period. There was a thick volume of Roper survey material. Why give the press only a few hours to wade through it and write their stories? I prevailed. Philip Morris did not hold the conference but simply sent out the materials well in advance of a release date, giving the press time to write their stories. Virginia Slims wound up with more coverage and better in-depth stories.

When Not to Seek Attention: The Single Dumbest Congressman

Frazer Seitel, veteran PR executive and teacher, in a column headed "Press Conferences Kill," told this story in *Ragan's PR Intelligence Report* (December 14, 1998):

> Many years ago, a now-defunct prickly little magazine called *New Times* published an article called "The 10 Dumbest Congressmen." The piece, as you might expect, listed in graphic detail the exploits of the 10 individuals in the halls of the U.S. Congress who, in the publication's judgment, were even dumber than the rest.
>
> At the top of the chart stood Sen. William Scott of Virginia, whom *New Times* dubbed the "single dumbest Congressman."
>
> Sen. Scott, understandably, was outraged. And to vent his wrath, two days after the article's publication, Sen. Scott called a Capitol Hill press conference to deny that he was "the single dumbest Congressman"—thus proving the point.
>
> Beware the press conference. It is truly a public relations practitioner's biggest nightmare—unwieldy and uncontrollable.

Low-Key Alternatives to News Conferences

If the subject does not warrant a full-blown news conference but is worth more than a release, the news briefing is a good alternative. The news briefing is less formal and confrontational than a news conference. It is usually held off-premises, often in a hotel meeting room or suite. The spokesperson need not be as high-powered as the star of the news conference, but can be just somebody who answers questions. The press kit should be prepared just as carefully as the press kit for a news conference. The informality of the occasion makes it more of a get-together than a presentation or confrontation. Thus— unlike the news conference, which should not be connected with a lot of food and drink—the news briefing works well at breakfast or lunch. It is a chance for a company person to schmooze with reporters, and for both sides to get to know each other better.

There is an even lower-voltage alternative to the news conference: the news availability. This, as Peter Hannaford says, "is informal in tone, held in your office conference room, and called on relatively short notice." It is usually shorter than the news conference, running approximately ten minutes, as compared to twenty minutes for the news conference.

Hannaford suggests that the news availability is a good way of keeping contact with media while a negative story is breaking. The atmosphere is less heated. The spokesperson is usually seated, rather than standing. The exchanges are lower in key. And expectations are lower on both sides. The reporters know that a news availability will help them get up-to-date but will not produce any bombshells. The organization does not expect major coverage.

One injunction holds true for the news conference, news briefing, or news availability. *Be careful.* The informality of the lower-key get-togethers does not make them off the record. An unwise comment at an availability can be just as damaging as if it happened at a conference.

Basics of the News Conference

If a full-scale news conference is the best way to get the message out, a number of logistical questions must be addressed.

Location

Rent a meeting room in a hotel with a convenient location—convenient for the media, not for the people holding the conference. Hannaford says it is best to stay away from meeting rooms at clubs, unless it is a press club. Clubs (university or otherwise) may convey an elitist image. And some clubs are regarded as discriminatory against women or minorities. Maybe that inference is inaccurate and unfair; maybe whatever discrimination existed in the past has been banished. It does not matter. The location should not be a potential problem in any way.

Setup

Arrange chairs facing a low-rise platform with a dais. Make provisions for television and radio; there should be ample electrical facilities. If necessary, says Hannaford, "obtain, from a communications supply dealer, a 'mult' box that permits many [recorders] to be plugged in and your spokesperson to speak from only one." This eliminates the forest of mikes with a tangle of spaghetti wires that festoon many news conferences.

Eats and Drinks

There is a notion in some quarters that reporters at a news conference should be plied with food and drinks. This may go back to the stereotype that these ink-stained wretches are always starved for a decent meal, and that they are inveterate boozers. Even if this were the case—and it is not—the conference should not take place at a meal, nor should it be a party. (Parties for the media have their place, but they are not news conferences.) The event should be crisp and businesslike, respecting the time demands on the reporters and conveying the idea that this is an important happening.

Not that the doings should be Spartan. There should be a table at the back with good, hot coffee and maybe hot water, tea bags, juice, and snacks.

Timing

In setting a time for the news conference, the convenience of the media is all-important. A midmorning news conference is usually best. It makes the evening news, and it lets reporters write their stories for the next day's papers.

Announcement

The announcement or advisory of the news conference should be sent—faxed, if possible—to all appropriate media. Except in unusual circumstances, it should be addressed to program directors or editors rather than to reporters. Let the editors make the assignments; they tend to resent usurpation of that function.

Besides giving the time, place, and sponsor of the news conference, the announcement should—unless it is obvious—hint at what is going to be presented. This is a "sell" document; media professionals have to be sold on devoting their time to the conference. Follow up with phone calls the day before the conference.

Press Kit

The press kit distributed at the news conference should be a real help to reporters in writing their stories. It should contain the opening statement, biographies of all participants and relevant people, background material, photos, and any other relevant information.

Rehearsal

Hold a dry run before the news conference. Make sure that the lights and mikes work, all visuals are present and operative, computers and Internet connections have been checked, and there are no bugs.

Media professionals notice whether a news conference is run well or badly. A professionally run event denotes professionalism all along the line. An amateurish news conference is harmful. It can erode credibility. It can have an unconscious effect on those attending. Even if the content is solid, sloppy packaging tarnishes the perception.

Opening Statement

The news conference starts with a brief opening statement. This statement must be carefully crafted. It lays out the essentials of the message. The written statement should be handed out at the beginning.

The spokesperson should be well rehearsed, of course, and part of that rehearsal must be emphasis on the role of the statement. First of all, the opening statement does not set the ground rules. Reporters may well ask questions that have little or nothing to do with the topics covered in the statement. This is particularly true if the organization is in any way involved in newsworthy activities that are not covered in the statement.

Reporters may also ask questions that are already addressed by the statement. It is not a good idea to simply instruct the reporter to refer to the printed words, as if the spokesperson were a teacher telling a student he did not do his homework. The thing to do, rather, is to answer graciously, winding up with a reference to the statement ("which gives some details on the matter").

Negative News

News conferences are a part of any good crisis plan. In Chapter 10, my discussion of responding to crisis covers the overall strategy and the ways in which the conference fits into it. Here it is worthwhile to emphasize the importance of role-playing and preparing for all conceivable questions (no matter how "unfair" some may seem).

The very fact that you are holding a full-scale news conference says that you take the situation seriously. If the strategy is to minimize the importance of what happened, it may be better to hold an informal news briefing or a news availability.

Ground Rules

The ground rules for the news conference should be as few and as clear as possible. The media will want everything to be on the record and will want no limitations on questions. The organization holding the conference should make every effort to conform to these wishes.

It takes more preparation and there is a greater risk, but it is worth it. Willingness to handle any question greatly enhances credibility.

Sometimes, however, it may be necessary to impose some limitations. The PR professional—not the spokesperson—should intervene to handle this part and take whatever heat must be taken. Media representatives should be subtly advised, in advance, that there may be reasons for indirect responses to certain questions—and the media should be given the reasons.

For example, the PR professional and spokesperson may have agreed beforehand that, if a question about a pending move comes up, they do not want to answer "no comment"—a ridiculous and provocative answer from someone who called a conference—or, even worse, to lie. (This is to be avoided at all costs.) One way to handle it is to go "off the record." This device is to be used sparingly, and only in small groups of trusted reporters. Another nondirect response is "not for attribution"—in which an answer is given but is not to be connected to the person who gave it. This may be useful when the reporter seems to have the facts anyway and is just trying to confirm them.

"Background"—or sometimes "deep background"—means the person giving the interview can't be named but can be given a general label, such as "a White House official." News briefings or advisories are often done on a background basis.

Overselling the News Value

"What is your guy going to say?" That is the question the arranger of the news conference hears from reporters. Of course, the logical answer is, "Show up at the conference, and you'll hear it." However, unless the news value of the conference is obvious, you must give media representatives a reason for attending. The more important the media outlet, the greater the sales resistance. The *New York Times,* the *Wall Street Journal,* the network news shows—they do not show up without assurance that there is something in it for them.

Here is where the PR professional's credibility comes into play. Public relations pros who are trusted can say, "There's going to be some real meat here. I think you'll get a good story out of it." (It is best not to say things like, "I *guarantee* you a great story," unless the content is absolute dynamite.)

If there is doubt as to whether there will be a story for the major media, then the PR counselor should be candid about it. Some people think attendance at news conferences is a matter of prestige. If the big papers or TV stations are not there, the sponsor feels slighted. That is a harmful point of view. If you sucker reporters or editors once, they will never trust you again.

Press Parties

Press parties are quite different from news conferences. These are *parties,* put together to introduce the media to an organization or some people in the organization. The food and drink should be first-rate. There should be no effort to cover serious topics.

Robert J. Wood (in *Confessions of a PR Man,* NAL, 1988) explains the media's mind-set:

> People review a press party in the same way they might review
> a play or a book, and it is by no means unusual for reviewers
> to have sharply different opinions.

The organization putting on a press party must be ready to be judged on the basis of its lavish hospitality, not its wonderful products. Therefore, the party is a tool that should be used only on appropriate, light-hearted occasions.

Giving Favored Media a Break

A dominant media outlet—the biggest newspaper or broadcaster—may ask for an early look at the statement, if it contains a significant announcement. Should PR practitioners give such big-time media a break?

That depends. Let us say a company's chairman is going to announce an important and dramatic merger with a big competitor. This is a story that will have wide ramifications in the industry, on Wall Street, and even in Washington. The *New York Times* asks to be given the story early. The *Times* often does this. And the *Times* often gets away with it, the same way that a 600-pound gorilla gets to sleep wherever she wants.

The *Times* says it does not want the premature disclosure so it can break the story early, but rather so it can have full-fledged coverage, including sidebars, ready to go. The story will run; that is not the issue. But the PR professional would like the *Times* story to be as complete as possible, laying out all the angles and presenting the company's point of view fully, if not sympathetically.

Some argue it might be advisable to give the *Times* a break. The other newspapers will not like it, but they are used to it. Be careful. You do not want to antagonize the other media. The TV stations are not particularly affected; they will have the story that evening in any case. The trade-off is better handling in the *Times* versus avoiding getting the other papers annoyed. Public relations practitioners are paid to make these calls. The individual handling this news conference might well decide the best course is to cooperate with the *Times* and mollify the others to the extent possible.

Sometimes you can play a "reality game" with a smart reporter who wants a beat on the announcement and who has some ideas about what the announcement might be. The reporter guesses at the content, and the PR pro indicates by some indirect means that this is an accurate guess.

Here is how it worked in one episode of the fantastic Watergate saga. In 1974, damaging stories were coming out about President Nixon and his associates, but Nixon was still confident that he could retain the support of Republican members of Congress along with enough Democrats to stave off impeachment. At this time, James Buckley, a conservative Republican, was the senator from New York. (Buckley's brother William called him, affectionately, "the sainted junior senator from New York.")

Obviously, the continuing support of Senator Buckley was essential to Nixon—and Nixon took it for granted. But Buckley, increasingly troubled about Watergate and what it was doing to the country, at last concluded that the nation would be better off if Nixon were to leave office. This was heresy for a man who had seconded Nixon's nomination at the Republican convention in Miami two years earlier.

Buckley thought about issuing a statement. I persuaded him that a statement was not sufficient for such dynamite and that a news conference should be held. I had to operate in absolute secrecy. If the White House staff suspected what Buckley was going to say, they would do everything possible to hold it up. And Buckley would find it hard to defy a direct appeal from the president of the United States.

How do you get people to a news conference when you cannot give them a clue about what is going on? I put out a news alert the day before:

> Senator James L. Buckley (R.-N.Y.) will hold a news conference on Watergate in the Senate Caucus Room at 10 A.M. on Wednesday, March 19.

Short and sweet. The phones started ringing. What was Buckley up to? Was the conference worth attending? Roger Mudd, covering Capitol Hill for CBS, reminded me of what I already knew: there were only so many TV crews available. Mudd could not assign a three-person crew unless he thought the news was worthy of being broadcast on network news.

I told Mudd I could not divulge the contents of the Buckley statement, but I assured Mudd that what Buckley had to say would surely be on top of the news in that evening's broadcast. I made the same pledge to other media representatives, putting my reputation and credibility on the line. In my six years on the Hill, I had never exaggerated the news, and that stood me in good stead in this case.

Fifteen minutes before the conference was to start, the historic caucus room was overflowing with reporters, camera crews, and broadcasting equipment.

And now an enterprising reporter played a game with me. As I was going to get Buckley, a call came through from Carl Leubsdorf, then of the Associated Press. Leubsdorf said he was about to go with a story that Buckley was going to call for Nixon's resignation. "Would I be wrong?" he asked.

If it had been earlier, I would have had to ponder the question more deliberately. Should I give the nod to the story, letting the AP beat the others, or should I withhold assent and leave it up to the reporter to go with it or not? Now, though, with just a minute to go, I felt it did not matter, and I might as well do the AP a favor. "You wouldn't be wrong," I told Leubsdorf.

The reporter put out a flash on the "A" wire, and it was read seconds later in the White House, which reacted quickly enough to make it a very close call. As I walked past the desk of Dawne Cina, Buckley's secretary, to bring Buckley to the news conference, a call came in from General Alexander Haig, the White House chief of staff. Haig wanted to talk to Buckley, and so did the president. I told Dawne to say that Buckley had already left for the news conference.

Buckley dropped his bombshell. The three networks all led with the story, using a combined total of forty minutes.

It is vital never to mislead a reporter by seeming to deny accurate speculation. The response is to be noncommittal (which will usually be taken as confirmation) or to confirm by some indirect word or action. (A reporter may say, "If you don't say anything, I'm going with this story.")

Interesting Settings and Visuals

Some announcements—like Buckley's call for Nixon's resignation—are so strong they need no props. In most cases, though, the subject matter can be helped by slides, charts, props, and visuals for the benefit of TV camera crews and photographers.

It might be worthwhile to supply videotape, too, since news conferences do not produce good video. News directors do not want talking heads on the 6:00 P.M. news. And chances are, a head shot of a speaker at the podium will wind up in the wastebasket. This is true even when the speaker is a celebrity. Dolly Parton announcing a Marlboro Country Music concert at Lincoln Center would not make an acceptable photo. However, when we posed her with two horses wearing caps, the picture made the AP and UPI wires.

Sometimes, the news conference can be spiced up by coaching the central figure to put on a performance—what is called a shtick. When I was campaign manager for New York State Senator John Marchi, in Marchi's race for mayor of New York, crime in the streets was (then as now) a big issue. I called a news conference and equipped Marchi with the *New York Times* as a prop and with charts showing rising crime statistics. Marchi was to use these statistics against his opponent, Abe Beame. I suggested that the usually dignified, soft-spoken candidate get mad at Beame for visual purposes.

Marchi threw himself into the role. He rolled up the papers in his hand, waved them, and started shouting. Everyone in the room was startled, including Marchi's daughter, who thought he would have a heart attack. The candidate threw the *Times,* containing a quotation from Beame, on the floor. His flailing arm hit the easel, sending the boards with the crime statistics sailing into a roomful of press.

Marchi was on all the TV newscasts that evening.

This is a tricky tactic. The subject has to be able to carry it off. But it can be worthwhile. A burst of action can make all the difference in getting on TV.

17

Building and Running a PR Firm

People, Policy, and Procedures

Public relations is now a mature discipline, involving a variety of techniques. It is useful in setting corporate policy, making and executing plans, and handling many of the most fundamental challenges facing the company.

That is the premise of this book, and that is what an objective assessment of the current state of public relations will find. However, the PR professional fighting it out in the trenches knows very well that not everyone has reached this state of enlightened respect for the discipline. There is still a lot of misunderstanding of public relations, a lot of underestimation of it, and no small measure of contempt for it.

Here is a set of observations and tips for the PR practitioner who goes to work in an environment replete with the attitudes of a bygone day, or for the PR practitioner who does not have the luxury of a large, well-placed department, but who has to act as a kind of one-person band in a smaller organization.

Let's say you answer a want ad like the following:

Writer/PR

Writer, quick and facile, to handle PR function in growing organization. Deadline-oriented materials needed include news releases, feature articles for trade and media outlets, brochures and collaterals, newsletters, research, some statistical analysis . . .

You get the job. You are the company's public relations department and also its on-site writer. You will write, or be involved with writing, just about everything that comes out of the company except for advertising and technical writing.

The first thing to note is that the job, as characterized by the want ad, is production oriented. Nobody expects the occupant of this job to do much strategizing. The emphasis is on writing to order. And this leads to one of the major problems facing the public relations professional in a lot of places.

The Wordsmith Syndrome

The wordsmith syndrome implies a kind of literate odd-job person who is summoned, like a janitor, to make quick alterations or do quick repairs. Everything is short-term. The wordsmith is judged on the basis of personal ability to turn out a release fast, revise a product pamphlet against a deadline, create a quick form letter to be sent to complaining customers.

The biggest trouble with the wordsmith syndrome is not that it makes PR practitioners do a lot of work. There is nothing demeaning about writing. It takes drive and skill to meet tight deadlines with well-written material.

The trouble is that the PR professional becomes a wordsmith and nothing else. Under the pressure of deadlines, there is no time to create coherent public relations programs or to set up the kinds of relationships with other departments that will give the company a strong, unified PR presence. If the PR practitioner tries to do some conceptual work, there are complaints: "What about the leaflets that sales is waiting for?"

Then, too, efforts by PR practitioners to do conceptual work are likely to be greeted with skepticism and derision. Why is this trained monkey rattling her chain? Why is she not pounding away at the keyboard? When the PR function is seen as all *doing* and no *thinking*, then much of the potential of the function is wasted.

Of course, one simple answer is that the PR professional should not be the company's all-around writer. But, in smaller organizations, that all-aroundness is a fact of life. There is no inclination to hire more PR staff. The tendency is likely to be the other way. The PR function is on trial: what does this spot produce that makes it worth keeping?

So, the PR professional who is trapped in a wordsmith role is not likely to get anywhere with pleas to be allowed to do it the way they do it in the giant corporations, or with complaints about the writing workload. The answer, rather, is to use the wordsmith role to carve out a meaningful PR function.

Carving Out a Role

The wordsmith can find writing assignments that will get influential officers of the company hooked on PR. One way to do this is with speeches. The want ad that started this section does not mention speechwriting, but the individual who gets this job will surely have many opportunities to write speeches.

It can start with a chore that has nothing to do with the company. The president remarks that she has to give a talk to the local chapter of her club. She had written out her speech, but it needs a few touches—maybe a funny opening, maybe a graceful ending. In other words, some wordsmithing is needed.

Now, this is the kind of assignment a lot of PR operatives hate. It is, to them, the equivalent of the secretary being sent out to buy the boss's Christmas presents. The PR professional finds some excuse not to do it or, being unable to refuse, does the bare minimum.

The speech is an opportunity to bring the PR function into some of the more important policy functions of the organization. An astute PR professional will make a specialty of writing good speeches, long and short, for all occasions. And this should not be just speeches to clubs; the idea is to get into a position where you are working on important policy speeches by the CEO, president, or senior officers.

Working on speeches is a way to gain entrance to the policy tent. At the very least, the writer gets a better sense of what is going on in the company and, even more important, what is about to happen. Then the PR professional can begin to suggest shadings and modifications—not in content, but in how things are said. Let me make an important point: *When you are involved in the way policy is articulated, you are involved in the way policy is made.*

Here is an example of how wordsmithing segues into discussion and then into subtle influence. The president of a large company that distributes to retail stores is to make a speech to a group of retailers. The president wants to send a message: "We need to get paid on time." He wants to say it bluntly:

> Today's conditions do not permit us to carry delinquent accounts. From here on in, we are going to require full payment in 12 days for Class A status, and full payment in 30 days for Class B status.

The PR professional working on the speech says, "This is an important speech. It will not only be heard by this group, it will be reported in the trades. We can send this same message, along with an important related message, by saying it a little differently":

> We all know what conditions are like today. Everybody is talking about getting more lean and mean. We see it a little differently. We want to get leaner—but we are not going to get mean.
>
> Here's what we're going to do. First of all, we are going to tighten up our own situation by requiring full payment in 12 days for Class A accounts and full payment in 30 days for Class B accounts. That's just good business. You and our other customers want to pay on time, just as we want to be paid on time. So you want to get leaner—if not meaner—too.
>
> We're ready to give you some concrete help. Today I'm announcing our new "Lean, Not Mean" program. Through this program, we will help you in a number of specific ways. We'll make a complete review of your inventory and stocking patterns, and work out a plan to save you money. We'll use

our knowledge of what's new and hot in retail merchandising to help you pull in more traffic and sell more lines. And we'll sit down with you and work out payment schedules that will make sure you always qualify for the highest possible discount.

The PR practitioner has simply described things the distributor's drivers and customer service representatives are supposed to do anyway. The new language gets the "pay on time" message across—but, without adding new programs or services, it sells the distributor's willingness to cooperate and its ability to provide concrete assistance.

This is more than wordsmithing. It influences policy by putting the company's ancillary services in a new light. Customers who did not take advantage of these services before will do so now. And the distributor is glad to oblige, because these activities bind customers more closely and help customers pay their bills on time.

The PR professional is doing something else: making public relations a two-way function, as it is supposed to be. The PR pro automatically thinks about how various populations are going to react to messages, and about ways to maximize the effectiveness of messages. By feeding the results of this thinking back in the form of a concrete suggestion, the PR professional makes a contribution that goes beyond writing to order.

And let's face it: most people welcome help in cutting a more impressive figure. Most people know they could be more effective speakers. When the PR professional provides help in being more compelling on the speaker's platform, he or she is acting as a kind of personal image consultant. This is the quid pro quo for becoming more involved in policy matters.

It is a trade-off. The PR professional, trying to create a more substantial role for the function, uses PR skills to help people who can, in turn, be of help. This is the best way to deal with the wordsmith syndrome. Rather than resisting it and resenting every "unnecessary" call on the PR function for writing chores, you exploit the fact that other people know they cannot write and will welcome the help of a professional writer. Writers of news releases must try to think like editors, says marketing veteran Peter Gorman. This is the coin that pays for greater stature and influence. It is better than sending cases of Scotch.

Developing Public Relations Power

A number of tactics can be used to make an undervalued public relations function into something closer to what it should be.

Generate Ideas

Public relations practitioners should give away "free samples." When something is happening in the company, or is about to happen, volunteer ideas about how it can be used for public relations. Maybe put it in the form of a release or an outline for an article.

Get Around

The PR practitioner should become familiar with every aspect of the company, even the most mundane and ignored parts. Talk to people. Collect facts. Develop a sense of how the departments relate to each other.

Read, Read, Read

Public relations practitioners should be voraciously inquisitive, eager to learn about everything, and omnivorous readers. Dick Weiner sets a good example:

> I have always been a library buff. I have spent many days in the Mid-Manhattan branch of the New York Public Library and confess to spending an hour or two in libraries even when I'm on vacation; for instance, in the headquarters of the Miami Public Library, which is within walking distance of the hotel at which I regularly stay. . . . When I retire I hope to find a library near the beach.

I usually read a half dozen newspapers every day and skim a couple of dozen magazines each week.

Be a Fly on the Wall

What is going on? In many companies, public relations is left out of the loop. Plans are made and decisions are reached—and then the PR practitioners are told to do something with it.

In building their functions, public relations practitioners should do everything possible to be allowed to sit in on high-level meetings. Not necessarily to participate, at least, not at first—just to listen. The astute PR professional will develop ideas about the implications of what is being discussed, and see angles that other people do not see. (Some of these thoughts can be shared after the meeting, perhaps in a summary the PR professional undertakes to write.)

Develop a Network

People working in various places in the organization can be valuable sources. Often they are not people with resounding titles or big salaries. They are veterans in production, executive assistants, supervisors. They see the results of high-level policy in action. And, sometimes, they can warn about things that are about to go wrong. Above all, they are the sources of nitty-gritty detail, which give credibility and texture to stories.

Volunteer Comments

Without being assigned to the job, the PR practitioner can make points by circulating brief memos commenting on the public relations aspects of recent events in the company or the industry. Of course, these comments must have a point and must not be just hot air. But when they are sent out regularly, they can at least help senior management to see that the PR function is more than just wordsmithing. And these ideas can help others to develop more of a public relations point of view, which can help when decisions are being made and implemented.

Take Inventory

Begin collecting facts that may be useful. Find out about the backgrounds of people in the company. Get the human resources department to help you. Learn the history of the company's products or services: who started them, when, why, and how have they fared? Make a file of the company's most important successes. The PR function should build and maintain a storehouse of facts. The facts may not be applicable immediately, but they can come in handy later.

Work Up Some Public Relations Ground Rules

One of the attributes of a successful public relations program is that everybody sings from the same page. The executive vice president does not make a public statement that contradicts what the president said.

No PR professional can prevent goofs and mental glitches. However, the public posture of the organization can be given greater consistency and coherence, and the PR function can help a lot.

Work up some acceptable ways of saying things that are said over and over again. Here is an example. A factory process pumps a certain amount of waste material into the local sewage system. What do you call the stuff? The head chemist calls it *effluent*. The department head calls it *sludge*. The vice president for production calls it *liquid waste*. A technician calls it *outflux*.

It is probably a good idea to get some uniformity into how the stuff is described internally. Misunderstandings and mistakes are reduced when there is a precise, standard term for everything. But the PR professional is more concerned with how the material is described for external consumption—in formal statements, documents that become public, or in informal talk. The choice of a word can condition—to some extent—how the community sees the process and the company.

So the PR function tries to come up with a useful term that describes the material in at least a neutral fashion. The idea is to find words that are not ridiculous euphemisms, but also not self-condemnatory.

Perhaps public relations decides that the best term is *runoff*. The PR professional probably should not go around the place haranguing one and all about semantics. Usually, it is better to go to a senior line executive, explain why the right term is important, and suggest ways in which that senior executive can help to promote consistency.

In the same way, public relations can gradually build a set of principles and practices that should be familiar to all relevant people in the organization.

Make Contingency Plans

In Chapter 10, where I discussed handling emergencies, you will find examples of detailed contingency plans and training scenarios through which firms train people to handle potential emergencies, such as severe product failures or accidents.

Even if it takes a while for a fledgling PR operation to be able to mount elaborate contingency plans, public relations can start building such plans right away.

The PR practitioner is in a good position to work up emergency programs. Most people in an organization accentuate the positive. They look on the bright side. They should, as a matter of common sense, think about negative possibilities, but they like to look at the upside. Public relations practitioners, in contrast, can look at the enterprise and ask, "What if it goes wrong? What if the product fails, disastrously, injuring or killing someone? What if we have an explosion or fire? What if we are accused of serious illegalities?"

While the rest of the company is working to achieve positive goals, PR practitioners can quietly think thoughts of disaster—and then start making plans to do something about it. It may well be a good idea to keep this activity secret, especially for a function that has yet to establish itself. Those who harbor enmity for public relations should not be given ammunition, and the news that public relations is contriving disaster scenarios might be used as ammunition. It is all-important that contingency plans be kept top secret. The leaking of such plans can, in itself, be disastrous.

Look Ahead

Public relations should be prepared to deal with change. It helps when the change does not come as a complete surprise. In a well-run organization, where public relations has established the proper weight and status, top management will trust the function enough to share thoughts about long-range plans. In many places, however, line management tries to keep the lid on important plans right up until the last moment. This includes keeping public relations in the dark. That may not be logical; PR professionals may deplore it; but it is the way it goes in the real world. Worse, in such organizations, new developments are suddenly sprung on public relations, and when the function does not respond instantly with a detailed and effective plan, the critics ask, "What good is public relations anyway?"

Savvy PR professionals should develop sensitive antennae. Tune in to the grapevine. Find out what is happening in research. Find out about new applications and modifications, unusual personnel moves, or allocations of money.

Most speculation about the future is wrong. But PR practitioners should be aware of the possibilities and spend a few moments thinking about the PR implications. Then, if there seems any possibility that a development may be more than idle rumor, public relations ought to start roughing out appropriate plans.

Sometimes, PR practitioners can find out interesting things about their own operations from people outside the operation—PR counterparts in other companies, suppliers, customers, and members of the trade press.

The idea is to get around, to keep your ears open to the maximum possible extent, and to think about the possibilities. That way, when a new development is revealed, public relations can do more than just write a few releases. The PR professional can recommend new ways to exploit the development and suggest how marketing can be helped to make more sales. Marketing, which should be the natural ally of public relations, is often its biggest rival. Forewarned about an important change, public relations can help significantly by being ready to help marketing cope with change.

Coordinate

All too often, the individual who is trying to establish a PR function says, "I'll show them what I can do," then labors in isolation to generate publicity. The effort is reasonably successful. Stories appear in places where they are likely to reach the logical target audience. The PR practitioner then says, "Hey! See what I did?" And the disappointing answer is, "So what?" The achievement, of which the PR practitioner is very proud, is shrugged off by others, because it does not seem to have much to do with their own concerns.

One of the most important tasks for the new PR function is opening channels to other departments—sales, for example. Sales should be a natural ally. Instead, the relationship between sales and public relations is sometimes indifference, occasionally downright hostility.

So it is not enough to "go out and prove something" by generating publicity. Unless it is obviously hooked up to other departmental efforts, the publicity is looked upon as a stunt. The PR practitioner should talk to the people in sales about their needs and problems. Maybe a product story in a particular local paper will help the rep to land a key retailer. So, the PR practitioner works on getting that story printed. It is still a demonstration of what the function can accomplish, but it has more point.

By working this way with sales—frequently a maligned and neglected entity—public relations can forge useful bonds. People in sales often feel that they are slighted by the advertising and merchandising folks, who take credit for everything the soldiers in the trenches accomplish. Some attention from public relations can pay off.

However, it is not just a matter of applying TLC to people and departments that feel neglected. Public relations must *connect*; by itself, it does not work. The function can be of help to a number of divisions in the organization. Human resources wants to attract better people in certain categories; public relations can direct a message at that audience. Research wants more recognition for its achievements, not by the broad public, but by peers in the discipline; public relations can help with speeches and articles in relevant journals. Production is proud of the strides it is making in conserving energy; public relations can translate that pride into publicity.

In establishing connections with other departments, public relations should be receptive and adaptable. The key question is, What can we do for you? That is not always what public relations is saying internally. Some public relations departments are fond of circulating summaries of the stories they have placed. That is not a bad idea, but it ought to be combined with requests for ideas and recommendations about how public relations can use its skills to help the other folks.

By actively seeking partnerships, the growing PR function not only shows what it is capable of doing, but shows how that capability translates into concrete help for others, the kind of help that makes people look good.

Connect. Then show off.

Trade Association Public Relations

Corporate PR practitioners can learn some tricks from those who work for trade associations, especially the less high-powered trade associations. Some associations—in industries like oil, tobacco, and automotive, to name just three—are fairly high-powered operations. They do not do marketing per se. Their skills are employed in the areas of pressure and advocacy. Some groups, usually Washington-based, are essentially lobbying operations. They deploy various elements of the discipline—releases, news conferences—primarily to influence legislators and regulators.

Other industries marshal formidable PR resources to carry on defensive actions—staving off unwelcome restrictions, trying to correct negative perceptions. Such industry associations employ articulate and skilled spokespersons who have become familiar sights on television, arguing the merits of their constituencies against equally familiar spokespersons from opposing groups—perhaps consumer associations.

Most association public relations is low-profile work. The work done by such groups often involves a high degree of quiet professionalism, because the associations do not enjoy the resources that many corporate groups can draw upon, and they do not work with the kind of spectacular subject matter that grabs media attention. In fact, they would shy away from spectacular subject matter if it were offered.

One exceptionally professional association executive is Larry Aasen, who for years tended the public relations needs of the Better Vision Institute. Aasen, like some other top-notch people, prefers association work to corporate work for a number of reasons. For one thing, the institute is truly and consistently putting forward a beneficial cause. The Better Vision Institute's mission is to get people to take better care of their eyes. True, when people take better care of their eyes, it means better business for those who check eyesight, work to improve eyesight, make eyeglasses, and other aspects of the business. The well-being of the membership is in harmony with the well-being of the population at large.

In one respect, association public relations gives its practitioners chances to get involved in areas rarely trod by their corporate counterparts—for example, advertising. Obviously, the frontier between advertising and public relations in corporate enterprises is sharply demarcated and jealously guarded. Advertising and public relations may work together. But they do not perform each other's tricks.

Larry Aasen and other association professionals will choose to advertise when, as in the case of the Better Vision Institute, the association focuses on a cause that lends itself to public service announcements. Aasen produced numerous PSAs for the Better Vision Institute, working with a range of celebrities who donated their time to the making of the commercials. Some PSAs are quite elaborate and are done by advertising agencies pro bono. (Image- and award-conscious agencies will pour more creative resources into these freebies than into their bread-and-butter work.) Some very simple and highly effective PSAs are simply done by the public relations arm of the association.

But the basic means of communication for pros like Aasen is the release. Aasen explains it this way:

I know I'm up against a lot of competition when I send out releases. And I know I rarely have something that causes somebody to grab the phone and yell, "Hold page one!" So I have to be extra careful about what I send out. I fine-tune releases, distill them, work over even the simplest story until it is practically a "turnkey" operation. The editor just has to slug it and send it along.

Aasen is equally rigorous with his lists:

Credibility is my stock in trade. When an editor gets a release from me, I want him to know that it's been thought through. I've done my best to make it useful for him or her. When they yawn at the sight of your logo, you're sending out too many releases.

Small-association PR practitioners are sharpshooters on a battlefield filled with heavy artillery. They succeed by superior craftsmanship in their output and by high selectivity in their targets. These are attributes that could be emulated by a lot of PR practitioners with bigger budgets who wonder why they are not placing more stories.

The Multinational Public Relations Firm

In the 1970s, public relations went global. American firms began to expand into the United Kingdom and, then, continental Europe. In the 1980s, public relations began to develop in a number of Pacific Rim countries. The former Iron Curtain countries are now in areas in which public relations is developing along with the other disciplines of capitalism. In the 1990s, most of the major PR firms in the United States had either offices or strategic alliances throughout the world.

Globalization and consolidation are two dominant trends in the PR business of this era. Consolidation will continue worldwide, with the few multinational giants coming out on top. There will, increasingly, be a host of thriving niche firms, along with specialist agencies.

Edward M. Stanton, former CEO of Manning, Selvage & Lee, Inc., has some keen observations on patterns for success in the worldwide operations of major public relations firms. Among Stanton's key points is the principle that *"Public relations operations in each country should be run by nationals of that country."* This relates to a key question that has been thrashed out in other industries: When a company is moving into a foreign country, which is more important, skill or "feel"? One approach is to have the foreign operation headed up by a nonnative expert, who will try to develop expertise among the nationals on staff. Manning, Selvage & Lee opts for foreign operations run by nationals.

I agree. When filling the top jobs in newly opened overseas offices, some firms tend to overestimate the uniqueness of their homegrown PR savvy and underestimate the importance of an operation rooted in the local culture. It is possible, as well, to drift into the belief that public relations is very difficult for foreigners to understand. (This brand of inadvertent chauvinism is progressive. Europeans are considered easier to teach than Asians.)

The new public relations is sophisticated, but there are no national or ethnic bars to mastering it. The national of the country in which the operation is located will give the theory and practice of public relations the angles and twists that will make it most effective there. A foreigner might take too long to pick the local nuances— and might never pick them up.

Staffing by nationals makes it easier to put into practice Stanton's dictum that "local requirements must be factored into public relations programs and their execution." He makes some other telling points:

- A regional manager and close coordination of units on a regional basis are important.
- Equity relationships offer two-way benefits.

It is commonplace to observe that political developments like the European Union, along with sophisticated communications technologies, are speeding us toward the ideal of "one world." Stanton says public relations professionals "must be alert to the effect these economic and political developments may have on the strategies we propose to our clients, and on the implementation of the strategies they direct."

But Stanton has an important caution, lest the PR community get swept away by one-worldism:

> We must beware the temptation to treat global projects as single projects. We must be sensitive to the sensitivities of different nationalities and of different groups within nations. For example, the people we call "Eastern Europeans" see themselves as "Central Europeans."
>
> In the global public relations programs we will carry out more frequently during the 1990s, we must be responsive to such nuances, both among the general public and among the media.
>
> We must be staffed abroad with people who can tell us when NOT to use mass mailings; when NOT to hold a press conference. And, who can tell us—on the positive side—how to bring a trade group to Moscow.

Stanton adds the following conclusion:

> Public relations by independent European agencies has been catching up with American methods and practices. . . . What comes next, in the 2000s? A further emergence of public relations as an increasingly effective tool for management, participating in strategic decisions concerning marketing, image, and public and governmental affairs.

American PR professionals may find, to their surprise, that their counterparts abroad have gone through the same evolution as the American PR industry, but have done it much more quickly and have reached a point at which they not only are abreast of American public relations, but in some respects have pulled ahead.

The Glut of News Releases

In mid-1991, the *Bulldog Reporter*, a public relations newsletter, said out loud what a lot of people in the business had been saying privately: that PR agencies were turning out a mindless glut of releases, alienating media sources, and demeaning the industry's reputation.

The *New York Times* of July 1, 1991, got hold of the story and presented it to a wider audience. This pained the public relations industry, which naturally prefers to air its dirty linen in private. The *Times* quoted authorities pro and con on the question. Joe S. Epley, president of the Public Relations Society of America and of Epley Associates, of Lexington, Kentucky, felt that the criticism was justified: "If we in our profession don't recognize that we're creating this problem, we're really shooting ourselves in the foot." However, Richard Edelman, president of Edelman Public Relations Worldwide, said, "One of our functions is the mass dissemination of news. You don't always know exactly who will be interested. . . . There's nothing pejorative about mass mailing. It's part of what we do."

I beg to differ with this view. "Mass dissemination of news" is *not* a function of public relations professionals. Mass dissemination of news is the job of mass media. In public relations, we are supposed to define our targets more precisely. And, sure, PR agencies "do not always know exactly who will be interested." But that is the challenge of the business. Public relations experts are supposed to have at least a pretty good idea of who will be interested.

In all fairness to Edelman, there are frequent situations in which broadscale mailings are thoroughly justified. For example, as the *New York Times* reports, "An Edelman survey of mobile telephone use for the Nynex Mobile Communications Company was sent to about 400 editors and reporters, along with press releases that highlighted aspects of interest to business editors, women's publications, and communications-industry publications." The campaign worked well and displayed strong legs, with articles still being published a year after the mailing. This campaign is not just a mindless broadside. It was part of the strategy to get the message—about a new and growing product area—into a number of different types of publications, each aimed at a particular interest.

The main problem is not with campaigns like this, but with the seemingly pointless grinding out of releases that are duplicated in the thousands and dispatched all over the place, without any thought about whether anybody on the list will be interested. It is happening more and more, and it is something that self-respecting PR professionals should worry about.

Why is it happening? One reason is money. When an agency gets paid on the basis of activity, rather than through a flat fee, public relations becomes a form of piecework. The paymaster has to count the pieces, and the agency needs to accumulate the pieces to count.

In some cases, agencies actually qualify for part of their compensation through a formula that focuses on the number of media organizations contacted (rather than, for example, the time involved, the number of stories that actually ran, or the number of people reached). That is not a very good way to pay a PR firm. It encourages pointless activity.

Most compensation schemes are not like that. However, when the billing scheme is on an hourly basis, there is often a scramble to show activity that justifies the charges. As the influential *Jack O'Dwyer's Newsletter* asks, "What do the beancounters count when there are no beans to count?" Multiple mailings can be a ploy to harvest what looks like a bumper crop of beans. But are those beans edible?

Another factor that works to encourage broadcast distribution of releases is the technological convenience of it. As the *New York Times* remarks, "Computers, data bases, optical scanners, and laser printers have made mass mailings of press kits far easier than ever before." The promotional material for all kinds of electronic communications systems emphasize that you can shoot duplicated material to enormous lists through the touch of a button. When the technology exists, it gets used—even when it makes no sense.

And then there is what we might call junk think—the equating of releases with direct mail. In the direct-mail business, a response rate of 1 percent is often a resounding success—which means that 99 percent of the mailing failed.

The difference is that direct-mail people—at least those with something on the ball—choose their lists very carefully, cull those lists continually, and work hard to avoid sending mail to places where there are no prospects. They work on razor-thin margins; if 1 percent is success, ⅞ percent may be disaster.

Whatever the reasons, it is unfortunately true that media sources are being deluged with releases. Some important publications throw away—unopened—releases from PR agencies. As a result, the good goes out with the bad. A public relations team builds a sound strategy and crafts releases that are precisely on that strategy. The distribution list is carefully honed down to a select few—programs and publications that are especially apt for reaching the target audience. Moreover, the releases carry real news and are written to be eminently helpful to the publications at which they are aimed.

But it all goes to waste. The good releases slosh around in the slush bucket with the multitude of junk releases, and nothing gets read with any care. This situation calls for creativity from PR professionals.

The proliferation of stories is growing and will continue to grow. As the *Wall Street Journal* of July 25, 1991, observes, "Clients want more ink and pared-back papers want more items." Newspapers need ready-to-go copy, and placement services like News USA, Inc., and North American Precis Syndicate, Inc., deliver stories to papers. Many of these stories are furnished by companies; for example, the *Journal* mentions that GM used Precis to circulate two fuel-economy stories and "got back a six-inch stack of clippings." A Chrysler airbag story was picked up by 300 papers.

For the most part these are smaller papers—small-town, suburban. These papers work on tight budgets. When they receive legitimate ready-to-run stories of interest to their readers, they are ahead of the game. And this applies to larger papers as well. There is, increasingly, a symbiotic relationship between organizations wanting publicity and newspapers looking to fill their columns. (A similar relationship exists between publicity-seeking organizations and TV stations. Here the medium of exchange is the videocassette.)

The distribution services make it easy for papers to use their stuff. News USA ships out floppy disks, which editors can insert right into their PCs. The output of the services is occasionally used by large papers as well as small ones. The trend toward prepackaged news and features will continue.

Obviously, PR professionals want to take advantage of the trend. But using the distribution services is not the same as sending out huge amounts of releases to all kinds of addresses, many of which could not care less about the product. The stories beamed to the papers by the placement services will be used only if they are legitimate stories: well written and containing material of substance, not just puffery.

The receptivity of the press to such stories is a good opportunity for public relations practitioners. However, an indiscriminate avalanche of releases is not the way to take advantage of it. Editors (and, as we have seen, this is already happening) will stop looking at releases coming from anything but trusted sources. They will simply ignore the kind of release that is generated automatically, without reference to appropriateness.

The glut is one reason to mistrust broadscale mailings. Another reason is what this practice does to the PR function. Huge mailing lists should carry warning labels: "Danger! Multiple mailings can be hazardous to your professional health!"

Mass distribution of releases is a substitute for thinking. Some of the most rigorous thinking in public relations goes into the fitting of the message to the medium. Public relations professionals do not get stories placed by taking editors to lunch. Editors use stories because the stories are crafted to fit the publication and say something meaningful to the publication's readers. Slicing out one-size-fits-all releases is the lazy way to do it. Public relations practitioners who are worth their salt are proud of their ability to match up message to medium.

When a large number of duplicated releases are sent out, there has to be a reason. The strategy calls for the widest possible dissemination, and the story is one that appeals to the readers of the class of publications on the list. As a rule, public relations should be ready to justify every addressee on a list. If a PR practitioner does not know much about a particular addressee, then that practitioner has the job of finding out whether the publication in question should receive the story.

Sheer activity—including, particularly, the number of mailings sent out—should not be a criterion for evaluating the public relations effort. If anything, mass mailings ought to be a cause for suspicion by whoever is paying the bills.

Mass mailings and similar make-work activities are, in many cases, symptomatic of a deeper problem—a problem that should be of concern to the agency and the client. The agency knows that there are better ways of carrying out a PR campaign, and it should develop those ways and sell the client on them. As for the client, if management is judging the public relations function on the basis of busyness rather than effectiveness, then the client is, to a good extent, picking its own pocket. Bean counting is lazy management, just as mass mailing is lazy public relations. Both sides have to focus on what is really important—and the assessment and compensation of the PR functions should be geared accordingly.

Mailing Lists

One of the most important jobs in a PR department or agency is one that is never recognized or appreciated. It is the preparation of mailing lists. The job is thankless and often assigned to the summer intern or to the executive secretary's secretary.

Up-to-date mailing lists are the lifeblood of public relations, yet mistakes such as the following are commonplace in agencies of all sizes:

- Mail is addressed to an editor who has been dead for years.
- News releases are sent to defunct newspapers.
- A pitch letter goes out to Ben Bradley at the *Washington Post*. (It's Bradlee, and he is no longer at the *Post*.)
- A letter to Tina Brown at *Vanity Fair* opens with "Dear Mr. Brown." (And besides, she's left *Vanity Fair*.)

Richard Weiner, as the head of his agency for many years, had a lot on his plate day by day. Yet mailing lists were a priority. He perused all lists before a big mailing (and corrected an average of 15 percent of the names), and he ordered his mail room to bring to him personally all undelivered mail. The envelopes went back to the person in charge with a note on them from Weiner.

Just grinding out releases for widespread distribution, either by mail or on the Internet, is a cop-out. Clients deserve better than that. And Power Public Relations demands better than that.

18

Building Strategies

Thinking Big

One way to tell that a discipline like public relations has grown up is that everybody talks about "strategy." Once, not all that long ago, strategy was an alien word. As Thomas L. Harris says, "Public relations plans of the past focused almost exclusively on tactics—the trick was to come up with a Big Idea that would generate headlines." Today, the word *strategy* is commonplace in public relations. But that does not mean everybody understands what a strategy is—and what a strategy is not.

Strategy is the articulation of overall objectives along with general guidelines on achieving those objectives. It is where we are going and how we are getting there. At this point, however, it might be useful to take a look at an actual strategy statement. This one happens to be for Weight Watchers:

Overall Business Objectives

To strengthen leadership position in the weight-loss service field.

To maintain dominance in the reduced calorie food product category.

Move current users to trial and usage of other Weight Watchers products and services.

Communications Objectives

Project a consistent image for the entire brand as a provider of weight loss/control products and services which are satisfying to consumers and consistent with their lifestyles.

Assure Weight Watchers perspective is considered in media coverage of weight control/loss and food choices for better health.

Improve the quality and volume of media coverage to reflect more key messages about the brand and maintain visibility outside of traditional dieting seasons.

Be proactive in shaping media coverage on trends affecting weight control and better health.

Prepare Weight Watchers to anticipate and respond effectively to problems affecting the brand image.

Strategy statements vary. This one is longer than some. It designates several objectives; some strategists insist on honing it down to one objective. A number of the objectives overlap. The two categories of objectives are basically different; the business objectives are "where we are going," and the communications objectives are "how we are getting there." The format of the strategy statement is not of great importance, as long as it does the job.

Tying In with Larger Goals

The business objectives in the Weight Watchers strategy are not pure PR objectives. They are broader goals, applicable to advertising, sales, and other divisions. This is as it should be. Public relations does not operate in a vacuum. The use of public relations must always be dedicated to reaching broad organizational goals. In this particular case, those goals are marketing goals. That is often the case—but not always. The objectives may be to influence government policy, to win community cooperation, to enhance stock value, to persuade a legal opponent to settle a lawsuit.

The Strategy Is a Litmus Paper

The basic strategy for a campaign serves as a litmus test for the steps, large and small, that will be taken to carry out the campaign. Every time something is considered—the wording of a release, the appearance of an executive on television, sponsorship of an event—it should be sized up by applying the strategy.

The first question is, Does this step conform with the strategy? If, for example, the particular step would violate the strategy, then, of course, it must be ruled out instantly. Take an extreme case. Let us say Weight Watchers got the chance to have "before" pictures of some of its customers on a zany TV show noted for making fun of fat people. This would be publicity for the Weight Watchers name all right, but it would definitely not fit in with the strategy.

The "litmus test" function of the strategy goes beyond just the negative. When activities are contemplated, they should be judged in the light of the question, Is this the best way to carry out the strategy?

This last question calls for consideration of alternatives. There are always other ways to deploy resources. Reference to the strategy should make people think, at least to some extent, about these other ways. This kind of thinking irks some impetuous souls. They chafe when brilliant ideas are called into question by the question, Is it on strategy? The asker of the question is denounced as a nitpicker.

Measurement of tactics against strategy is not nitpicking. It is a professional practice that gives coherence and purpose to every part of a campaign. To defend against strategy-based objections, the PR practitioner should make the comparison first. No matter how bright the idea looks, if it does not fit the strategy, it should be modified to make it fit. If that does not work, the idea should be shelved.

Strategy vs. Tactics

Most people know the difference between the dictionary definitions of *strategy* and *tactics:* tactics are the measures taken to carry out a strategy. In practice—among PR practitioners and a lot of other people—the words overlap. Strategy has come to mean a discrete activity that, strictly speaking, should be called a tactic. A public relations professional talks about strategies—meaning news conferences, releases, and other practices.

If this were just a semantic mix-up, it would be of little significance. But it can be more than that. When we think of an event as a strategy—rather than as a way of carrying out a strategy—the event can become an end in itself. This kind of thinking can lead to big trouble, as the PR function goes off on tangents instead of sticking to the course set during the strategy-making stage. The tactical tail can never be allowed to wag the strategic dog.

Five Key Questions

While developing a public relations strategy, the strategists should ask themselves five key questions:

1. Does it track with corporate goals?
2. Can we do it all on schedule?
3. Can we change it if it does not work?
4. Could we do something else that would work better?
5. Can we afford it?

The last of these questions may be the most irritating to creative spirits. Nevertheless, it must be asked—not once, but over and over.

Strategic planning of a public relations campaign must never be permitted to develop into an ivory tower exercise. The nagging questions must be addressed at every step. Time and money are two constant considerations.

Cost Considerations

A lot of planning processes defer the matter of cost until later. The strategists design, on paper, a great plan. They focus on it, discuss it, fine-tune it, perfect it. Then somebody says, "Now let's cost this out."

Enter the despised bean counters, who proceed to spoil it for everybody. It turns out that the program, or at least important elements of the program, cannot be done without spending more money than has been budgeted—or is likely to be budgeted.

But by now, everybody is committed to the program. They have long since stopped thinking about alternatives. They insist on getting enough money to carry out their plans. Usually, they fall short. Then the optimistic planners try to achieve the hoped-for results on the cheap. They project what is, in effect, the same program for less money.

When the bargain-priced campaign fails to work as the PR planners hoped, they blame it on inadequate funding. Not only does the campaign produce poor results, it creates suspicion and bad blood between public relations and other functions, which has a negative effect on future efforts.

The unwelcome—but necessary—art of bean counting should be injected into the strategic process at an early stage. Whenever sentiment begins to coalesce around a certain course of action, the question, Can we afford it?, must be addressed. And it must be addressed in a realistic fashion, not brushed off or deferred with hopeful assurances that the money will be found someplace.

Budget planning should proceed parallel with program planning. If the budget is inadequate for a particular step, maybe resources can be reallocated. If, however, the money is inadequate, that fact must be faced. If you cannot afford it, you come up with something you can afford.

PR professionals who conduct strategy sessions have to walk a fine line. Good ideas should not be crushed instantly by the no-money objection. If a proposal has possibilities, it ought to be developed— up to a point. Then the planners must shift gears and examine the resources.

Let us say, for example, that a group planning a product introduction has hit upon the notion that the best way to do it is with half a dozen big media events in different parts of the country. The logistics are explored, the benefits assessed, the ramifications discussed. Then they start hanging the price tags. The budget is not adequate. At this point, the planners look at alternatives. Scale down each special event. Switch funds from other parts of the PR budget. Cut the number of events. Finally, they come to an optimum solution, involving fewer events but an enhanced use of communications channels to spread the effects of each event to a wider audience. Ingenuity has been brought into play to make up—to a good extent—for the shortage of money. Without a parallel and continuing consideration of the budget, the planning process is in danger of becoming a wish list.

Scheduling Considerations

Another question that should be asked over and over is, Can we do it all on schedule? It is easy to lose sight of time lines when you are riding the crest of creativity. The strategy looks good. The elements fit together. The total effect is satisfying. Only later, when the strategy has to be executed, do the planners realize that it cannot be done in the time frame allowed. The result is an inefficient scramble.

Building a strategy is a combination of big thinking and practical thinking. The constant infusion of practical questions of time and money keep the strategic process on track. They also combat one of the biggest dangers of the strategy phase—overconfidence. When you are confident and enthusiastic about the plan, you tend to believe almost anything is possible—and to promise that impossible things will be accomplished. Overpromising sours the whole process. An otherwise successful campaign can be deemed a failure because it did not reach unrealistic goals.

Monitoring Progress

The strategy works best when it includes measurements that indicate whether the execution is on track, as well as enough flexibility to switch tactics. It can answer the question, What happens if we find this strategy is not working?

The built-in measurements should be practical and meaningful. For example, if breadth of coverage is important, then subgoals should be set so that coverage can be measured at points along the way. If coverage starts to lag, then Plan B should be on tap.

All parties should agree on the validity of the strategy beforehand. Otherwise, when one element needs adjusting, the naysayers emerge from the woodwork proclaiming that they never bought the initial premise. Revision of tactics is not an admission that there is something wrong with the strategy. Flexibility is a positive attribute. Public relations is often the art of possibilities. When an opportunity opens up, the PR function is ready to go after it—*if* it furthers the strategy.

Selling the Wrong Strategy

Public relations people are good with words—sometimes too good for their own good. Some of their best wordsmithing is used to sell to the person who is paying the bills, who to them is the most significant public of all. Many of us are familiar with the public relations professional who is indomitable at meetings. This person dazzles the assemblage with graphics, spins word pictures of magical beauty and promise, and dispels doubts and objections with an easy command of the debater's art. This kind of performance is useful when it is employed to present an idea clearly and forcefully. It is not so good when it obscures major problems.

Superb selling technique can be used—and has been used—to sell the organization on approving the wrong PR strategy. The result? A PR strategy that strikes off on its own, rather than conforming to organizational objectives. For example, one star of the public relations industry had just been hired by a large chemical company. The company's long-term strategy was to move out of the consumer products area and concentrate on industrial products, with particular emphasis on selling to developing countries. The PR giant, however, came in with a seductive plan for endearing the company and its products to the American consuming public. There would be stories in major media. The company's senior executives, good at their jobs but not widely known, would be made into public figures. The PR star sold the strategy. There were some objections, but they were overridden.

The PR strategy was put into play. A number of the company's top brass found themselves getting more ink and airtime than ever before. The company's name became more widely known than ever before. Through a number of ingenious devices, including support of causes and big special events, the company was "humanized" to a considerable degree.

All this cost a lot of money. It sucked up all the resources available for public relations. Certain special publics, important to the company's long-range plans, were neglected. The momentum of the consumer-oriented PR effort pulled marketing along with it. More marketing effort was put into the consumer area than was justified.

The PR strategy that the company bought was fulfilled to a great extent. Some of the results were quite showy. But ultimately the strategy was a failure, because it was not rooted in the corporation's overall objectives.

Strategic planning for public relations must start with the stated objectives of the organization. The PR operative who sells a program that diverges from corporate objectives is selling snake oil. As public relations becomes a mature discipline, and as public relations assumes (rightfully) a more important and respected position, some PR practitioners chafe under this burden. They find it irksome to have to defer to the company's long-range plans. This means that they cannot use some of their brightest ideas. Besides, PR practitioners may conclude that the company's strategic thinkers do not know what they are doing, so it is all right to ignore them.

No matter how attractive a PR program looks or how shortsighted corporate policy appears, PR policy must be subordinate to corporate policy. But it does not always happen that way. One reason is that the PR professionals do not know what corporate policy is.

Give Your Ears a Chance

The formulation of a public relations strategy properly begins with listening, not talking. Public relations practitioners find out all they can about where the company is going and how it wants to get there.

Corporate officials are sometimes to blame for aberrant PR strategies. They are busy men and women; they do not have time to talk to the PR practitioners. Thus, the PR strategists have to learn their ideas about overall corporate policy from various sources— some written, some oral, some out-of-date, some just plain erroneous.

When public relations is being used as a marketing tool, there should be a clear-cut marketing strategy, available to the PR practitioners. And most of the time, there is. But, occasionally, you run into situations in which the senior marketing people are, themselves, cloudy about the mission and the strategy. Or they may be very clear on the strategy but unwilling to share it with an outside public relations agency.

When the larger corporate policy is not clear, it is up to PR to keep at it until it is clear. Sometimes, outside PR professionals find themselves helping to forge a corporate policy. A public relations viewpoint can clarify and catalyze the broadscale strategy process.

Only when PR is thoroughly integrated in the larger picture can it develop into the best possible program. The problem of developing the best possible public relations strategy is particularly acute when the agency has been newly hired. Typically, agencies make pitches for the business. Agencies that are on the ball make it a point to study the prospect's situation and to tailor the pitch, at least to some degree. Then they make presentations that seem to fit the company's needs.

The agency is hired. *And the pitch becomes the strategy.* This is a waste. The pitch is no doubt very good, but a better strategy can be created after the agency has a chance to get to know the client organization from the inside. Neither agency nor client should take it for granted that the ideas put forth in the proposal are the last word. Clients should insist on an in-depth approach. Some clients, unfortunately, do the opposite. If the agency suggests a modification of the ideas in the proposal, the client says, "Aha! You promised, and now you are trying to weasel out of it!"

The newly hired agency should have the guts to say, "We are proud of the proposals we gave you, and we are glad you appreciated them. We want to see if we can do even better. Let us do some fact-finding and then come to you with some new ideas, which we will be prepared to discuss."

The strategy stage, though hard, unglamorous work, is essential and should be carried out with integrity and diligence.

Specializations Within Public Relations

One of the liveliest developments in public relations is the growth of specialist organizations that focus on a particular market segment. One such firm is Cultural Communications Consultants of Westport, Connecticut, which advises cultural and educational institutions on marketing and public relations, and advises corporations on strategies involving cultural programs, sponsorships, and community affairs.

Fritz Jellinghause, president of Cultural Communications Consultants, built a track record at large, mainstream PR organizations before establishing his company. He provides consultation along with PR chores:

> Arts groups live or die on the basis of how the public sees them. I run full-day or half-day roundtables with their people to help them sharpen their own public relations skills. Most of the groups I work with cannot afford a full-time PR operation. But, by following a sensible public relations plan

which a number of people contribute to, they can do what they need to do.

The availability of professionals like Jellinghause will be of great help to smaller nonprofit organizations and corporations, which will benefit from partnerships that have a valuable public relations dimension.

Targets of Opportunity

While strategy is essential and PR successes are carefully planned, sometimes there are spur-of-the-moment gut impulses or targets of opportunity.

Late in August 1991, while Mikhail Gorbachev was on vacation in the Crimea, a group of plotters seized power. Roy Leinweber, president of Gannett Outdoor Company (a billboard firm), was driving to work to his Detroit office. On the radio, he heard that the coup had failed and Gorbachev was returning to Moscow. Leinweber called his office on the car phone, ordered a billboard, and actually came up with the copy while in the car. That night, Gannett's PR department sent out a release announcing the sign.

The next morning the billboard appeared, proclaiming, "Welcome Back Gorby! Next Time Vacation in Michigan." It made virtually every newspaper in the United States, as well as network television.

Every strategy needs leeway for the brilliant coup.

19

Evaluating the PR Program

Yardsticks to Be Welcomed, Not Feared

"Compared to what?" This is the key question in evaluating a PR program. Public relations does not fit into a convenient slot. It contributes to sales (or at least it should!), but it does not generate the concrete numbers that can be used to assess sales performance, hand out bonuses, and set quotas. Public relations is most readily compared to advertising. Sophisticated methods have been developed to test the impact and retention of advertising messages, the effects of repetition, and other advertising tactics. Some marketing professionals feel that the same—or similar—criteria should be applied to public relations.

There are problems with this. First of all, reasonable people can question the validity of some of the more exquisite forms of advertising research. It is possible to come up with elegant charts showing advertising effectiveness carried out to four decimal points, but do these numbers and graphics represent what is really happening? Second, to the extent that advertising research is valid—and plenty of it does work—it is designed for advertising, not for public relations. Public relations does its job differently and must be measured differently. The development of public relations is moving parallel to that of advertising, but several decades behind it. We now have useful research resources to help us *shape* and *direct* public relations programs; we have yet to develop reliable and universally accepted means of measuring what public relations does.

When a PR professional raises this argument about evaluation, it is sometimes derided as a cop-out. Mean-spirited people make snide comments to the effect that the flacks resist testing because they are selling blue sky. In the face of this, the PR professional has to be able to do more than simply fend off unwelcome evaluation measures. The best approach is to build commonsense evaluative criteria into the program.

The Nuts and Bolts of Evaluation

These criteria will vary from company to company, industry to industry, program to program. Here are some issues to consider in crafting an evaluation procedure that works.

Goals

What is the program supposed to accomplish? This, of course, is a fundamental question, not only for evaluation, but for planning and implementation of a program. It goes to the very heart of the public relations effort, so it might be reasonable to think that the goals, long- and short-term, are spelled out before the program starts. Those with experience in the trenches know better. In a surprising number of cases, public relations lacks clear objectives. It becomes a process that seems to be carried on for its own sake. Public relations agencies are tempted to collude in this folly. Vagueness makes it easier to get away with lackluster work.

The lack of clear goals is a malady besetting other corporate disciplines. Training is an example. Training can go on, year after year, with a lot of activity and expenditure but not much happening. Nobody notices that there is not much happening because nobody knows what is supposed to happen. Everybody knows, however, that training is something you have to do.

In setting up a PR program, as well as a training program, it is important to ask, "When this program ends, how will things be different from the way they were when the program started?" The search for answers to this question can be a forging of useful goals. The goals can usually not be quantified precisely. But in the case of public relations, it should be possible to make statements like these:

- People who are important to us will know our name and what we do.

- Our new product will be familiar to more prospects.

- The company's position will be understood and respected, even if it does not receive universal acceptance.

Here it is useful to note that the evaluation method starts with an understanding of objectives.

Quantitative Measurements

The number of releases sent out is not a useful criterion of effectiveness. The number of messages delivered has some value as a yardstick—but with qualifications.

Sometimes, a PR department or agency can mount an intriguing presentation featuring the number of impressions registered on various populations or markets. This is a legitimate means of measurement. However, it may not give the evaluators much feel for the depth of the impressions made.

While too much may be made of getting the company's message on big-time shows like *Good Morning America* and the *Today* show, or onto the front page of the *New York Times* or the *Wall Street Journal*, there should be agreement on the media that are most desirable. "Impressions" can be weighed with regard to the authority and aura of the medium.

Compatibility

All the impressions in the world will not help if the PR program is not working in harmony with the other relevant departments, notably advertising, marketing, and legal. While compatibility is a subjective measurement to a degree, it can be made by reasonable minds. To make this judgment, those who make the assessment should spend some time actually observing the interaction between public relations and other areas of the enterprise.

Coherence

Activities and accomplishments of the PR program cannot be weighed in a vacuum. They must be evaluated as to how they fit in with the initial objectives and the agreed-on process. Sometimes, PR programs go off on tangents because they spot a "target of opportunity." For example, the main objective of a particular campaign was to reach and influence a relatively small segment of the financial community. The process has concentrated on exploiting the channels that lead to this population. But there is a curious development that makes it possible to generate human interest stories for a much wider population. The stories go out, and they run in the newspapers and on television. The PR professionals can, with some justification, point to this as an example of their skill. But they must be ready to answer the question, How does it help us reach the target audience?

The answer to that question should be candid. Here is one reasonable response:

> It helps us in a number of ways. First, it gives our message broad visibility. True, it is not aimed precisely at the target audience. But that target audience does not exist in a vacuum. A favorable message to a broad population reaches, to a greater or lesser degree, the narrower population that we care about.
>
> Second, we do not exist in a vacuum, either. Our biggest concern is our primary target market. But we can use favorable recognition among opinion makers, politicians, regulators, and so on.
>
> Third, it is useful to get our name and message known more widely, because we are a growing organization. As we move into new areas, it helps to be already well-thought-of in those areas.
>
> By taking these targets of opportunity, we achieve these goals with a minimum of time, cost, and effort. We are skim-

ming the cream of our primary campaign and getting the most out of it, without in any way interfering with our main objectives.

Coherence requires that the various aspects of the PR process tie in with basic objectives—or, in the case of targets of opportunity, that they not divert the main effort. Coherence is not a straitjacket. The program should have the flexibility to take advantage of opportunities without being criticized unfairly by those who are evaluating the program.

Boldness

A play-it-safe PR program never makes any mistakes—except the biggest mistake of all: futility. If assessment focuses too much on things that go wrong, it will stultify creativity. Things can go wrong in any area of the business. Risk is everywhere.

Public relations practitioners should take appropriate risks and be prepared to defend those risks. The first consideration is to see that risks and mistakes are evaluated in the context of what was intended and what is being accomplished overall.

Here is an analogy. A company spends years and invests millions on developing a new product. The product goes on the market. There are some problems and failures. The company has to recall some products, fulfill some guarantees, or whatever. But the company does not junk the new-product program because of these bugs. A savvy organization anticipates that there will be bugs. The more ambitious and innovative the program, the greater the likelihood of problems, especially right after the program kicks off. These difficulties are an inevitable part of growth in business.

Some public relations programs are judged by a different standard. When there is a problem or error of any magnitude, people from other areas of the company question the whole program. A release goes out with an unfortunately worded paragraph, resulting in a negative response by several long-standing customers. Instantly, voices are raised: "We can't take the risk of this happening again! We have to stop right now!"

Public relations professionals can help to protect themselves from this kind of sniping by discussing the risks and rewards in advance. Make it clear right up front that PR professionals have not achieved a state of perfection, so there will be errors. Put it in perspective:

> We are doing everything we can to eliminate any problems we can anticipate. As for those we cannot anticipate, we are ready to do a fast and effective job of damage control.
>
> So the question is not, Will everything go perfectly? It will not. When did it ever, for any of us? Here are the questions: Are the goals worth the effort and the risk? Are we doing a good job of keeping problems at a minimum and cutting down the fallout when problems occur?

Evaluation of the PR program should assume that there will be problems and the evaluation should judge how well those problems are handled.

Alternative Uses of the Resources?

Another legitimate yardstick for measuring just about any activity, including public relations, is to compare the benefits of spending on the PR program with alternative uses of the resources. The evaluation asks, "What else could we do with the resources?"

Public relations practitioners should welcome this measurement—if the question is applied fairly. The unfairness comes in when the evaluators slide off into talking about how *other* objectives could be accomplished.

Here is an example. The typical alternative is advertising: "For what we spent on public relations, we could have done three more flights of broadcast commercials and run more than a dozen half-page ads in the *Times* and *Journal*." The facts may be accurate—but the argument is based on the premise that advertising and public relations achieve the same objectives. So the question is where the money will buy the most.

Public relations professionals set themselves up as targets for this falsely premised assessment when they do not make sure that all relevant parties understand that public relations is different from advertising, and important in its own right. Sure, in a broad sense, public relations and advertising aim at the same objectives—as do manufacturing, research, finance, and every other department. But the subgoals of public relations are different, as are the means public relations uses. The evaluation should never be based just on the notion that something else could be done with the money. There has to be a clear understanding of what public relations does, along with agreement that it is worth doing.

When that understanding exists, it is legitimate and useful to judge the program through informed speculation about alternative use of resources.

Can It Be Done with Less?

There is an old story, perhaps apocryphal, about John D. Rockefeller the elder. Visiting one of his refineries, the great mogul watched a workman nailing tops on barrels. Rockefeller counted the number of nails the man was using: twenty. "Can you do it with eighteen?" he asked.

They tried. They could not do it with eighteen, but they could do it with nineteen. A tiny savings on one barrel, a substantial savings on 50,000 barrels.

Public relations professionals should continually ask themselves, "Could we do it with fewer nails?" Then, when the question comes up in evaluation, the PR team will have a convincing answer. A PR operation that does not ask such questions about economy and cost-effectiveness is a legitimate target for criticism.

Is Public Relations Pulling Its Weight?

Since public relations is an activity that almost always works best in combination with other activities, it is difficult to judge it in artificial isolation. Perhaps the best commonsense approach to structuring a sound evaluation process is to base it on two questions:

1. *How is public relations fulfilling its role in the larger effort?*
   This goes to competence, communication, cost-effectiveness,
   creativity, proactiveness—the qualities, not all of them
   quantifiable by any means, on which a creative staff program
   depends. It is legitimate to ask whether public relations
   achieves its goal within the bigger picture. It is not legitimate
   to give public relations too much credit if the overall effort
   succeeds, or too much blame if it fails.
2. *How is the larger effort working?*
   If the message—promulgated by advertising and PR—is
   getting heard and the product or service is selling, then
   its elements are working (even though they could be
   improved). If the bottom line is not benefiting, then the
   whole apparatus needs fixing, not just the PR part.

Research in Evaluating Public Relations

As I have remarked, some PR agencies tend to go overboard in tout-
ing the effectiveness of research in all phases of public relations.
I urge a balance between instinct and process. Neither should
dominate.

This is true in evaluation as in any other area. There are good
tools for evaluating certain aspects of public relations. There are also
indifferent or downright bad tools, which are adopted because they
are fashionable or because they sing the siren song of ultimate precision—a state that cannot be achieved in the real world.

Here is an evaluation and tracking system used by a large and successful PR agency:

The process utilizes print clips and broadcast manuscripts, identified through clipping services and searches of computerized databases. The service employs four methods to analyze the quantity and
the quality of media coverage. It first assesses the volume of a placement effort by quantifying circulation, clips, messages, and media
vehicles. It next measures gross impressions for a specific target audi-

ence. The third method establishes whether placement messages were on strategy, and identifies areas of confusion or negative coverage. Finally, the system examines the quality of each placement, based on seven characteristics:

1. *Publication or media outlet*—The quality and nature of the publication or media outlet, with respect to the target audience
2. *Information highlights*—The headline, subheadlines, captions, pictures, or anything special, other than copy, that would gain attention or communicate. (For broadcast placements, video segments and special promotions are assessed.)
3. *Placement copy points*—The extent to which a placement contains key copy points derived from the campaign strategy statement
4. *Information location*—The communications influence of the location of key copy points within the placement
5. *Placement length*—The influence of placement length in communicating the message to the target audience
6. *Placement timing*—How timely the placement is, relative to the campaign schedule
7. *Merchandisability*—Those qualities which make a placement useful for other purposes, such as direct mailings, management presentations, and lobbying

This approach is a sensible combination of scientific measurement and common sense. It is a good framework on which to hang a PR evaluation process.

The Right Attitude Toward Evaluation

The assessment process just described uses four measurements: volume, gross impressions, conformity with strategy, and quality of placement. These are reasonable criteria—as far as they go. They are not the be-all and end-all of evaluating the total contribution of a good PR operation. When properly used, public relations makes a substantial contribution to strategic thinking and planning, and this cannot be measured by volume. Good public relations makes everybody in the organization better at saying and doing things in a way that enhances the public image of the organization. An effective PR operation can make the difference between survival and debacle when misfortune strikes. And so on.

Nevertheless, within limits, these yardsticks are helpful in providing an idea of what the function is doing and how well it is doing it. Public relations professionals make a mistake when they scorn such measuring devices because they are not accurate. No measuring device is perfectly accurate. Besides, the PR industry—by its recent emphasis on the scientific method—has invited this sort of scrutiny.

Public relations practitioners should agree to cooperate with the evaluation process. The important thing is to be involved with the process from the beginning, rather than resisting it. When the PR function is involved in setting up the assessment machinery, that machinery will work more fairly and practically.

It is important in building and running an evaluation program to have everybody understand how much of it is objective measurement and how much is subjective. Volume is quantifiable; gross impressions are a softer measurement, but at least one that is accepted as standard in media circles.

When we move on to the other methods, we move further away from precision. "On strategy" is a judgment call in many cases. A blatant departure from strategy is not debatable, but most cases of possible divergence from strategy are more subtle. Smith says the story does not agree with the strategy document. Jones can demonstrate how it really does conform. Brown is not sure.

There is even more subjectivity in judging quality of placement. In general, certain shows and publications are considered the crème de la crème of the business. But, to reach a certain audience with a certain message, a story in *Electronics Quarterly* may be better than a story in the *New York Times* or a segment on the *Today* show.

The more subjective measurements are likely to be more important than the more quantitative ones. Quality of placement—most people would agree—is more important than simple volume.

So who makes the judgment calls? Line management is apt to insist that it should be the ultimate judge. After all, line management has the responsibility for running the enterprise. Public relations professionals retort that others do not understand the subtleties of the profession, so they are the only ones capable of realistic assessment. Line managers retort that this would be like putting the fox in charge of the hen coop.

And so on.

Neither side should prevail, at least not totally. The evaluation of a public relations program should not be altogether in the hands of non-PR professionals. The craft may not be as complicated as nuclear physics, but it requires understanding and insight. Nor should PR practitioners be given unchecked freedom to assess themselves. Even with the best will in the world, those within the craft will be tempted to fall into errors. One prevailing error in evaluation—in public relations as in advertising—is to judge by the "artistic" criteria of insiders, rather than by results. Advertising people often toast each other—and confer awards on each other—for advertising that they like but that does not sell the product. Often, they like it because it is different, or daring, or titillating to their jaded sensibilities. They are bored with advertising, so they go wild over stuff that seems to flout the rules, even if it does not do what the ad is supposed to do.

The same thing happens among PR insiders. A practitioner scores a clever coup in getting a story on network news. The PR professionals know the details. They know how tough it was to get this story on. Therefore, they applaud the progenitor as a genius. The actual story may not have done much good. Perhaps it would have been far more cost-effective to get a number of stories in other, more conventional media. But this does not thrill the insiders.

Evaluation of the public relations function should be done by a task force comprising PR professionals, people who work closely with PR (e.g., marketers), and senior managers who have no particular experience with public relations, but who have judgment and common sense. The most important consideration in deciding who does the judging is *attitude*. Individuals who resent or oppose the whole idea of public relations should not be assessing it. The judgment that public relations is a useful function should be made at the time it is adopted. Once that battle has been decided, the fight should not be carried on in guerilla skirmishes. This ruins the evaluation process and diverts energies that could be used better elsewhere.

The evaluation process should be carried forward with the understanding that public relations is an integral part of the mix. The purpose of the assessment, then, is not to give a thumbs-up or thumbs-down to the function, but rather to make it more effective, more coherent, more cost-effective. When evaluation is rigorous but fair and soundly based, public relations has nothing to fear. The process is a healthy one.

20

How PR Is Sold—and How It Should Be Bought

"Can This Marriage Be Saved?"

Asked about the turning point of the game, the losing coach said, "It came five years ago when we scheduled it." Some agency-client relationships are doomed from before day one, because the client picked the wrong agency.

Any firm with anything on the ball at all is good at presentations. The senior people and the top agency talent spend a lot of time and effort on new business, sometimes giving short shrift to existing clients. The new-business team will have developed a polished dog and pony show. The basics of all effective new-business pitches are pretty much the same: demonstrate a dazzling flair, show extraordinary sensitivity in responding to the client's concerns, promise enduring cooperation and high-level results.

The medium is the message in new-business presentations, at least to a large extent. The team descends on the battlefield with a lot of "smart-bomb" paraphernalia: video, multiscreen audiovisuals, leave-behind gifts. (Pitching Ciba-Geigy and its arthritis drug, Voltaren, using Mickey Mantle as a spokesperson, one-time Porter Novelli executive vice president Bob Seltzer chose baseballs autographed by the former Yankee slugger.) The speakers are polished and impressive; after all, they have rehearsed for days. The handoffs from one speaker to another are smooth. It is a show with impact and persuasiveness.

And that is as it should be. The public relations agency ought to be able to demonstrate that it can put on a good show. But it should demonstrate a lot more than that. Prospective clients should ask the right questions and make the right moves to get behind the sell and make sure the fit is going to be right. And it is in the agency's interest to encourage this. Too many new-business pitchers feel triumphant when they dodge the bullet because the client did not bring up a potential trouble spot. The agency should *help* the client ask the right questions; disclose, not hide, the trouble spots; and work to make a sale on the basis of substance. This is not only a matter of ethics, it is a matter of common sense and survival.

Some Good Questions to Ask

The best PR agencies do it that way, at least most of the time. But now that we are in the new millennium, there will still be a lot of razzle-dazzle in selling PR services, so potential clients should ask a lot of tough, sophisticated questions and weigh the answers carefully. Here are some useful questions.

Who Runs the Agency?

Is the top executive a solid public relations practitioner or someone with a different background—financial or advertising, for instance? In my opinion, clients are best served when the PR agency is headed by hands-on practitioners who not only keep up with the state of the art, but who practice what they preach at new-business meetings. Top-notch PR professionals get a thrill out of plying the craft of their discipline. Non-PR professionals, no matter how good they may be in other respects, do not feel this thrill.

Executives who are active in today's public relations are better equipped to hire and evaluate good people, and to assign the right people to the client's business. All PR firms want to make money. It may be important to the client to know that the agency is driven, at least in part, by considerations other than money.

What Kind of Turnover Does the Agency Have?

Public relations agencies are like advertising agencies in that they add people to service accounts and lay people off when they lose the accounts. Turnover at the margins may look high. But the prospective client ought to know if there is relative stability at the core, among the senior associates and the key creative and research people. If not, why not? Have people resigned, or have they been fired? What happens to the account when a key individual leaves?

Prospects should note with interest the way in which the pitching agency talks about turnover. Some will be candid: "He quit because he thought he had a better opportunity over at Burson Marsteller." Others will have a battery of alibis—the person who left was just not cutting it, or whatever. Others may hint at client pressure: "They changed marketing VPs and asked that we shake up the team."

Public relations agencies that seem overly susceptible to client pressure are agencies to beware of. The savvy client wants an agency that will fight to keep a professional in place, in spite of problems, if they are convinced that the professional is right for the job. "Yes-persons" who seem to promise that the client will have extensive personnel control are not to be counted on as strong counselors.

What Accounts Have You Lost, and Why Did You Lose Them?

After nodding through the usual litany of clients, the prospect should ask about the ones that got away. Since every agency loses clients, the agency must have lost some accounts. How many did it lose in the past year? Who were they? Why did it happen?

These are tough questions. Some PR new-business presenters will try to slide past them, saying that, of course, there is always flux in the business, and that it is complicated to find the reasons for partings of the ways, and that often the separations have been by mutual agreement, etc., etc. Prospects ought not to be satisfied with agency representatives who merely parrot the words of the innocuous press releases that may have been sent out at the time of the change. Agencies should be willing to admit that they are not perfect and talk about their own share in the responsibility for losing accounts.

What Have You Learned from the Accounts You Have Lost?

All that some PR practitioners "learn" from losing an account is that the client was unreasonable. Good PR practitioners should be willing and able to analyze their shortcomings, draw principles from them, and demonstrate how they have translated those principles into action.

Clients should also beware of PR agencies that seem to indicate they will continually be uptight, constantly feeling that they are on the verge of losing the account. The agency that runs scared is as bad as the one that ignores client concerns.

Do You Mind if We Talk to Some of the Accounts You Lost?

All agencies have success stories—happy clients who will attest to good working relationships and good results. Many of these stories are no doubt true. Clients need to look at the downside as well. Astute clients will conduct fruitful interviews with accounts the agency has kept and accounts the agency has lost. (We will get to that in a moment.)

In talking with the agency's new-business presenters, the prospect should note how they react when this question comes up. They are not going to be jubilant—nobody would be—but are they evasive? Do they try to talk the prospect out of it? Or do they try to discount, in advance, what might be said, by making comments like these:

- For some reason, they like to bad-mouth us.

- Their in-house people knifed us.

- There were some personal problems with one of our staff who has since left our agency.

- You have to take anything they say with a grain of salt.

A secure, professional PR agency knows that some former clients may say things that are less than complimentary. The presenters will take this as a matter of course, and go on trying to sell their agency's strong points.

Are These All the Accounts You Have Gained or Lost in the Past Year?

Agencies that censor the list of lost accounts have something to hide. If they say, "Well, no, there are a few others," that is a cue for the prospective client to pursue vigorously. Get the names of all the accounts lost, and check with the ones that were held back.

May We See Your Client Lists from Last Year and the Year Before?

How does the prospect know the agency is leveling about the comings and goings of accounts? Most agencies hand out client lists that are updated periodically. By obtaining those from one and two years back and comparing them with the present list, the prospect can, perhaps, spot some areas that need further investigation: departed business that was not mentioned, long-term accounts that left, a shift in the nature of the client list—for example, toward a heavy concentration in one particular industry.

Prospects should not buy the excuse that old client lists no longer exist. They do exist, and if they have been expunged, then the prospect is entitled to ask why.

Agencies need not go into new-business pitches with an urge to flaunt their failures. But they should be ready to talk fully about their total client experience.

May We Visit Your Agency?

Some PR agencies, especially the larger ones and those that have invested heavily in "front," are eager to have prospects come to see them. They may want to have the pitch meetings at their premises.

This is not a bad idea for the prospect. In the agency headquarters, prospects can ask to see documents and people and not be pushed off with the answer "We will get back to you on that."

But a visit to the agency should be more than a stage-managed affair, which can take on the aspects of a Potemkin village. When the client has narrowed agencies down to a short list, the client should make some short-notice—or even unannounced—visits. The idea is to soak up impressions. Are they busy? Do they seem purposeful? Is there an air of excitement? If they have made a point of their research or information systems, what do they seem like in action?

The informed visit to the agency is part of a process of getting to know each other before entering into matrimony. Both parties should feel comfortable with each other.

Who Will Be Working on My Business?

The key question, of course, is who will be doing the actual work on your account. The new-business pitch will be made by a star-studded lineup, the top—at least very senior—people in the agency. The makeup of the team that will handle the day-to-day affairs of the client is another matter.

Some agencies tend to overpromise the everyday services of their top executives. Agency executives spend a certain amount of time on administration and a substantial amount of time on new business. What time they have left over—and it is usually very little—is likely to be spent on their biggest accounts.

Prospects should get a feeling of how they will rank in the agency account list. The agency cannot be expected to open its books, but if there are, for example, twenty-five clients, and five of them are billing well into the millions, a $150,000 account is not apt to get the undivided attention of the top brass.

This is not necessarily bad; it is just a fact of life. And the PR practitioners who are pitching for the business ought to be honest and matter-of-fact about it.

In handling the question, Who will be working on my business? agencies are often tempted to use certain standard evasions:

- I'll be personally keeping an eye on things.
  (Eye-on is not hands-on.)

- When you have a question, call and ask for me.
  (To ask is not necessarily to receive.)

- Every one of us at this table will be actively involved in your account.
  (Until the contract is signed.)

The agency should be forthcoming about who will be working on the business and what they will be doing. As contacts progress beyond the initial dog and pony show, the designated team should be more and more prominent. If the team members are too busy to talk before the deal is made, what assurance does the client have that they will have sufficient time afterward?

Big numbers do not necessarily spell good service. A larger agency may parade half a dozen or more people before the eyes of the prospect. The prospect should concentrate on the one person who will be the captain of the team. One person with brains, common sense, guts, and know-how is better than ten Ivy League drones.

The agency's professional who is assigned to the account ought to function as practically a member of the client firm. When the client sizes up this person, it should be, in many respects, like sizing up a potential recruit for a key job. The person can be a young, bright practitioner or a veteran of many PR wars. Age should not be a dominant factor in judging who has been earmarked to handle the business. The person assigned to the account should draw enough water in the agency to be able to call upon the agency's ancillary resources (like research) when necessary. However, this consideration is not nearly as important as the person's ability and personality.

The agency, and especially the designated account person, should be able to talk comfortably about where to get additional staff as needed. Large agencies can point to a lot of bodies and say that they are right there on hand when needed. This is not a big deal. People are not ordinarily needed on a moment's notice—they certainly should not be, if planning is adequate. A savvy one-person band, operating out of a telephone booth, can get freelancers or moonlighters when necessary, and these people can be a lot better than available staff people in a larger organization.

The designated hitter from the agency should be introduced to the prospect company's lower-echelon employees who will be involved day to day in the management of the firm's PR program. Those employees should go along on visits to the agency and then be debriefed about their impressions.

And here is an important point. I have talked about how vital it is for the company to meet the agency people who will actually do the

work. The reverse is true as well. The agency should be eager to get
to know their counterparts in the company. An agency that shows no
curiosity about the day-to-day functioning of the account—should it
be signed—may be an agency that is desperate for any business or,
at least, an agency that does not think far beyond the sale. A high-
quality public relations agency will be somewhat choosy. The prospect should welcome this, not be offended by it.

What Are You Going to Do for Us?

Some firms, when asked what they will do for the prospect, answer
with a genial generality: "Our objective is to make you number one
in your industry." But the discussion of what the PR agency will do for
the client should go a lot deeper than slogans or broad promises. An
agency that has made a real study of the prospect company should
have some definite ideas about how its particular strengths can be
harnessed to the benefit of the company.

When asked what they hope to accomplish, PR firms should talk
about process, not promises. Public relations, by itself, cannot make
anyone "number one." But the agency can draw the general outline
of a good working relationship.

Here is one way a pitching agency might respond to the question:

> We want to become your strategic and tactical arm in the
> areas of influencing the audiences and markets you want to
> influence. We also want to be able to influence *you,* to pro-
> vide you with an input that gives a public relations dimension
> to the important moves you make.

In spelling out this general prospectus, the agency describes *process:*
how it will work in coordination with the firm.

In describing the future relationship, the agency ought to
demonstrate a reasonable familiarity with the company, not an all-
purpose scheme. Many presentations have an unfortunate one-size-
fits-all aspect.

In Working with Us, What Would You See as Your Biggest Problem?

The next question to ask is what problem the agency anticipates it may encounter in working with you. Confronting this question, certain new-business presenters may brush it off with a salute to positive thinking: "We don't anticipate problems, so let's not spoil our day by talking about them."

Most presenters are likely to be more realistic, and they may make an answer that acknowledges that even the course of truest love does not always run smooth. In this case, the temptation may be to say something like, "I don't see any problem situations at the moment. No doubt, difficulties may crop up along the way, but you can be sure that we'll move fast to straighten them out."

Clients should not be content with such answers. They should press the PR practitioners for a discussion of problems. Pick out one of the agency's existing clients, one that bears some resemblance to the company being pitched: "What kind of problems do you run into with them, and what do you do about it?" Since the prospect firm may decide to talk to the client company, the agency new-business team is under some obligation to answer realistically.

Some answers are keyed to the size and nature of the challenge: "You're a small company, and it will take a strong and innovative campaign to position you. That's why we recommend . . . " This sales technique—in which the salesperson mentions an obvious truth and then bridges back into a recitation of benefits—may be good selling, but it does not help in the appraisal process.

Here is what should happen. The agency representatives should be candid about possible problems they see: "You have a long-standing relationship with your ad agency, and you might just think of us as spear-carriers." Or the agency might say, "There are always going to be problems, or at least things we perceive as problems. The best time to talk about them is ahead of time. At this point, what do you see as the biggest problem in working with us?"

The company should welcome this opening, raising possible concerns and expecting substantive answers. But it should still require the agency, for its part, to suggest potential hang-ups.

The nature of the possible problems (or the problems experienced with other companies) can be revealing. With some PR practitioners, it always boils down to personal problems: "The chemistry just is not right." Clients should be leery about agencies that take the obsequious stance that the customer is always right, seeming to promise that people who give offense will be pulled off the account. A more credible comment on problems might go like this:

> First, there will be the problem that you don't agree with everything we recommend. Our recommendations will be strong and sometimes unusual. You're not going to like every one. We don't expect you to. We do expect a chance to show you why we think you ought to buy our proposals.
>
> Then there will be friction in the process of working together. We are not just a little appendage. We aim to work as an integral part of your organization. That will mean affecting, and sometimes disturbing, existing relationships. That's always an interesting situation, and sometimes a tough one. But we won't shy away from what is right because it's tough.
>
> Finally, we will make mistakes. We are not perfect. And we don't plan to play it safe. When we see risks, we spell them out. But that doesn't mean it will always be pleasant when something doesn't pan out.
>
> In short, our objective is to be a productive, functioning element of the company, with all the rewards and drawbacks that will entail.

What Is the Biggest Thing Wrong with Our Public Relations Now?

Pitching agencies may be shy about directly criticizing the existing agency, if there is one. Nevertheless, the agency that wants the business should be able to make some shrewd comments about the existing situation. An agency that is unable to do this has not really studied what is going on.

The discussion of what is wrong with the company's current approach should be conducted with candor. Clients should note whether the aspiring PR firm is pulling its punches or is really being professional in its analysis. A response like, "You're not making the most of all the great things that can be said about your company," may be flattering and pleasant, but it is probably not an incisive analysis.

The agency may say it is not prepared to suggest detailed correctives to the problems it raises. This is fair enough. But the client wants to hear honest, perceptive observations.

Honesty and perceptivity are keynotes of a good presentation. Sure, the agency is selling. But at times selling should stop, and professionalism should take over. The agency representatives should be secure enough in their craft to have a frank give-and-take, forgetting about making selling points. Of course, some new-business whizzes are able to give the impression of being frank, to the point of self-damage, even while they are still selling hard. Nevertheless, free discussion is the most fruitful form the sales pitch can take.

Can We "Roll Our Own"?

At some point in the process of evaluating PR agencies, the prospect company should ask itself, once again, if its needs can best be met by hiring someone as a member of the firm, or a single consultant, rather than by retaining a PR agency.

That is a basic decision—do it in-house, hire a consultant, or hire an outside firm. The typical progression is that a company carries on a PR function, such as it is, in-house until it becomes big enough or smart enough to get good PR help. By and large, this is the best route to go. Public relations is a mature discipline, and a freestanding, professional PR firm can ordinarily provide the best in public relations counsel (if the company hires the right agency and works with it the right way).

This is not true in every case. Sometimes, it would be better to hire one individual with brains, experience, and know-how than to hire an agency with fifty people. This might be true in the following circumstances:

- The public relations job to be done is narrow and well defined. This might be true in the case of a small specialty firm selling to a limited number of customers. The firm has a small but important "public" and a limited number of channels for reaching that public.

- The public relations job—at the moment—is very broad and ill defined, to the point that it is still not clear that the services of a PR firm will be useful. The company has a sharply defined PR mission and is looking strictly for someone to execute it.

- The company has good reason to feel that people already on the payroll have sufficient PR flair, and that what is needed is the marshaling of these talents.

- The industry is so highly specialized that thorough familiarity with it is an absolute must.

Any of these conditions may make in-house PR a reasonable proposition. But the condition has to really exist. Take the last one. Most companies feel that they are unique—and it is true that all companies are different and that all industries differ significantly from each other. But the intricacies can be highly overrated. A lot of organizations, when hiring agencies, set great store by the question of whether the agency has experience in the particular field.

So let us take that up right now.

The Trap of Experience

Picking a PR agency primarily because it has experience in the company's specific industry can be a fatal mistake. This experience can take a number of forms: the agency actually has, or has had, clients in the industry, or the agency produces staff members who can boast of specific experience. Since the idea of a client in the same or a similar business may raise questions of conflict of interest, an agency going after a new account may scour the payroll for people who have toiled in the vineyards occupied by the target company. If someone with the requisite experience is found, that person is trotted out as an asset.

Such "experience" should be discounted substantially, if not ignored entirely. The client company should be far more interested in getting the services of keen, gifted people rather than those who happen to have already been around a particular track. There can be far more benefit in getting the fresh thinking of a professional who comes with a new slant than in getting the well-worn wisdom of somebody who knows the industry. Good PR practitioners are quick studies. They can learn the relevant essentials of the business in a remarkably short time.

So experience in the actual industry should be given little weight.

The Value of Media Contacts

While we are at it, let us dispose of another issue in evaluating public relations agencies: "media contacts." Time was that certain PR professionals made much of their ability to call editors by their first names. They projected the idea that public relations was done largely over lunch and cocktails, that by buying meals and drinks for editors and program directors and buttering them up, it was possible to "place" almost anything.

The whole idea of placing stories is largely invalid in public relations. You place advertising, because you are paying for it. You try to get editors and program directors to accept your stories.

Does it help if you know the editor? Sure. You can, possibly, get through a little faster with your idea. Does it help to buy a lunch? Sure. You can always tell your story better eye to eye. But does a cordial relationship with an editor enable the PR practitioner to get a banal story accepted or to win media cooperation with a lackluster campaign? It does not. Editors with anything on the ball make up their own minds about stories.

Good editors and program directors are likely to keep in touch with certain PR professionals, not because they like them or enjoy being wined and dined, but because these PR professionals are good at providing interesting material. This applies even when the two do not get along. Editors will talk with PR practitioners whom they loathe, if they think they can get something good out of it.

Another factor that minimizes the importance of contacts is turnover. Editors move around and get reassigned. Personal contacts are not much use when that happens. In fact, if an editor has demonstrated partiality for a certain PR practitioner, that editor's replacement may lean over backward not to deal with that person.

The media come to rely on PR firms as having a creative, cooperative approach, no matter who the people involved may be. When an agency demonstrates that it has the will and the skill to work with the media and to not waste the media's time with irrelevant ideas, then that firm finds acceptance.

Contacts are therefore not much of a factor in selecting an agency. They should not be boasted about, and they should not be required.

Checking References

Prospective clients should check the references (i.e., the client list) of an aspiring agency, just as they would check references in filling a high-level job. This usually means a phone call to the highest-ranking executive who actually works with the PR firm. It does not help much to talk with a remote chairman of the board who provides bland generalities.

In contacts with present clients of the agency, it is important to listen to what Samuel I. Hayakawa called the "meta-message"—the meaning behind the words. People tend to be uniformly laudatory about their PR agencies, as they are with their advertising agencies and their consulting firms. After all, to criticize them would reflect on the company. If there is something wrong, why continue to retain them?

The reference checker is not looking for judgments; the judgments are going to be favorable. The thing to look for is a picture of how the PR agency works with the company and how important it is in the scheme of things. If, for example, the top marketing executive is only marginally aware of the PR firm and has trouble thinking of important things it has done, that should tell the reference checker something.

Does the agency contribute to the formation of strategy? Does it meet deadlines, react quickly, collaborate well? The process need not be invariably smooth—in fact, there should be occasional frictions, if the agency is doing its job.

Probably the most positive comment on the value of a PR agency is the evidence that the client relies on the agency to do important things—almost taking for granted the agency's professionalism and vital role in the making of policy and its execution.

Talking with Accounts the Agency Lost

These days, managers are more reluctant than ever before to say anything bad about anybody—ex-employees, ex-suppliers, ex-agencies. There is always the chance of a lawsuit. So, clients who fired the agency are apt to be highly cautious.

The caller can draw some useful inferences in spite of the caginess. Why was the relationship severed? If the answer is obviously phony, then there must be a story behind it. If the answer seems to be reasonably truthful, but general, then the company might be asked, "Why did you hire them? What did you expect from them?" A recitation of expectations may give a clue as to where the agency fell short, because in this context the respondent is likely to think first of the expectations that were not met.

It is usually a good idea to say to the former client, "We're not interested in just focusing on the negatives. We'd just like to hear your impressions of how the agency worked with you, day to day." Out of this may come some fairly positive things about the agency, things that have a certain credibility because they come from a former client.

Lower-echelon people at the former client company, if they can be reached, are apt to be more candid than their bosses. So, unlike the situation with existing accounts, where it is most important to talk to the highest-level executive who works hands-on with the PR firm, the best sources at the former accounts may be in the lower echelons.

The Written Proposal

In pitching for new business, the public relations agency submits a written proposal of substantial length. Such proposals tend to fall into a pattern. They state goals and objectives, give a terse recap of strategies, discuss target audiences, and then spend a lot of space on tactics, or the nuts and bolts of implementation. Then there is a fact sheet about the agency.

Too often, the new-business proposal becomes cast in concrete. The people putting together the new-business presentation are busy at other jobs, so they save time where they can. One way to save time is by using off-the-shelf material for the bulk of the proposal.

A written proposal that seems truly fresh and innovative, and that is truly aimed at the client, without a lot of boilerplate, speaks well for the agency. However, the prospect should not write off an agency just because the proposal seems blah. Many agencies are better than they look in their formal new-business prospectuses.

Agencies should be more original in doing written proposals. Make them shorter, give them visual impact, shake up the conventional order. Write something other than the pablum-prose in most such documents. If the new-business pitch is really important, turn the writing of the proposal over to a highly creative person who is not necessarily one of the heavyweights in the organization. Writing good, fresh proposals should be a rite of passage for ambitious juniors.

The client can use the table of contents of the written proposal as a kind of outline for the proceedings. However, there should be some healthy skepticism about the written pitch. One good question: "Will you please show which parts of this proposal were created exclusively for us? Parts that have never appeared in any other proposal?"

After an agency has been chosen, some clients use the proposal as a kind of yardstick, watching closely to see that the agency performs every little chore mentioned in the paper. That can be a big mistake. As we have just said, the document may be the weakest and stalest part of the presentation, the place where the agency gives the weakest account of itself. It stands to reason that, once the agency is working closely with the client, new and better ideas will emerge. To hold an agency to the ideas it had *before* becoming familiar with the clients is a formula for obtaining stereotyped work.

In the final analysis, the choice of an agency ought to be based, to a considerable extent, upon gut feelings, guided by experience, rather than on the reputation of the agency, its client list, or the promises it makes. And once the selection is made, the slate of specifics should be wiped clean. Let the PR professionals do the best job they can, without being referred back to specifics that may no longer apply.

21

A Look Ahead at Power Public Relations

What Now?

Power Public Relations is still learning to use its muscles. And these muscles are still growing. As we look ahead in the new millennium, here are several implications I see.

The Rise of Public Relations—Driven Businesses

The advertising-driven business is now familiar, but it is of relatively recent vintage. Half a century ago and more, a business came into being as a product-driven or service-driven entity. The company made the best tools or cars or shoes that it could make, then tried to sell them, using various means, including advertising.

Then, as advertising reached maturity, we began to see a new phenomenon—companies that went into business making things strictly because they could be advertised effectively. (This is not to imply that the products were poor; it just means that advertisability was the primary thrust in deciding to make them.) Alberto Culver comes to mind as one company where advertising has been a primary driving force from the inception.

Now public relations is reaching maturity. We are going to see more and more enterprises in which public relations is a primary component—perhaps the most important component—in the viability of the company, rather than just another aid to promotion.

I started a PR-driven enterprise when I became a proud founder, along with a friend, Margo Mayor, of Hollywood Fantasy. Hollywood Fantasy gave even the most jaded travelers a chance to have a truly new and different kind of vacation by starring in a film with real Hollywood leading actors.

Margo Mayor and I created the notion of Hollywood Fantasy as a way of ushering ordinary people into the dreamworld they see on television. Alice went through the looking glass; the Hollywood Fantasy vacationer went through the TV screen. Here is how we described it:

> Imagine starring in a film with Hollywood actors Elliott Gould and Maxwell Caulfield while on a one-week, luxury vacation.
>
> For a week, Hollywood Fantasy vacationers live the life of a Hollywood star. They are pampered and preened like screen legends and taught the "tricks of the trade" by the best in the business.
>
> Using original script material, vacationers rehearse roles with a film crew and a top-name Hollywood director. Throughout the week, professional drama coaches give voice training and acting lessons as participants run through their scenes. Make-overs and wardrobe tips are provided by fashion and beauty experts. It is amazing to see how quickly basic acting skills can be developed.
>
> Although there is plenty of time for lounging by the pool and attending lavish cast parties, the focus of the week's activities is appearing in a production with the talented screen actor Elliott Gould and TV star Maxwell Caulfield. When the vacation is over, and it seems like it was all just a dream, participants will receive a keepsake videocassette of their starring role.

The first Hollywood Fantasy vacation took place at the Palm Springs Marquis Hotel in January 1991. Vacationers paid $7,500 to spend a week taking voice, acting, and beauty lessons; rehearsing; and making a short film with the stars. Back home, instead of slides, they could show their friends the video of their performances with Elliott Gould and Maxwell Caulfield, two recognized film and television actors.

The movie fantasy motif was kept constant throughout the week. Indulging in a bit of fantasy ourselves, Margo and I played the part of the traditional movie moguls. Various celebrities from Hollywood, like Tony Martin and Cyd Charise, and the late Sonny Bono, chatted with our "stars." I saw this as a PR-driven venture. Hollywood Fantasy made the *CBS Evening News* with Dan Rather. *A Current Affair* actually paid to send someone to our fantasy camp; her experiences were filmed and used for two shows. There was a lot of newspaper coverage. Hollywood Fantasy offered travel-page editors something different, and they latched on to it.

The success of the first Hollywood Fantasy was assured when it made the *New York Times* travel section. The *Times*'s immense power proved itself once again.

The second Hollywood Fantasy vacation experience was scheduled for the luxurious La Mansion del Rio Hotel in San Antonio in May 1991. Looking for an available star who would attract the media, I signed Zsa Zsa Gabor. Gabor seemed ideal. She is almost a figure of folklore rather than an actress. Making a movie with her would be fun. The only trouble was that Gabor pulled out at the last minute, demanding more money. I sued her for more than a million dollars, making sure that this suit was well publicized.

Publicized it was—in years 1991 through 1998. The lawsuit went to trial in San Antonio in 1991 in federal court. Gabor was a no-show. The judge heard the case, and the jury awarded us $3 million.

That publicity got a rise out of Gabor. She hired famous attorney Melvin Belli and filed for a new trial. It was granted. The venue was changed to Midland, Texas. The world's press were in attendance. Belli was in his glory as he examined Gabor before a jury of conservative West Texans. To no avail. She lost again, but this time the verdict came in under $1 million.

"Appeal," she told her attorneys. Soon they were in a federal court of appeals in New Orleans. Along the way she delayed everything by filing for bankruptcy, even though her assets exceeded her liabilities both real and contingent. Finally, in late 1998, the appeals court released its verdict—another win for Hollywood Fantasy, though the financial award was cut some more, this time to actual losses. More national publicity followed.

Because Gabor had been a resident of Palm Beach at one time, Thom Smith, the very popular "people" columnist for the *Palm Beach Post,* had been following the story since 1991. After the appeals court verdict, in a column headlined, "Zsa Zsa Tries Her Best but PR Wizard Wins in Court," Smith wrote, "Good things come to those who wait . . . and wait . . . and wait. Just ask Len Saffir."

In mid-1999 Gabor's attorneys were trying to settle or go to the Supreme Court. Or perhaps a made-for-television movie written and directed by Oliver Stone?

Mark Twain for President

Having used PR techniques to create a business, I decided to create a president.

Mark Twain had done great things for me in my cigar industry campaign. I decided to run Mark Twain for president of the United States in 1992.

With me as his campaign manager, Twain (a.k.a. actor Roger Durrett) began testing the political waters in New Hampshire late in 1991. We got more coverage than all the Democratic candidates combined. Front-page color photographs with headlines that proclaimed, "Mark Twain Considering '92 Run for President as Mugwump Candidate." We garnered excellent television and radio time. We got out a press kit and did all the things presidential candidates do: speeches, news conferences, walking tours with mayors.

Clinton and Our Campaign

During a break in Twain campaigning, we both went to St. Paul's School in Concord to hear candidate Bill Clinton speak. After his speech, I walked over to the former governor of Arkansas and shook his hand. "My name is Leonard Saffir, and I am campaign manager for Mark Twain."

The soon-to-be president at first looked at me as if I were crazy, but after losing only a few beats, he responded, "Oh, I like Mark Twain. Good luck to you."

I gave him a Twain for President press kit. He tucked it under his arm, and I watched him as he exited the school building. He stopped to talk to his aides before entering his limousine and gave one aide all his papers, but I saw that he kept the Mark Twain press kit.

A few days later, I read an AP story reporting on a stump speech by Clinton in another New Hampshire town. Clinton quoted Mark Twain, a quote taken from one of our press releases. And through his two terms as president, he has continued to quote Twain, but I will not take credit for that.

Results of the Experiment

One thing that set Twain off from the other presidential candidates was his fearlessness; for example, his willingness to take part in a display of banned books in Portsmouth, New Hampshire. (And why not? *Huckleberry Finn* was on the banned-book list.)

Another unique part of Twain's campaign was his willingness to puncture sacred cows and take potshots at the absurdities of both parties.

One purpose of the Mark Twain campaign was to attract speaking engagements on the lecture circuit. Inquiries flooded in, along with invitations to appear on TV shows in various areas. A bonus result was Public Broadcasting System's agreement to produce two half-hour specials featuring Twain on politics. Another purpose of the campaign was to say some things that needed to be said about politics and society in America.

I had a third reason for running Mark Twain: to serve as a kind of laboratory experiment in applied Power Public Relations. The results further validated my feeling that we have entered a world in which people *welcome* the workings of public relations. They are willing to suspend their disbelief to enjoy the sensation of acting, and then are willing to feel as if something is true when they really know it is not true.

The people in New Hampshire and elsewhere on Mark Twain's campaign trail (with, I suppose, a few weird exceptions) knew that Mark Twain was not really up there on the hustings. Nevertheless, they listened as if it were Mark Twain; they received the opinions as if they had been actually uttered by Mark Twain; and they responded to Mark Twain as if he were a real person, expressing their sense of what this country ought to be and can be.

Ronald Reagan was only the beginning. Before long, we may see shoals of actors running, successfully, for the highest offices, because they are able to embody people's ideas of what leaders in high office should be like.

Mark Twain and Hollywood Fantasy are finger exercises—warm-ups. We look forward to the creation and growth of all kinds of enterprises that will exist primarily as manifestations of public relations power. In a way, it is how we PR professionals, who have had sand kicked in our faces all these years, are showing off our Charles Atlas strength.

Public Relations Executives Running Advertising/ PR Agencies

On September 26, 1991, Ketchum Communications, Pittsburgh, named a new president and CEO: Paul H. Alvarez. As the *New York Times* reported, Alvarez's "primary experience is in public relations." This background information was worthy of note. It was quite unusual for a PR professional to take over a major advertising agency.

Ketchum would still be identified by most as an ad agency. As Ketchum, McLeod & Grove, it had been one of the big ad agencies. Like practically all major ad agencies, Ketchum set up a public relations division. Essentially, when PR arms have been established, they have been regarded as emphatically inferior to the advertising function. Certainly, traditionalists would never contemplate that a PR practitioner could head up such an organization. This would be standing the natural order of things on its head.

Since then, a number of ad agencies have tapped PR professionals for the chief executive positions. In 1998 Young & Rubicam, the giant advertising agency, picked its top public relations executive, Tom Bell, to head the agency. On September 25, 1998, the *Wall Street Journal* wrote that the appointment of Bell "underscored the escalating demands of clients for marketing help beyond just thirty-second commercials and print ads."

Bell had no prior Madison Avenue experience, having spent most of his career trying to influence public opinion in Washington. He had previously been president and chief executive of Burson-Marsteller Worldwide, the big public relations firm owned by Y&R. Peter Georgescu, the top man at Y&R, Inc., the ad agency's parent company, said, in discussing the Bell appointment, "The game has changed from selling an ad campaign to a client to creating results in the marketplace."

Actually, these are very logical developments. Public relations practitioners are, all things being equal, better qualified to run such agencies than advertising people. While advertising still boasts the bigger budgets (and will continue to do so for a long time), public relations is a more rounded discipline, and those who are good at it are better able to run organizations than their advertising counterparts.

Make Way for the "Sell Shop"

Sure, PR professionals will run firms that are now called advertising agencies. But the changes in the business will be a lot more profound than that.

"When," asked a *Wall Street Journal* article in October 1991, "will the beleaguered advertising industry turn around?" The answer, as provided by executives gathered in Phoenix for the annual meeting of the Association of National Advertisers, may be "never."

Declining billings, slashed budgets—to a degree, these phenomena could be attributed to a recessionary economy. But in the last decade of the twentieth century, it began to dawn on advertising people that, as the *Journal* said, the recession "masks a fundamental change in the structure of the marketing business. Advertising may never bounce back to its previous levels, because the business of both agencies and clients has changed for good." Even when the recession was over, many companies continued to lay off employees because of mergers.

The increasing freneticism and weirdness of a lot of advertising is both a cause and a symptom of this evolutionary development. David Ogilvy, a legend at the age of eighty, told the *Journal* that present-day advertising is "pretentious and incomprehensible nonsense. . . . It's highbrow, obscure . . . and it doesn't sell."

Advertising is going through the agonizing throes of transition from one phase to the next. The transition is painful because traditional advertising becomes less important under the new marketing concepts that will dominate the twenty-first century. It will still be very important, but not dominant in the way it has been for most of a century.

Marketing will be just as important as it ever was, but the mix of disciplines that make up the marketing effort will change. One of the most significant changes—and it is already happening—is the marked increase in public relations as a factor, especially as compared to advertising.

But wait a minute. Why should advertising and public relations continue to have a wall separating them? As it stands now, the two are quite distinct disciplines. In modern marketing, they are being used, to a much greater degree than before, to complement each other. But each discipline functions by itself.

And, in many cases, that is probably the way it should continue to be. The differences between the two are obvious. But maybe we have all been focusing too hard on the differences and not paying enough attention to the similarities. Public relations and advertising take creativity, writing ability, visualization skills, and, above all, mastery of the tools of persuasion.

Persuasion. That is what both disciplines are about. In each discipline, the tools of persuasion are used in different ways to influence perception.

I predict that the similarities between public relations and advertising will become more important than the differences, and the result will be a gradual blending of the specialties. Right now, of course, the two do not mix. An advertising agency and a public relations function may work under the same roof and under the same company name, and serve the same clients, but they have their own separate organizations. And in-house functions are even more separate. The in-house PR department, as Dick Weiner points out, functions like an independent public relations firm, dealing with various brands and company departments as if they were clients. But advertising and PR work separately.

That "separate but unequal" notion does not make sense anymore. What is going to happen is that the two disciplines will combine. Ultimately, instead of separate advertising agencies and public relations firms (or internal departments), we will see a combined operation devoted to the influencing of perception. This combined entity will no longer be called an ad agency or a PR firm. The term I like is *sell shop*.

At a sell shop, the marketing task will start as it does now in advertising or public relations. The job is to sell widgets. The widget market is studied, widget buyers are dissected, the levers that move the perceptual machinery are identified.

But then the sell shop goes about selling the widgets by a mix that includes, for example, TV advertising, print advertising, special events, mass-market public relations, and trade public relations. A copywriter might work on a thirty-second commercial one day and a PR release the next day. Why not? The copywriter knows what it takes to sell widgets. The selling message must be adapted for public relations channels—just as it must be adapted for print and broadcast.

Obviously, there will still be specialists. Advertising media work is quite different from public relations "placement." But the job of serving the account, distilling the selling message, and transforming it into persuasive form, will be handled by the same teams and, often, the identical people.

In the twenty-first century, separate advertising agencies and public relations firms will gradually disappear, to be replaced by sell shops that do both. Looking back, people will feel that there was no more reason for separation of public relations and advertising than there would be to completely separate print and broadcast advertising and have them done by totally distinct organizations.

Public Relations People Running IBM, GM, GE? Why Not?

The public relations function will be a large and powerful entity in the corporation of the twenty-first century—influential throughout the organization, much more important than advertising, essential in planning and policy direction. Along with this, executives with public relations backgrounds will be serving as chairpersons and CEOs of corporations that make all kinds of products and sell all kinds of services. There is no fundamental reason why a PR professional should not head up IBM or General Electric or General Motors.

Now, on the face of it, this statement seems so exaggerated as to be preposterous. How could a PR practitioner ever hope to run an enterprise like Intel?

Here is why. People who rise to the top of companies, big and small, all come out of some specialized background. There is no such thing as an all-around executive who is equally trained in all disciplines and practices all disciplines to the same extent. No, you are a marketing manager, a financial manager, a production manager, an engineer, or whatever. Traditionally, the road to the heights has been trod almost exclusively by line executives. For decades after the rise of large corporations, staff executives were virtually barred from leadership.

That has changed. Lawyers, research scientists, human resource managers—practitioners of these and other staff specialties can and do become CEOs of large organizations, although the bulk of these top jobs are still filled by persons from the conventional line backgrounds.

The point is that every CEO started as a specialist in something and then, having demonstrated a grasp of broader management areas, was given greater responsibility. It is reasonable to think that most top executives go about their jobs with approaches that have been shaped by their specialties. Marketing executives look at plans and decisions in terms of their effect on selling. Financial people are keenly conscious of the money aspects of what is going on. And so on.

Advertising specialists do not become heads of giant companies. Maybe they should. Good advertising people must understand the public and know how to sell the company's wares to that public. This is by no means an unimportant skill. But advertising, powerful as it is, is a sharply defined discipline, devoted strictly to the use of paid-for time and space to sell things.

Public relations, in its mature form, is a broader discipline than advertising. As the range of topics covered in this book might indicate, public relations now penetrates a surprising number of important areas. It is a two-way discipline. Companies of the future will have well-rounded PR functions that provide input on all major moves the organization makes. And why not? The reaction of the public at large—and of all the discrete publics—is a paramount consideration in most corporate planning. The likely reactions of relevant publics—customers, communities, legislators, and others—will be probed and evaluated, not in a seat-of-the-pants fashion, but through an array of opinion-measuring techniques. This job will be done by public relations.

Nor does the task of public relations in shaping policy in the modern corporation stop there. If it is necessary to change the viewpoints of certain publics before a corporate policy is put into effect, the assignment will be entrusted to public relations.

So public relations will, before we have gone very far into the twenty-first century, be taken for granted as a major element in just about any corporation, as are marketing, finance, and human resources. The work of PR practitioners will be influential and sometimes decisive in molding policy.

That being the case, there is no logical reason why executives who come out of the public relations discipline cannot run big companies just as well as executives who come out of the traditional mainstream disciplines. Indeed, it can be argued that someone who is gifted in the analysis and influencing of public opinion is a more likely choice to run a corporation than an engineer.

Public relations practitioners have certain important qualifications for high corporate office that are not necessarily possessed by other specialists. For one thing, the PR professional looks realistically at what a company does and asks tough questions about it. Public relations practitioners cannot settle for inadequate answers, fuzzy explanations, or assumptions that a thing is OK because "we have always done it that way." They have to be able to put things into plain language, so that reasonable people can understand them. A good rule for CEOs is, If it cannot be explained, it should be fixed or abolished. Public relations professionals see a lot that is difficult, at best, to explain. As it stands now, they have to grit their teeth and make the best of it. Empowered as CEOs, they could change things.

But would a company president from the PR ranks understand finances? Sure; as well as anyone who did not come out of a financial background and, probably, better than most. Because one of the attributes of good PR practitioners is the capacity to understand every phase of the operation, so its story can be told.

In terms of planning and decision making, public relations is as good a training ground as any of the traditional disciplines. And in some other important aspects of the top job, it is better. One of the things a leader must do is get others to carry out decisions. The most brilliant plan fails if the leaders cannot communicate it effectively and persuasively. In the twenty-first-century corporation, the PR function will increasingly be charged with this responsibility, because public relations is the persuasion department. Public relations executives who develop all-around management skills will have an advantage in senior line positions because they are skilled at persuading others to do things. And when it comes to decisiveness, resourcefulness, and the ability to function under pressure, public relations is a good training ground.

Public relations executives can and should be considered equally with those from other disciplines as candidates for top corporate jobs. It is only a matter of time until we see a public relations practitioner at the helm of one of the world's biggest companies.

"Insanity," you could argue. You might check it out with George Weissman, former chairman and CEO of Philip Morris, who started as a PR professional.

Or how about a former PR professional, who never sold an insurance policy in his life, becoming president of John Hancock Mutual Life Insurance Company? That happened in January 1998, when David F. D'Alessandro was promoted after joining the company as head of PR in 1984. D'Alessandro majored in public relations at Utica College, in upstate New York (I went there for two years), and then worked for Edelman Public Relations.

Business Week (June 2, 1997) reported, "Traditionally, top insurance honchos come up either as agents or actuaries. D'Alessandro never had heard of an actuary until he joined Hancock as PR chief." He is best known for saving the Boston Marathon from extinction when he talked Hancock's brass into sponsoring the race. As a sponsor of the 2000 Olympics, he led the corporate charge to clean up one of the worst stains on the modern Olympics, the Salt Lake City bribery scandal. Now that's the kind of innovative leadership you will need to make it to the cover of *CEO* magazine.

Public Relations Power Will Be Taken for Granted

"Street smart" has gotten to be a cliché. For a while, it seemed that just about every high-profile executive was so labeled. Successful businesspeople like David Mahoney boasted about their street smarts.

Being smart is great, but an objective look at the business picture these days shows that it is a lot better to master public relations.

Some people have tremendous public relations instincts; others fall far short of mastery. Between the two extremes is a continuum of PR perspicacity. Many people have the potential to master PR but are wasting that potential, because they do not think public relations is all that important or do not know the right things to do to build their PR power.

Losing the Art: Donald Trump

Donald Trump is this era's most interesting character, by far, from a public relations perspective. Trump performed the extraordinary feat of dropping from PR mastery to PR disaster almost overnight.

In this book I have described PR-driven companies, industries, and people. Donald Trump's deliberate use of personal promotion as a titanic tool for success is not exactly unprecedented, but his rise and fall is almost a laboratory demonstration of how far public relations mastery can get you, and how badly public relations maladroitness can hurt you.

Trump is not just a big operator who decided his image needed refurbishing, as tycoons have been doing from John D. Rockefeller to Bill Gates. Nor is he simply a highly successful personality for whom celebrity is one of the principal perks—like Michael Eisner or George Steinbrenner. Donald Trump is more than that. Trump has deliberately and specifically used inflation of his personal image as a business tool. Some headline-grabbing executives rationalize their activities by saying there is a business advantage; Trump has actually used it as a strategy. One observer said of him, "His image *is* the strategy."

Trump's idea is that by becoming famous—and even somewhat notorious—he adds value to his holdings. Ordinary people will have some of the glamour rub off on them when they shop at Trump Tower or gamble at Trump's Castle. He even thought business travelers would bask in the glow of his success when they rode the Trump Shuttle.

The strategy went beyond beguiling ordinary folks with the magic of the Trump name. Donald Trump operated on the assumption that his high profile was a strong plus in getting bankers to lend him money, suppliers to extend him credit, and government regulatory agencies to do what he wanted.

In the 1970s, the 1980s, and part of the 1990s, it worked. Maybe not as well as Trump thought it worked, but it worked. Supposedly hardheaded financial giants were willing to lend Trump incredible amounts of money, despite the cold evidence of the printouts that showed the flamboyant developer to be leveraged to the breaking point. In judging Trump's ventures, like the completion of the Taj Mahal in Atlantic City, it did not take a financial genius to see that, even if the economy continued to boom to an unprecedented degree and everything went absolutely favorably, Trump's chances of squeaking through were, at best, fifty-fifty. Practically anyone else who asked lenders to take such chances would have been thrown out on an ear. The Trump magic carried the lenders along. And that Trump magic had been built and fostered by a shrewd mastery of public relations.

Then things started to happen. Some of them were things over which Trump had no control. But even a person totally lacking PR savvy could have seen that some of the things that happened were land mines. A respected financial analyst was less than enthusiastic about one of Trump's proposals. Trump called up and demanded that the analyst be fired and, in fact, did get him fired—temporarily. The analyst went public, the company was forced to reinstate him, and Donald Trump looked like a bully and, what was far worse, an ineffectual bully.

The lurid divorce proceedings between Donald and Ivana Trump—in which both sides rolled up the big guns of high-priced PR batteries—did a great deal in a short time to erode the Trump image. And a series of ludicrous events centering around Marla Maples made Donald Trump look more like a well-dressed sideshow geek than a colossus who had once thought about running for president of the United States.

Trump became a figure of ridicule. His superb mastery of public relations had turned to grotesque clumsiness.

In the nineties Trump started getting his personal and financial lives back in shape. He began talking big deals and getting the extraordinary PR only he could muster. He announced plans to build a world-class tower near the United Nations headquarters, and he renovated the former Gulf & Western Building in New York's Columbus Circle to open Trump International Tower to go with Trump Plaza, Trump Tower, Trump Parc, Trump Palace, and Trump Taj Mahal. He also wanted to expand one of his Atlantic City casinos to build a parking lot. Then, when he seemed to have it all made, on June 1, 1998, Trump demolished his rebuilt image with a disastrous appearance on ABC's *20/20* television program:

HUGH DOWNS: There's something Donald Trump wants really badly. It happens to belong to someone else. But that's not going to stop him. Donald Trump wants an elderly woman's house in Atlantic City. And John Stossel tells us he's convinced the state to take it away from her and give it to him. How could that be legal?

JOHN STOSSEL, ABC NEWS: Your home is your castle, right? It's yours. Once you paid for your property, no one can just take it from you, can they? Well governments can use your property for public use.

That's what Trump convinced the state of New Jersey to do: take over the home of an elderly widow in Atlantic City who lived there for thirty years right next to the Boardwalk. He wanted it for a parking lot for his Trump Plaza Casino across the street. She thought she could live out her life in her handsome three-story home.

VERA COKING, HOMEOWNER: He don't care. He only care Trump and Trump and Trump. That's all. Heart, he doesn't have a heart, that man.

TV REPORTER: Yesterday the Casino Reinvestment Development Authority voted unanimously to use its power of eminent domain to acquire Coking's property.

DONALD TRUMP: Everybody coming into Atlantic City sees that property, and it's not fair to Atlantic City and the people. They're staring at this terrible house instead of staring at beautiful fountains and beautiful other things that would be good.

Trump had slipped so low as to square off with an elderly widow on national television.

And how did that all come about? Power Public Relations. John Kramer, the able director of communications for the Institute of Justice, lawyers for Coking, arranged it. "Most all legal cases we take on," says Kramer, "we fight in court and the court of public opinion."

Trump very well might have won his case if he had kept himself off TV. Instead, Coking won when a judge in New Jersey blocked the state authority's effort to condemn the property and turn it over to the Trump organization.

And so, as we view the leading figures of the end of the century we see none who has plummeted so far with such cataclysmic flair as Donald Trump.

Other Disaster Stories

Certainly, there are other prominent figures who have failed at PR. Mike Tyson is the heaviest hitter in these ranks. As just one example, take his statement following his indictment for rape: "My only problem is that I associated with the common people."

It takes something special to go from the heights to the pits. Gary Hart was never quite perfect at public relations, but he had major PR ability. He plummeted by making the most rudimentary mistake in the book: challenging the media. "OK, stake me out and see if you can catch me!" is an unforgettable PR blunder.

Of course, it is all too possible for organizations to qualify for a collective award for PR disaster of the year. One of the surest ways to do this is to try covering up major bad news. In September 1991, AT&T's circuits broke down, shutting down New York airports, breaking off stock exchange information, and in general raising hell. The problem was that alarms went off when no technicians were around to notice. AT&T insisted for an unconscionably long time that it was adequately staffed. The truth of its inadequate staffing inevitably came out, casting a dark shadow over the kickoff of the company's multi-million-dollar We Want You Back campaign.

A particularly notorious PR blunder was the 1998 Abercrombie & Fitch magazine-catalog of the trendiest clothes that college students can wear at their back-to-school parties, which incorporated a primer on how to get drunk. The catalog's drinking games, complete with recipes for libations like a "Woo-Woo" and a "Brain Hemorrhage," outraged groups throughout the country. Said the Center for Science in the Public Interest, "The Abercrombie & Fitch promotion callously exploits a college drinking culture that is dangerously out of control." Dallas-based Mothers Against Drunk Driving asked the retailer to send an apology to everyone who received the catalog. The company's stock dropped nearly $1 after an article about the catalog appeared in the *Wall Street Journal*. The media had a field day on that one before Abercrombie dropped the promotion.

Just as bad was the District of Columbia Housing Authority's news release announcing a drug bust—the night before the raid was planned. Naturally the drug bust was a bust, as drug dealers heard about it on the radio and disappeared.

At the Other Extreme

Managers with PR savvy are better managers. They say it is better to talk about bad news than keep quiet about it. "Get it all into the open at once," says Warren Cowan, chairman of Rogers & Cowan in Los Angeles. "Periodic revelations stretch the story out and get it rehashed with each new detail."

This is a good tactic in handling the PR aspects of a disaster. And it is a good management approach in general. Managers who are inept at PR cover up when things go wrong. The PR-savvy managers get the facts out and face them.

There are other significant ways in which Power Public Relations improves management capability across the board. Public relations professionals evaluate moves in terms of how people will react to them. Some old-school executives tend to denigrate this tendency. They maintain that decision making is a pure exercise, which should be undertaken without being adulterated by thoughts about how others are going to react. The dominance of computer technology has given new vigor to this kind of thinking. The computer assists in coming up with a "pure" solution, taking into account numbers, trends, resources—but leaving out the human factor.

That is fine, as far as it goes. But the purest decision will not work if people do not execute it properly. Logic does not always translate into motivation.

Let us say a CEO devises a strategy in which two major divisions of the company take a backseat to a third division, which will spearhead a new campaign. The logic is flawless, but the plan fails because the two supporting divisions do not do a good enough job.

A manager without PR skills will fume about this and blame the laggard division. A manager with PR savvy would have anticipated the problem. Such managers know that these phenomena are not deliberate sabotage. They are natural human reactions. People do not like to work against their own self-interest. Even when they do their dutiful best, their hearts are not in it. So the PR-savvy manager would try to find ways to persuade the divisions in question to give it their best shot; these ways would include modifying the plan if necessary.

Here is another way PR skills are an asset in general line management. Part of the Power Public Relations approach is to explain things well. Public relations frequently involves the translation of the complex into the simple, so that nonexperts can understand it. And good public relations means translating functions and features into benefits. How a new machine works is of interest to a few mechanically minded souls, but the good things that machine will do for humankind may be of very wide interest.

Now, these skills are second nature to accomplished PR practitioners. They are, however, skills insufficiently practiced by a lot of non-PR professionals. The ability to turn complicated things into simple things is a considerable asset to any executive in finance, production, research, whatever.

And, of course, the ability to translate features into benefits is universally recognized as a necessity in marketing, but a surprising number of marketing managers do not seem to know how to do it. When you have the PR mind-set, you do this as a matter of course.

Part of the nitty-gritty of public relations is finding story angles. Handling public relations for a company often means looking for ways to make the people and processes of the company interesting to those outside the company. To do this requires that the PR pro learn all about the organization and the products and services it turns out, in depth and detail beyond what most executives do.

Some of what goes wrong in corporations today happens because the managers are too remote from what is actually happening. The PR approach involves actually seeing things and talking to people— "getting your hands dirty"—as opposed to keeping in touch by remote control through reports, charts, printouts. Of course, senior executives, who have a great many concerns, cannot get overly involved in day-to-day operations or play hooky from planning and decision making by hanging around the factory floor. The tendency today is for them to spend too little time on the factory floor, or its equivalent.

Managers with good PR instincts have an interest in, and feel for, the fabric of the organization—the threads, stiches, and knots—as well as the large designs printed on that fabric.

Public Relations Literacy as a Motivation Tool

Motivation is a major task of management. One of the prime tools of public relations can be adapted as an aid to motivation for managers in all disciplines.

The standard approach to motivating workers concentrates on similarities. The patron saint of motivators is Dr. Abraham H. Maslow. Maslow's hierarchy of human needs, published in 1954, is the underpinning for modern motivational techniques. Maslow said the most basic needs are physiological—food, shelter, sex. Then come safety needs—survival against danger. When these needs are satisfied, we seek love, friendship, and affection—social needs. Then, Maslow said, we are concerned with the need for esteem—self-esteem and the good opinion of others. Finally, there is the need for "self-actualization," or self-fulfillment.

Another shaper of modern motivational theory is Dr. Frederick Herzberg, who distinguished between what he called true motivators and "hygiene factors." Hygiene factors cannot satisfy. They can merely keep a person from being dissatisfied. They include working conditions, supervision, interpersonal relations on the job, company policy—and compensation.

Herzberg's most controversial precept was that money is not a motivator. He said real motivators—those with the power to satisfy— are achievement, recognition of achievement, advancement, responsibility, the work itself. While it seems to go counter to common sense—people, after all, are always saying that they work for the money, and they fully believe this—training and motivation practices used in the corporate world today follow Herzberg's dictum. And, on the whole, it seems to work.

However, motivation is still too much of a hit-and-miss undertaking. What motivates one person or group does not motivate another. And since the ability to motivate is a universally recognized attribute of leadership, improvement in this area would be most welcome.

One of the hallmarks of public relations discipline as it has now evolved is segmentation. Public relations practitioners do not think of "the public"; they think of publics. They are used to the idea of having to address multiple audiences and package the message for each audience.

This approach is badly needed in motivation. Take the case of a company that wants to expand. The company is dealing with multiple publics: stockholders, customers, community, government, bankers, its own workers. Beaming pretty much the same message to all is a losing strategy. If the company is skillful with PR, it will tailor separate messages and deliver them through the channels best adapted to reach each public.

An individual manager is usually dealing with a number of publics: staff, top management, colleagues, the industry as a whole. The public may consist of one person—a boss, let us say. We often go wrong by beaming a single message to all, because it saves time, money, and effort; we do not know how to do it differently; others have always done it that way; and we do not realize it is a mistake.

Managers of whatever discipline who are proficient at PR are automatically aware of multiple audiences. Segmentation, to them, is the norm. And they think in terms of the appropriate channels to reach each segment.

Motivators know that the basic doctrines of motivation work differently with different people, but they have not had a world of success in putting that knowledge into practice. Motivation is still too much of a generality expected to work the same with everyone.

The manager skilled in PR takes Maslow and Herzberg for granted and goes beyond, segmenting, analyzing individual publics, and beaming the most effective persuasion to each.

Fear and Loathing of Power Public Relations

As I have mentioned, savvy public relations practitioners tend to play down the giant strength of the discipline rather than draw attention to it. The less the public knows about public relations techniques, the better they work. Another reason for soft-pedaling PR's real power is fear of backlash.

Public relations is already involved in controversies that are unique to the business. Hill & Knowlton has drawn a lot of fire. The company has worked for a highly varied array of clients, including antiabortion Catholic bishops and the Church of Scientology. Critics don't complain that Hill & Knowlton does its work badly, but rather that it works only too well.

Early in 1992, the *Wall Street Journal* reported on a lawsuit that has interesting implications. A group of depositors in the scandal-ridden Bank of Credit & Commerce International (BCCI) filed a lawsuit charging that Hill & Knowlton painted BCCI as "a legitimate business and helped publicize 'the false information necessary to conceal (BCCI's) reckless, improper and illegal business activities.' " The lawsuit, filed under the federal Racketeer Influenced and Corrupt Organizations Act—commonly known as RICO—held Hill & Knowlton responsible for the information it disseminated and suggested that it was the public relations firm's efforts that made depositors think BCCI was safe and respectable.

The idea of "public relations fraud" chills the hearts of professionals. One observer said, "If PR firms are strictly liable for the words a client wants spoken, that would be awful." But the threat is real. In a way the lawsuit is a tribute to the power of the discipline, like the law that designates the fists of a professional boxer as lethal weapons. However, those in the business would be just as happy to pass up the tribute. For one thing, if the idea catches hold, public relations companies, and even individual practitioners, will have to carry expensive insurance similar to the malpractice insurance load borne by physicians and surgeons.

Near the beginning of 1992, Hill & Knowlton was embroiled in another significant controversy. When Iraq invaded Kuwait late in

1990, Kuwait financed a group called Citizens for a Free Kuwait, which retained Hill & Knowlton to work toward U.S. intervention. Focus groups indicated that there was no American groundswell for war on Kuwait's behalf, but that the American people were sympathetic to the Kuwaitis, and their sympathy could be heated toward the point at which they would support action. An effective way to accomplish this would be to let Americans know about atrocities committed by Iraqi soldiers. One of the most dramatic moments of the resulting Hill & Knowlton campaign came when "Nayirah," a fifteen-year-old Kuwaiti girl, tearfully told the Congressional Human Rights Caucus that she had seen the invaders pull babies from incubators and leave them on the floor to die. Hill & Knowlton played it to the hilt, distributing widely-aired video news releases of Nayirah.

Later, a number of on-the-scene authorities would cast doubt on this story. But the real furor erupted when it turned out that Nayirah—who had not been otherwise identified—was in fact the daughter of the Kuwaiti ambassador to the United States and related to the Kuwaiti ruling family. The chairman of the caucus, California congressman Tom Lantos, knew the witness's identity. Most of his colleagues did not. Some of them were less than thrilled with Lantos when the story hit the headlines. It was a natural for TV shows like *20/20* and *60 Minutes*. Hill & Knowlton was depicted as a Machiavellian force, bending the minds of government and the public.

The public relations firm defended itself vigorously. Nayirah's identity had been kept secret to protect her. Just because she was the ambassador's daughter, it need not be concluded that she didn't see Iraqis throwing babies out of incubators. And so forth. Overall, though, this imbroglio was not good for Congress, Hill & Knowlton, or the public relations industry.

It's time for the industry to use its power and skill to better acquaint the public at large with the true nature of the discipline. People fear what they don't understand. They rebel at the thought that unseen forces may be manipulating them. While public relations was still growing, general ignorance about its nature was irritating but not all that harmful. Now it is damaging and can be disastrous. Public relations professionals need to pool their formidable resources to influence the perceptions of PR held by businesspeople, government officials, and the public. They say the shoemaker's children go barefoot; public relations has done a poor job of PR on itself. As the power and stature of the discipline grow, it is essential to do better. The public relations industry must take itself on as a client.

As for Congress—and indeed all public officials—the woefully low level of public relations literacy in government has to be raised. Senators and members of Congress are usually highly regarded by their own constitutents, but those same constituents despise Congress as a whole. This is not good for the country. In 1998, Congress was at its lowest level of approval in decades. Yet in elections that year, most incumbents were reelected. Congress should establish its own office of public relations. Of course there would be complaints. But there were plenty of complaints when Congress raised members' own salaries, and the raises went through. (With intelligent public relations counsel, our elected representatives might not be cursed and reviled when they ask for reasonable wages.)

Controversy will continue to swirl around public relations as it looms larger in business, government, and society. The more people know about the discipline, the more the controversy will be based on informed judgments rather than on blind fear and revulsion.

Let's Hear It for Public Relations Literacy

As we move along in the new millennium, we must foster the spread of PR literacy. Everyone who aspires to business success should be literate in today's (and tomorrow's) Power Public Relations. Here is why.

Few executives arrive at or near the top without a decent working knowledge of every important discipline in the company's operation. There was a time when management was considered by some to be a totally pure art, uncontaminated by nitty-gritty. Persons who mastered the tools could move from one industry to another without skipping a beat.

The pendulum has swung away from that extreme. Today, managers need a healthy mix of universal skills and particular knowledge.

Self-defense is one reason the aspiring executive needs all-around familiarity, especially as disciplines become more complex. Not that executives are expected to do it all themselves. They depend on experts.

Depend is the key word. It is one thing to depend on your chief information technology director or research chief or data processing guru. It is quite another thing to be at that person's mercy. But that is where you are if you do not understand what the expert is talking about. You do not know if you are getting a snow job, you do not know how to apply criteria to performance, you do not know where the money goes.

Another reason for having a grasp of all the relevant disciplines is the ecology of the organization. People who do not know what ecology is all about can destroy nature. Farmers decide that certain birds are pests, so they kill them off and drive them away. Then it turns out that the birds eat certain destructive insects. No longer checked by the birds, these insects multiply and turn into far worse pests than the birds ever were. That is learning ecology the hard way.

Something similar happens in organizations. A seemingly small change in one department or division affects another. For the sake of streamlining a production process, a "minor" feature is eliminated from a product. It develops that this supposedly minor feature was important for selling the product in certain regions. Sales fall off. The sales force is disgruntled and demoralized. All this because the manager in overall charge did not have a sense of ecology.

Managers who are ignorant of some disciplines do not know how those disciplines affect other areas. Such managers fall too easily into the trap of thinking that change can be compartmentalized.

Public relations should be added to the list of disciplines of which managers have a working knowledge. Public relations literacy is important for two reasons. It is growing in stature; before long, just about any organization of any size will have a real PR function, either in-house, through an agency, or with a consultant.

Would the late PR guru Edward Bernays ever have believed that the International Monetary Fund would hire a big-name public relations firm to figure out why the secretive agency was most unloved just when its activities were the most visible? On December 18, 1998,

the IMF announced it had selected Edelman Public Relations Worldwide to strengthen public understanding and increase openness of
the IMF.

There are snow-job artists in public relations, just as there are in
other disciplines—maybe more. Managers who are PR-literate can
cut through the bull. Those who lack a basic grasp of the discipline
must just sit there and nod their heads, or try to bluff.

A working knowledge of public relations is helpful, too, in giving
managers a better grip on organizational ecology. A professional
PR approach to an organization calls for familiarity with the whole
organization.

Managers need to know what public relations is today and how it
works. Not so they can sit down and write releases, but so they can
manage the discipline effectively and make it work with other disciplines to add up to a more effective organization.

Public relations literacy holds an added bonus. Knowledge of
disciplines like data communication and finance are, of course,
important to the ambitious executive, but they do not help in self-
promotion. Those who know public relations have an advantage in
building their own careers, as well as building the strength of their
organizations. A manager with PR expertise can use some PR techniques personally and can, in subtle ways, use the organization's PR
arm to look better.

Now, strictly speaking, this may not be altogether kosher. But it is
part of the real world. PR-literate executives not only can do it for
themselves, they can also detect cases in which other people have
done it. And this is no small advantage.

Public relations literacy is spreading. Dozens of public relations
courses are taught at the undergraduate and graduate level in the
United States and a few other countries. Schools of journalism are
getting the message, albeit slowly. There are successful graduate PR
programs at Northwestern University, Boston University, Syracuse
University, the University of Pennsylvania, and other major universities. However, the graduate business schools have been slow to bring
public relations into their curricula. There are exceptions. Richard
Weiner started the first public relations course for MBAs at Fordham
University.

The inexorable growth in the importance of public relations will soon make it a standard subject in any curriculum that prepares people for business careers. Meanwhile, those who realize the crucial nature of Power Public Relations will have to seek public relations literacy on their own.

This book is my contribution to that vital process.

About the Author

Leonard Saffir's career spans public relations, marketing, politics, journalism, television, and the Internet.

Saffir joined Richard Weiner, Inc., in 1984 and rose to executive vice president before it was acquired by BBDO to become part of Porter Novelli International and Omnicom. He stayed with Porter Novelli, one of the nation's largest public relations firms, as executive vice president through 1990. In 1989 he was named to the additional position of president of Jay DeBow and Partners, a Porter Novelli financial public relations subsidiary. Saffir's responsibilities at Porter Novelli covered supervision of account groups in the areas of entertainment, sports marketing, special events, sponsorships, consumer products, crisis and litigation, as well as company management and new business.

During his career in public relations, Saffir's clients and accounts have included Philip Morris, Pepsi Cola, Michelin, MasterCard, Mattel Toys, Porsche, Johnson & Johnson, McDonald's, and several Internet companies.

He is the recipient of the Public Relations Society of America's Silver Anvil and Big Apple awards.

Saffir served as a chief of staff and press secretary to U.S. Senator James L. Buckley (R.-N.Y.) from 1971 to 1976. Saffir also served as Buckley's campaign manager in 1976. He was campaign manager for Senator John Marchi's 1973 New York City mayoral campaign and a consultant on other campaigns in the United States, the Philippines, and El Salvador. He has met and worked with Presidents Nixon, Ford, Reagan, and Bush.

Saffir was a founder of the *New York Standard* (an award-winning daily newspaper published during the 114-day newspaper strike in 1962–1963), a founder and publisher of the *Latin American Times* (a daily newspaper praised by President Lyndon B. Johnson), the founder and editor-in-chief of *The Trib* (New York's first new major daily newspaper in thirty-eight years) and *The Sun* (an award-winning weekly serving eastern Long Island and based in Bridgehampton, New York). Saffir also worked for Hearst's International News Service in New York, Dallas, and Tokyo before it became United Press International.

He was an associate producer of a one-hour prime-time television special on the Public Broadcasting System, *An Evening with Mark Twain,* and worked on other television and entertainment projects.

He has received numerous journalism awards, including a Sigma Delta Chi Professional Journalistic Society Award for distinguished journalistic achievement. He has been honored by a City of New York mayor, the New York State Press Association, the Overseas Press Club of America, and the Union League and Wharton Clubs of New York.

Saffir is a past president of the Overseas Press Club of America. He is listed in the 1997, 1998, 1999, and 2000 editions of *Who's Who in America.* He lives in Boca Raton, Florida, where he doesn't let a day go by without practicing Power Public Relations for some company, person, or cause.

Index

313